C.1

Baudelaire
PRINCE OF CLOUDS

Illustration by Leonard Baskin

C. 1

Baudelaire
PRINCE OF CLOUDS

A Biography by
Alex de Jonge

PADDINGTON
PRESS LTD
NEW YORK LONDON

Library of Congress Cataloging in Publication Data

De Jonge, Alex, 1938 —
  Baudelaire, Prince of Clouds.

  Bibliography: p.
  Includes index.
  1. Baudelaire, Charles Pierre, 1821-1867
Biography. I. Title.
PQ2191.Z5D44 1976   841'.8 (B)   76-3804
ISBN 0-8467-0137-5

Copyright © 1976 Paddington Press Ltd.
Photoset by Filmtype Services Ltd.
Scarborough, England
Printed in England by The Garden City Press Ltd.
London & Letchworth
Jacket illustration by Leonard Baskin
Designed by Richard Johnson

Published by PADDINGTON PRESS LTD New York · London

CONTENTS

The Poet is like the Prince of Clouds,
Who haunts the storm and laughs at the archer;
Exiled on earth, surrounded by mocking laughter,
His gigantic wings are fetters to his walk.

Le Poëte est semblable au Prince des Nuées
Qui hante la tempête et se rit de l'archer;
Exilé sur le sol au milieu des huées,
Ses ailes de géant l'empêchent de marcher.
                    —from Baudelaire's "L'Albatros"

INTRODUCTION

IN 1883 PAUL VERLAINE published a study of three French poets, Corbière, Rimbaud, and Mallarmé, under the title *Les Poètes maudits*—"The Damned Poets." Verlaine, a poet damned enough himself, once Rimbaud's lover, an alcoholic who died a pauper's death, picked his title not for its shock effect but for its accuracy. Indeed, as we look back on the major artists of the late nineteenth century, poets such as Rimbaud and Verlaine or painters like van Gogh, we can see a pattern of disaster, addiction, and insanity running through their lives. The art of that time was born of disaster, as if the artist who sought to capture its spirit could only do so by stretching his nerves beyond breaking point and building his art from the pieces of a shattered self. The figure of the damned artist, addict, neurotic or worse has come to dominate the history of Western art for the last 150 years: witness our own moderns—Fitzgerald, Sylvia Plath, Dylan Thomas and Billie Holiday. It is a tradition inaugurated in Europe by Charles Baudelaire.

Baudelaire was the first major writer to build his art from the process of his own destruction, the first of the damned. It is partly because he *was* the first that the story of his life is so absorbing, and sometimes so very painful. Painful because he lacked the reassurance that comes from inheriting a tradition—even if it is only a tradition of disaster linked to artistic greatness. He was a trailblazer who could not console himself with the thought that at least he was following in the footsteps of great and damned predecessors.

The artists of his own time—Victor Hugo, Hector Berlioz, Eugène Delacroix—enjoyed relatively settled and prosperous lives; at least they didn't starve. When the young Baudelaire decided to become a writer he felt that his private means and the much greater fortune that was his talent would suffice to guarantee success, prosperity, and a place in the sun. In one sense he was not disappointed, but it was neither the place, nor the sun that he had expected. In one of his most despairing poems, "De profundis clamavi," he describes his predicament:

> A sun without heat hovers for six months,
> And the other six months night covers the earth;
> It is a country more bare than the polar land;
> Neither animals, nor streams, nor greenery nor woods!

> *Un soleil sans chaleur plane au-dessus six mois,*
> *Et les six autres mois la nuit couvre la terre;*
> *C'est un pays plus nu que la terre polaire;*
> *—Ni bêtes, ni ruisseaux, ni verdure, ni bois!*

This arctic world was Baudelaire's regular place of residence. Life broke him as a man; as an artist it even denied him that greatest of all privileges: the serene, calm, and wise acceptance of life's patterns with which matured genius settles to wait for death—the mood of *The Tempest*. Baudelaire was never to know any kind of serenity or wise acceptance. Debt, failure, and disease haunted his final years. He died, at the age of forty-six, paralyzed and unable to speak.

Yet it was given to this luckless man to write the greatest poetry of his age, poetry born of loss and disaster which he turned into a strange beauty, sometimes savage, sometimes erotic, sometimes soothing—the swaying rocking calm of an adult lullaby. Baudelaire's writing inaugurated the language and the idioms of modern poetry. He was the first artist to fix the broken, neurotic consciousness of modern man, to pinpoint his dreams and fantasies. Every line he wrote rings with his genius and is colored by a temperament that draws his work close to our own times, our own aspirations, our own sense of the beautiful.

It is true that Baudelaire lived most of his adult life in a misery of hardship, tension and disease. Yet he never forgot that he embarked on that life as a dandy who cared passionately for beauty, both in his being and in his art. He never lost sight of his sense of beauty. In all practical respects, in all his dealings with men, women, and money, Baudelaire lost. But he was able to turn that loss into the words which he left us, words which remind us with a marvelous ringing insistence that he never lost his ability to reach out and find something which enabled him to sing and soar high above his own wretched, disaster-bound condition—that amid all his losses and disasters, the poet Charles Baudelaire was indeed the Prince of Clouds.

I

THE THIRTY-FOUR-YEAR-OLD widow and her six-year-old son loved their walks. Death had brought them together and they had only each other now. They would amble along the banks of the Seine or stroll through the Luxembourg Gardens, remembering the times when a third person had been with them—a white-haired old man who courageously drove away importunate dogs with a shake of his stick. The boy was delicate and fine-looking, with deep black eyes and a pale skin. He was sensitive, intelligent, and passionately in love with his mother. His father's death had made him extraordinarily affectionate, so much so that his mother found it almost disturbing. But the boy was all she had after the death of her sixty-eight-year-old mate, and she too appreciated the intimate companionship of her beautiful young child. Her elderly husband had been so dignified and composed, and her boy was so lively; no wonder they had grown close. Loneliness had amplified her mother's love, making it grow a trifle out of proportion—only to be matched, and more than matched, by the feelings of her son.

For the widow, however, loneliness was to be short-lived. Less than eighteen months after her bereavement, it would be dispelled by a handsome officer whose attentions would scar the sensitive poet-to-be, Charles Baudelaire, for the rest of his generally wretched and talented life.

Baudelaire was blessed—and cursed—with a complex, contradictory, and often puzzling character. To begin to understand it we must leave the six-year-old at the point that he is about to encounter his stepfather, and go back to the little we know about his parents' early life.

His father, Joseph-François Baudelaire, was born in 1759. He was of peasant stock, originating from Champagne. The name "Baudelaire" appears to have meant a kind of sword. We know almost nothing of his early life. He is first seen in Paris, where he enrolls at the Sorbonne in 1779. On May 24, 1781, he receives the tonsure, the first step toward Holy Orders. He takes minor orders in May 1782, and by December of that year he is subdeacon of the church of St. Denis. He receives an MA from Paris University in June 1786, by which time he is a full priest of the diocese of Châlons-sur-Marne. He has little or no money of his own.

He seems at this stage to have frequented Jansenist circles. Jansenism, with its uncompromising view of grace and salvation for a few, and damnation for the rest, may have left its mark upon Charles Baudelaire, the priest's son, and helped to shape his clear awareness of his own lack of grace. Yet it was the *idea* of a father once a priest, rather than the reality, which was to mark the poet. For Joseph-François was in no obvious sense a religious man. He was at one with his frivolous, impious age and its light-hearted treatment of affairs of the faith. Two pictures which his son inherited from him reflect his eighteenth-century sense of humor. One is a traditional rendition of St. Anthony in the desert, being tempted by the devil; the other, which Joseph-François painted himself, is a profane parody, featuring a bacchante in place of St. Anthony, surrounded by cupids.[1]

In the circumstances it is not surprising that the cleric did not survive the pressures which the French Revolution brought upon his vocation. He left Holy Orders on November 19, 1793, in response to a decree of the Convention, inviting persons in Orders to do so. Moreover, he accepted the invitation within a mere six days of the decree's being issued. The struggle between a sense of vocation and severe external pressures exerted by the revolutionary government to betray that vocation, a struggle which in a different way was to occupy much of his son's adult life, seems not to have been protracted.

At the time, Joseph-François was tutor to the two sons of the Duc Antoine César de Choiseul-Praslin, who had just been arrested by the Committee of Public Safety. It was part of the Baudelaire family mythology, if not its history, that Joseph-François saved the Choiseul-Praslin family from the guillotine.

The name Choiseul-Praslin is best known in France for a scandal that would shock the July Monarchy of Louis-Philippe some half a century later. A grandson of Joseph-François's employer was to murder his nymphomaniac wife, stupidly and brutally, stabbing her twenty-six times and beating out her brains with a pistol. Condemned to death, he killed himself in prison. The poet's mother would come to regard the family association with the now notorious name of Choiseul-Praslin as yet another addition to her long list of tribulations.

The family, however, was anything but a tribulation to Joseph-François Baudelaire. They felt indebted to him and they went to great lengths to ensure his prosperity when Napoleon placed them once more in a position to do so. The duke expressed his gratitude by securing for Joseph-François a post in the Senate. He lived in considerable style in a house at a corner of the Luxembourg Gardens.

He had married, in 1797, a certain Jeanne Justine Rosalie Janin. In 1805 she gave birth to a son, Alphonse, who, as the poet's half-brother, was destined to exacerbate Baudelaire's disastrous relationship with his stepfather in years to come.

In 1814, with the return of the Bourbons and the defeat of Napoleon, Joseph-François lost his post but was granted a substantial pension in compensation. His wife had died that year, and he was now fifty-four years old, quite well off, with a taste for fine living, comfort, and painting. It would seem however that such delights were not enough, for in 1819 Joseph-François, aged sixty, decided to marry again.

He chose Caroline Archembaut Dufays, the daughter of an émigré ex-officer of Louis XVI's army. She was born in St. Pancras, in London, in 1793. Both her parents had died when she was very young, and she was brought up in France by a prosperous lawyer, Pierre Pérignon, who was a friend both of her father and of Baudelaire.

In her youth she had acquired a taste for good living which she could scarcely expect to satisfy since she had no dowry. Although attractive, she had reached the age of twenty-five without finding a husband.

Caroline Dufays was, alas for her, not equipped to become the mother of France's most notorious and greatest poet. She was a limited person who would, in later life, combine a capacity for great affection with no less a capacity for taking offense. When her son was crippled by debts of his own making, she could mix generosity and meanness in various and seemingly arbitrary doses. She enjoyed luxury and was easily impressed by the trappings of wealth. But there is some reason to believe that she passed on to her spendthrift son Charles rather more than a love of high living and extravagance. She would display a certain capacity for sensuality, at least in her second marriage, and there are grounds for supposing that, if she herself was free of mental instability, she was nonetheless the carrier of a tainted blood line. In later life Baudelaire alluded to his mother's family in unflattering if somewhat Gothic terms:

My ancestors, idiots or maniacs, in solemn apartments, all the victims of dreadful passions.[2]

Caroline herself seems to have been free of this hint of lunacy which her son was to inherit, although, as we shall see there were certain suspicious aspects to her end. She was essentially a narrow, obstinate, somewhat stupid woman, easily impressed by externals, a stickler for decorum, but with a great capacity for feeling. Her character comes through clearly in her letter to a friend of her dead son in which she describes her first husband's courtship:

> I met M. Baudelaire in the house of my guardian M. Pérignon. . . . It was a large, extremely wealthy family. A princely establishment, luxurious and extravagant. M. Pérignon and M. Baudelaire were old friends. . . . He was well received in the house, spoiled, the guest of honor. Everybody used to praise him. This old man (he seemed old to me, and I was so young! with his gray curls and his brows as black as ebony) attracted me by his wit. . . .
>
> I remember that on high days and holidays, when there were a lot of guests at the Pérignon country house, I would see M. Baudelaire step out of a carriage with a coat of arms on it and a lackey with white hair, an imposing appearance and ornamental livery, who stood behind him at dinner. . . . M. Baudelaire seemed very grand to me.[3]

Her description explains why she agreed to marry the sexagenarian widower: she had no prospects; she loved luxury; she found the old man impressive. The couple were married in 1819, and on April 9, 1821, their only child, Charles Baudelaire, was born.

We know little of the boy's early childhood, except that it was the only extended period of happiness he ever knew. When he left it, he left a paradise which he was never, for all his efforts, to regain. In one sense his whole conception of art was an attempt to re-create the paradise of childhood. "Genius is only childhood rediscovered at will," he would write. Childhood lost, paradise lost—these are basic inspirations of his art:

> Any lyric poet, by reason of his nature, is fated to make a return to the lost Eden.[4]

We have glimpses of Baudelaire's Eden. He recalls his childhood in an eighteenth-century setting among his father's paintings and furniture:

> CHILDHOOD, old Louis Seize furniture, antiques, the consulate, pastels. Eighteenth-century society.[5]

Baudelaire's father died in 1827. In later years the poet could scarcely remember him. He was just the white-haired old man who used to take his family for walks in the Luxembourg Gardens and chase away dogs with his stick. But he was also a painter, and he described himself as such on his son's certificate of baptism. Baudelaire, who was to become the outstanding art critic of his age, had his own views about his father's indifferent talents. Yet there is no doubt that it was from his father that he inherited his passion for painting and visual imagery. Indifferent painter though he might have been, Baudelaire *père* was a profoundly cultured man with a love of fine arts, luxury, and creativity. When he died he left behind a considerable collection of paintings, a large, well-stocked library, and an apartment furnished with elegant eighteenth-century pieces—an atmosphere of refined luxury which left its mark on the poet-to-be. Indeed, part of Baudelaire's sense of vocation, his determination to be a poet and art critic, may have been motivated by that strange curiosity and admiration which a child may feel for the past of a parent he never really knew. Certainly Baudelaire would always remain most anxious to retain paintings that were by or had belonged to his father, as if they had a very special meaning for him.

In his adolescence Baudelaire recalled the remote old man with affection and was clearly interested in him. At the age of seventeen he wrote to ask his mother to send him his father's poems, saying he would be most interested to read them. Much later, as a broken man, he would pray that God should not punish him by punishing his mother; the prayer was also for the soul of Mariette, an old servant of his youth, and for that of his father.[6] Yet, just as he found a taint in his mother's ancestry, so too he suspected that the flaw he perceived running through his own wretched life and personality might derive from being the son of a senile father. In his short novel *La Fanfarlo*, a satirical self-portrait, he would write:

> A curse, a threefold curse upon the sickly fathers who made us rickety and of unwelcome birth, doomed to beget only still-born children.[7]

But set against this aspect of his parentage is his recollection of childhood as a world of sensual ecstasy. One of his poems mourns *"le vert paradis des amours enfantines"* [the green paradise of infant love]. It is essentially through the focus of a precociously evolved sensuality, a response to the odors and the textures of women's clothes, that Baudelaire recalls his childhood, the childhood of a poet and a cerebral sensualist:

> . . . my early taste for women. I confused the smell of furs with the smell of women. I remember. . . . Anyway I loved my mother for her elegance. . . . I was a precocious dandy.[8]

He describes his conception of childhood—a warm, sensuous refuge, composed of silks, scents, and maternal affection—as an unequivocally sexual experience:

> What does the child love so passionately in his mother, his maid, his elder sister? Is it just the creature that feeds, combs, washes, and rocks him? There are caresses and sensual pleasures as well. For the child is caressed, unbeknownst to women, by all the grace of a woman. So he loves his mother, his sister, his wet nurse, for the agreeable brush of satin and furs, for the smell of the bosom and the hair, for the click of the jewelry, for the play of ribbons, for all this world of femininity, which begins with the chemise and is even reflected in the furniture on which woman leaves the imprint of her sex.[9]

This is the atmosphere in which the young Baudelaire bathed; the atmosphere created by his luxury-loving and affectionate mother, with whom, at this stage in his life, he was passionately in love. He tells her years later what he once felt for her:

> In my childhood there was a period when I loved you passionately; don't be afraid, listen and read. I never told you. I remember a cab ride; you were coming out of a nursing home where you had been staying, and you showed me, to prove that you had been thinking of your son, some pen and ink drawings you had done for me. Do I not have a remarkable memory? Later, there was Place St. André des Arts and Neuilly. . . . Long walks, continual endearments! I remember the quays which were so melancholy in the evening. For me those were the good days of maternal tenderness. I'm sorry to call "the good days" a time which was doubtless bad for you. But I was still alive for you; you were all mine. You were both my idol and my comrade. You may be surprised to find me talking with passion of such a remote past. I too am surprised. Perhaps it is because once again I want to die, that the old days seem so clear to the mind's eye.[10]

As a child Baudelaire had already acquired his "unique, his dominant passion," the love of visual images. Even then he could never satisfy his greed for them.[11] At the same time he already had the sense that he was alone, cut off from humanity, from family and friends, in a privileged and isolated situation:

> A sense of *solitude* from childhood on. Despite my family—above all in the company of my friends—a sense of a future of un-

remitting solitude. With, however, a great love of life and of pleasure.[12]

This sense of being alone must have developed while living in the solemn atmosphere of an old-fashioned, dark, and dignified apartment, with a father who had lived the greater part of his life in another age, an age as remote as another world. This combined with Baudelaire's childhood sensuality and sensitivity to create a delicate introspective boy, over-responsive to the caresses and the praise of adults, with a precocious awareness of his own identity and tastes—a precocity reinforced by a father who had had no experience of young children for some fifteen years, and who treated his son as an adult. Thus Charles was never exposed to the moralizing platitudes of children's literature, "having as a child had the good or bad fortune to read only massive grown-up books."[13] This brief glimpse of his early reading completes the picture of a curious, sensual, sensitive, and precocious child, passionately attached to his widowed mother.

Joseph-François left a considerable fortune to his two sons. It was to be administered by a family trust, or *conseil de famille*, consisting of old friends, such as the Duc de Choiseul-Praslin and the painter Naigeon.

It was during the period immediately after his father's death that the family moved to 30 Place St. André des Arts, the period Baudelaire recalled in his nostalgic letter. They subsequently lived at 17 Rue du Bac still on the Left Bank, and it is there that we first meet the officer Jacques Aupick, who was to be Baudelaire's stepfather—and his mortal enemy.

Aupick had risen through the ranks of Napoleon's army, gaining most of his promotions on active service. He was a brilliantly successful careerist, who would serve two empires, two monarchies, and a republic with indiscriminate zeal. When he placed himself between mother and son, he had become a battalion commander.

He was also an extremely attractive man: a straightforward, forceful, and efficient soldier. Caroline Baudelaire fell very much in love with him, and he was the perfect match for that kind, pleasure-loving, and slightly limited woman. The intensity of their mutual affection is born witness to by the still-born child to which Caroline gave birth less than a month after the wedding.

It is hard to paint an objective portrait of Aupick. Baudelaire's view of him in later years renders the task impossible. Still harder is it to see what Baudelaire thought about him as a boy. At first sight the situation sounds like the basis for a Gallic *David Copperfield*. Certainly Charles's mother would marry again, and her son would be sent to a somewhat trying boarding school—for his own good. But Aupick was

15

no Mister Murdstone. He was a limited, but kind and well-intentioned officer who was anxious to bring up his stepson as if he were his own; the more anxious since his wife was never to bear him a child. Aupick, however, was ill-equipped and too busy to deal with the delicate sensitivities and searing jealousy of his stepson. But if Baudelaire felt evicted from his garden of Eden—and he did—there is little to suggest that Aupick threw him out by the scruff of his neck. Only once does an early letter Baudelaire wrote to his half-brother suggest that the young boy might have been "in the way": he was obliged to remain in lodgings for the summer holiday of 1832, although Aupick had promised to take him on a trip.

The mature Baudelaire was to enjoy contriving dramatic or erotic situations artificially, for the sake of the sensations which they might arouse. The distortion or contrivance of experience in the interests of more or less perverse sensation was to be an essential characteristic of his temperament, and the central theme of his art. It may be argued that Baudelaire imposed upon Aupick the role of a cruel stepfather, a role which did him grave injustice, but which he was too limited and conventional not to assume when provoked by his exasperating stepson. Yet neither provocation nor resentment were immediate. On the contrary, for some ten years Baudelaire's attitude towards his stepfather was to be characterized, at least on the surface, by a desire to please.

The stereotype images of Baudelaire—the impassive dandy, mulatto mistress on his arm, crushingly assertive; or the ageing and broken poet, who achieved a serene puritanism of mind and body through an ascetic's exploration of evil and vice—both these are very partial truths. From childhood on there will persist another Baudelaire: the Baudelaire who will write respectful, adulatory letters to celebrities; the Baudelaire who flatters the bourgeoisie in his art criticism; the Baudelaire who longs for public acclaim, and who wants very much to be liked. The desire for recognition and acceptance will sometimes be less apparent than the urge to shock and repel, yet the desire to please would never leave him and may be witnessed at its strongest in his school days, as will soon be seen.

IN DECEMBER 1831 Aupick was posted to Lyons on a strike-breaking mission, which he accomplished so successfully that he was given a permanent staff appointment there. Wife and stepson joined him early in 1832. In later years Baudelaire would describe Lyons as "A strange city, bigoted and commercial. Both Catholic and Protestant, full of mist and smoke."[1] Its impact upon the ten-year-old child was more immediate and less philosophical. The young Parisian disliked it intensely and missed the capital. In a letter to his half-brother he wrote:

> I have nothing to say except that I detest the Lyonnais, that they are dirty, mean, and selfish. . . . I loathe the *pension*, it is dirty, badly run, untidy, the pupils are unpleasant and dirty like all Lyonnais.[2]

The *pension*, however, was a temporary arrangement; Baudelaire shortly became a boarder at the Lyons Collège Royal. This was a school run on military lines. Instead of a bell being rung to mark the hour, a drum was beaten. The school also boasted a military band. It is obvious why Aupick should have chosen such an establishment for his stepson; equally obvious why Baudelaire would look back on his schooldays with revulsion, writing to his mother:

> . . . you know what a terrible education your husband wished me to have: I'm forty now, and I cannot think without suffering of the school or of the fear I felt of my stepfather. However I liked him, and know enough today to appreciate him. But he was obstinately clumsy.[3]

Apart from the occasional murmur, however, the young Baudelaire never made it apparent that he detested his school. Certainly it was not the calmest of places. In 1834, for example, there was a rebellion in Lyons, which lasted four days before being savagely repressed. There was violent fighting around the college, and the pupils were cut off. Several nearby houses were burnt and the boys helped to fight the fires. They were subsequently sent home while the damage was being repaired. Ten days after the college reopened, a school riot broke out. Baudelaire provides accounts of more mundane incidents:

> Dear Brother,
>   A lot of unrest in school. A master hit a pupil and gave him a pain in the chest. He is very ill and unable to get up. After half an hour of prep the pupil didn't know his homework and passed notes asking for help. The supervisor found out and was his usual stupid self. The pupil passed another note—for which he was beaten, and he replied with a few kicks. The supervisor wanted to end the fight at a blow and kicked him in the behind. The drum went for supper. The pupil took his usual place in the line. The supervisor sent him to the back, saying he didn't deserve to go with the others. After supper he put him in the coal hole for the same reason. Sometimes he came and slapped him; the pupil had a bad back and was not able to duck. . . . Two days later I . . . hear that he is in the sick bay, unable to stand, and that he had collapsed on parade. The nurse wants to get rid of the supervisor, but he is well in with the head.
>   We gave him a serenade in the yard that the head heard in his rooms. The supervisor laughed at what we were doing, on the wrong side of his face. I'm one of the rebels. I don't want to be one of those arse-lickers who are scared of offending the supervisors.[4]

Not the quietest of schools but, although he admittedly reacts against the discipline, there is no sign that the young Baudelaire suffers there or that he is actively miserable.

Indeed the dominant note struck in these early letters is an eagerness to please. He writes frequently to his half-brother Alphonse, who is in his late twenties, and his letters have a certain coy charm. Chiding "Monsieur Elder Brother" for not answering, they go on to tell of his scholastic successes or apologize for his failures. He wants, purely and simply, to be liked:

> Dear Brother,
>   I have received your letter; I see that you complain that I am a lazy letter writer. I write to you today to reproach you

in your turn. What! Not a word for three months—three months, no for much longer. But pray be silent, Monsieur Younger Brother, it is not for you to reprimand your elder, were his faults more serious still.[5]

He seems to have been as eager to please Aupick as he was Alphonse, and appears genuinely fond of his stepfather. Yet even now, in these early letters, we can detect a number of the tones and attitudes which would dominate both his correspondence and his outlook for the rest of his life. He is anxious to please to the point of being obsequious. For all his aloofness and his pride Baudelaire would never find it difficult to grovel; it is as if he purged himself through humiliation. His letters to his family throughout this period frequently strike notes of obsequious zeal. He claims to be full of schoolboy pride and ambition. The desire to please is there, even if his professed zeal is not always confirmed by results.

The Lyons schoolboy was already displaying the characteristically Baudelarian blend of high hopes and present idleness, an idleness which the school recognized and denied him a day out. Baudelaire was obliged to explain the embarrassing situation to his parents. Explanation was followed by a letter in which he pleaded his case with eloquence. Full of high hopes and self-recrimination, Baudelaire, as always, looked forward to better times:

The last time I promised not to give cause for concern any more, I meant what I said, I intended to work, and work hard, for you to be able to say we have a son who is grateful for the care we lavish upon him; but foolishness and idleness made me forget what I felt when I promised. It is not my heart that needs replacing, the heart is true enough, it is my mind that needs bracing, that must be made to think sensibly enough to produce sustained serious thoughts. You are both beginning to think me ungrateful; you are perhaps convinced of it. How can I make you change your minds? I know: I'll start to work at once; but whatever I do, the time I have wasted, by forgetting what I owed you, will always remain a black mark. How can I make you forget immediately three months of bad behavior? . . .

You despaired of me, as of a son gone hopelessly wrong . . . who is an idler. Flabby, cowardly, and unable to take a grip of himself. I *was* flabby, cowardly, idle. . . . But as nothing can change the heart, my heart, which despite its faults has its good sides, has remained the same. . . . The very idea that you might consider me ungrateful gave me a little courage. If you no longer have the courage to come and see me in college, write

19

to me and give me the advice and encouragement you would have given in person. . . . They are giving out the natural history marks on Thursday morning; I hope for a good one. Shall I tell you why? I recently had a very very bad one, but the desire to wipe out this insult made me take trouble over this morning's composition.[6]

We can already hear the voice of the mature apologetic Baudelaire, who begs forgiveness and promises to do better. There is no hypocrisy here. Just as he remained optimistic about his own prospects, so he would always believe that he was about to mend his ways. Thus he writes to his mother on February 6, 1834, begging her forgiveness. He has again been denied a day out, but it will be the last such denial; from now on he is going to work. But somehow things don't turn out quite as he had hoped. It took him longer than he had expected to get back in stride, and although his marks had improved, they were still not quite good enough, and a fortnight later he was obliged to write that he had been refused still another day out.

At the age of thirteen the tone of his mature letters is already there— a tone of self-justification and promising, with a minimal degree of anecdote and little or no desire to entertain the correspondent. Then as always Baudelaire would write from need: the need for self-vindication, a self-vindication accompanied by inveterate optimism. Baudelaire was perpetually convinced that he was about to do better, that something was about to turn up. Never allowing failure to erode hope, he would remain optimistic to the bitter end. Indeed, few men have attempted to live on hope to the extent that Baudelaire did, but then few men have had such a desperate need for some kind of hope to live on.

However, on this occasion, and for the last time, he kept his promise. He really did overcome his natural inertia, his dislike of routine, his lack of capacity for sustained, concentrated, and boring work. He completed his career at the Collège Royal with considerable distinction, winning various prizes including one for drawing. Aupick was pleased by his stepson's performance. When he was promoted and posted to Paris in 1836, he enrolled Charles as a border in the Collège Louis-le-Grand, informing the headmaster that he was giving him a "present," a boy who would do honor to his school. He was right, but it was not exactly the kind of honor that French *lycées* welcome.

Louis-le-Grand was not the right school for a sensitive boy already excited by the radical transformations which romanticism was bringing to French culture. Rather later in the century a former pupil of another school, the Lycée Condorcet, suggested that Condorcet boys who were day boys were much more sophisticated than their counterparts who boarded at the other great Parisian schools. The day boys prided themselves on being in the Parisian swim from an early age, while boarders seemed uncouth and unsophisticated in comparison. Certainly Louis-le-Grand did not encourage sophistication. The school seems to have been another stage in the toughening process which Aupick considered to be the most important feature of his stepson's upbringing. Another pupil, the somewhat abject man of letters Maxime du Camp, a year younger than Baudelaire and never appreciative of his genius, has left us the following picture of the school:

> The college is alleged to build character; I did not perceive anything of the sort, but I did see that it made me become bad-tempered, estranged, deceitful.[7]

Its strict discipline turned pupils into rebels, he says, as he describes its gloomy atmosphere. Homework was done by candlelight, although the supervisor had a wire-covered argand lamp, or *quinquet*, to help him keep order. It was known as the *"quinquet des révoltes,"* and every pupil dreamed of rebellion. The school even had cells for solitary confinement, cells which had held political prisoners during the Reign of Terror. When banished to a punishment cell, the pupil had to do 1500–1800 Latin lines a day. The "gaoler" would allow him to spend ten minutes in front of the stove—for a consideration of two sous. Pupils not actually confined to cells were allowed out once a fortnight.

Maxime du Camp reveals his indifferent literary judgment when he proudly mentions three boys expelled from his old school who made good in the world of literature. All are forgotten today. He fails to mention the most distinguished French poet to have been expelled from any school: Charles Baudelaire.

At first Baudelaire was a good student. He won various prizes and seemed set upon a distinguished school career. His letters contain few descriptions of school life; he would never be that sort of letter writer. However, we do get one glimpse. Should his mother come to visit him when he is ill, on no account should she go to the infirmary: "Because you will have to cross the yard, and pupils, running, might inadvertently knock you to the ground and kill you."[8]

The tone of Baudelaire's letters had not changed much since Lyons, but his character had. He was already developing his strange combination of delicacy and violence, the desire to please going hand in hand with the urge to shock. A contemporary observes:

> He was highly excitable, sometimes full of mysticism, sometimes immoral and cynical (in speech alone) to the point of excess; in a word he was an eccentric; passionately fond of poetry, reciting lines of Hugo, Gautier, etc., at the drop of a hat. I, and many of our comrades, felt his mind was out of joint.[9]

Although this is the reaction of a *"labadens"* or "swot," who, even in retrospect, had little sympathy for the scandalous poet, it suggests that there was more to the young Baudelaire than his letters reveal. Provocative and violent alternation of moods, lack of stability, went hand in hand with an enthusiasm for the new poetry.

Romanticism had developed late in France, and it was only in the 1830s that it began to dominate the literature. Writers such as Hugo, de Vigny, Musset, Sainte-Beuve, and, a little later, Gautier, brought a new kind of feeling-tone into poetry. They attached supreme importance to authenticity of emotion. The poet had become an aristocrat of feeling in an essentially hostile world.

The 1830s and '40s, the age of the July Monarchy, was the age of the banker and the speculator. It is summed up by Prime Minister Guizot's command to his electorate: "Get rich." In the face of the triumph of money over all other considerations, the romantic poets took refuge. They constructed for themselves royalist or republican political utopias, or hid in private emotion or in a feverish and violent world of Gothic fantasy. The poet was essentially out of harmony with his age, a fact reflected in the extravagant, dislocated, unstable, often desperate quality of his art and personality. This sense of being at odds with one's civilization would remain the dominant note in both the poetry and the personality of French writers for a hundred years.

It is also a quality which would come to dominate Baudelaire's own art—the reflection of an urgent quest for serenity and fulfillment conducted by a desperate and violently destructive personality. Failure to achieve serenity will lead to hysterical clowning, the striking of poses, and savage irony. These qualities can already be found in the schoolboy of Louis-le-Grand. His personality, his attitudes, are already in tune with the artistic spirit of his age.

It is not possible to say whether the fourteen-year-old Baudelaire was "really" like that or whether he was aping his elders. There is no doubt, however, that he was no longer the same boy he had been in Lyons. A contemporary who had known him there as being finer and more distinguished than his fellow pupils, found him in Paris—a rebel, "altered, sadder, more bitter."[10] This confirms du Camp's views of the effect of the Parisian school upon its inmates.

Baudelaire is already writing poetry, in imitation of his elders such as the critic and poet Saint-Beuve, whom he admired passionately. He imitates his tones of slightly low-key disenchantment and despair with considerable effect.

Although there is every reason to believe that Baudelaire enjoyed a "difficult" adolescence and was something of a rebel, his relationship with his stepfather remains smooth enough on the surface. He inquires anxiously after his health when Aupick starts to suffer from an old bullet wound in the knee that he incurred at the battle of Fleurus in 1815 (the offending missile, not removed until 1835, is preserved in the town hall of Gravelines, Aupick's birthplace). Young Baudelaire is very concerned about "papa's" state of health. "Papa" spends so much time entertaining the family when fit, that mother and stepson must do all they can for him now that he is ill.[11]

At the age of seventeen he continues to write with great affection to Aupick, and is still anxious to win the approval of both parents. In one of his rare, long and informative letters the future art critic describes to Aupick a school visit to Versailles, to see the royal art collection. His impressions are on the whole naive, but ingenious art historians have detected hints of his later critical attitudes. Admittedly the letter ends with a request to provide him with an extra tutor—an excuse to get out of school more often. This makes the whole piece and the sentiments expressed a trifle suspect; but, nevertheless, Baudelaire is able to end his letter with the words "I adore you," apparently without feeling that he is striking a false note.[12]

However, Baudelaire has started to slip down a slope which will only end with his death. His school reports are no longer flattering. He is not good at philosophy. In 1838 one of his schoolmasters, a M. Carrière, gives the following report:

Good behavior during religious practices, good behavior out of class. Had a long way to go before becoming unaffected and bearable.
He succeeded, which I think is commendable. Works but is somewhat disorganized.

As usual, though, he fails to keep it up. Three months later the same master writes:

. . . has recently readopted his eccentric mannerisms. I had to impose several rather severe punishments. It is tiresome that this pupil, who started on the right track this year, should enjoy setting a bad example.[13]

Another master describes him as follows:

Very flighty; lacks the energy to correct his weaknesses. Not good at classical languages, capricious and careless; a butterfly mind, lack of application in composition work.

A third writes:

> No stamina in his character. His behavior is excessively frivolous.
> His work as a result is not what it should be. A pity because he
> has what is required to do well.[14]

The reports isolate a vital aspect of Baudelaire's personality: a
total inaptitude for sustained and concentrated work. His loathing of
routine, of the everyday, made him unable to fulfill the normal demands
of a conventional existence, demands which most people carry out as a
matter of course. Baudelaire would always have to make a real effort
of will to conform to a routine; every day would require a renewal of
that effort, and steadfastness of will would never be, in any normal
sense, one of Baudelaire's strong points. Instead he was endowed with
great charm and enthusiasm, a passionate curiosity, a profound capacity
for artistic concentration; but he had no ability to concentrate on the
day-to-day business of survival. Never the sort who could face, let
alone read or check, a bank statement, small wonder that Baudelaire
the man would eventually go under.

Even during the period of his initial success at Lyons we can see
signs of this. His mother writes to Alphonse announcing triumphantly
that Baudelaire has regularly placed top or second out of fifty. He is a
far from ordinary boy, full of promise but:

> So frivolous, so mad, so fond of playing. . . . The only serious
> reproach we have is that he fools about in class instead of work-
> ing and always waits for the last moment before doing his
> work. . . . Tell him how important it is in life to do *what must be
> done* at once, and that *always putting things off* is a fault which will
> have the most serious consequences. This fault in your brother
> makes me despair.[15]

Rightly so. At this stage, however, Baudelaire would delay only as
long as possible before doing things. Within a few years he would still
be waiting to begin well beyond any possible last moment. This deadly
capacity for procrastination would be among the most serious of all
his shortcomings.

It is characteristic of Baudelaire's attitude to his weaknesses that
he would always admit them. In later life he was to set great store by
what he referred to as *"la conscience dans le mal"*—the conscious awareness of one's own evil. He would regard as his one consolation and pride
the fact that the wrongdoer who admitted and faced up to his evil was
at least superior to someone who pretended that his evil did not exist.
This belief in the value of clarity of consciousness was to be his lifeline.

24

It is a peculiarly Catholic trait, not unconnected with the practice of confession. Clarity of *consciousness* with respect to one's own weaknesses takes the place of *conscience*, and has the effect, if not of absolving, then at least of allowing one to live with one's weaknesses with a fair degree of comfort.

It is in just this spirit that Baudelaire writes to his half-brother:

> My only mistake, or rather mistakes, are caused by an eternal idleness, which makes me put everything off till tomorrow, even writing to people I am fond of. I have an absolutely insuperable reluctance when it comes to putting my thoughts on paper; and at school you may imagine how I detest copying out my work. I really don't know how people manage in jobs which require a lot of letter writing. . . .[16]

Yet for all his awareness of his idleness, he still seeks the approval of his family. It is only much later that Baudelaire the broken man will seek to ensure (controlled) rejection as a means of achieving peace: "When I shall have inspired universal disgust and horror I shall have achieved solitude."[17]

In 1839 Baudelaire experienced the first significant failure of his life. He had for some time been a difficult pupil. His posing, his extravagance of thought, his exotic literary leanings, his rejection of the values which his school represented, had long been apparent. Matters came to a head in the spring. Colonel Aupick received the following letter from his stepson's headmaster:

> Sir:
> This morning your son, called on by the Deputy Director to hand over a note which one of his friends had passed to him, tore it up and swallowed it. Summoned by me, he stated that he would accept any kind of punishment rather than reveal the secret of his fellow pupil, and urged to explain himself in the very interest of his friend, whom he exposed to the direst suspicions, he answered with a sneering impertinence which I cannot tolerate. Therefore I am sending this young man back to you; he was endowed with very considerable abilities, but has wrecked everything by a remarkably wicked temperament, which the discipline of the school has had to endure on more occasions than one.[18]

It is not easy to say why he was expelled. The actual reason appears to be a pretext, or the last of a series of comparable acts of insubordination. It has been suggested that beneath the episode lay what the French term a *"histoire de dortoir,"* i.e., a homosexual escapade. Biographers who wish to make Baudelaire's life as exotic and varied as possible are happy to entertain that possibility. But on the whole it seems unlikely, or at least irrelevant to the rest of his life. It is much more likely that Baudelaire indulged his readiness to rage against authority once too often and was expelled for his general attitude.

We have a letter from Baudelaire to his ex-headmaster, written on the same day. It is full of apologies and begs to be taken back for the sake of his mother, who is dreadfully upset. Although it seems likely that the letter was never sent, it is the kind of letter which Baudelaire, for all his raging, would never find difficult to write.

Even after his expulsion he still seeks his parents' approval, and appears to be on reasonable terms with them. He had not, of course, taken the *baccalauréat*, the exam which all French schoolboys take when they leave the *lycée* to qualify them for entrance to the university, and so he continued his studies as a day boy at the Collège Saint-Louis, staying in lodgings run by the parents of one of his tutors. From there he writes to his stepfather, thanking him for a fine, affectionate letter, and continuing:

> Here, frankly, is the reason why, for a week, I have put off writing to you: I have to tell you what I am doing, and I thought that before writing I would get back to work, so that I'd have some kind words to say about myself. But you chide me with such kindness in your letter that, my word, I'd rather own up than put off writing to you, or tell lies. Rest assured, the next time I write I'll have some kind words to say about myself.[19]

Baudelaire was eighteen when he wrote that. It is hard to know how much it tells us about his feelings for Aupick. Certainly he wanted to please, just as later he would often try to please writers such as Victor Hugo or George Sand, for whom he had little respect. He never found it difficult to write like that to anyone, and it may be that beneath his desire to please his stepfather, the young man already nursed a profound loathing for him. He was intelligent enough to understand how unsuited he had been for the education that Aupick had chosen for him. Moreover, precocious adolescent that Baudelaire was, it is not unlikely that his jealousy of Aupick had taken on a different, and better-informed, complexion as it grew tinged with his own developing sexual awareness. But this is all speculation. There is no direct evidence of any tension between the two, although one may imagine that Aupick, the good professional soldier and careerist, must have been appalled by his stepson's wayward behavior. Nevertheless when he passed his exam on the same day that Aupick was promoted to the rank of brigadier, Baudelaire was only too happy to congratulate his step-father and give him his own good news.

At eighteen Baudelaire was already beginning to pay the extravagant emotional price of his laziness and his inability to concentrate. Shortly after his graduation he wrote to his mother complaining that at school he at least had his work to do; now he was much worse off. His expulsion had made him buckle down at first, but now he did absolutely *nothing*; it was not a poetic or agreeable state of indolence that was burdening him, but a feeling of stupidness, a sickness at heart. Baudelaire would always remain incapable of self-delusion, even when unable to work or to concentrate. This paradoxical blend of indolence and lucidity was the mood he would describe as *ennui*: a condition of self-disgust, emptiness, waste, and above all of moral and physical paralysis, which, while it endured, seemed fated to last for all eternity. In its most acute form it would leave him with nothing but the awareness of time's passing—passing both with a terrible slowness and a fearful speed as the river of time threatened to wash him away before he had achieved anything. This *ennui*, or *spleen*, would later develop into a pathological condition and lead him to take recourse to the most desperate and self-destructive behavior in an attempt to jerk himself out of his sorry state.

It was generally assumed that after getting his *baccalauréat* he would study for the Foreign Office. But the young Baudelaire was in no hurry to "take the first job that came along." He writes to his half-brother:

> I've finished my final year and am to start a new kind of life; it seems strange, and of all my worries the greatest is the choice of a career. It disturbs and torments me, the more so since I feel no sense of vocation, and feel torn between one thing and another.
>
> The advice I request is not much help, for to choose you have to know what you're choosing, and I know nothing about the various careers that life has to offer. To choose you have to experiment, try out, so that it follows that before adopting a profession you must have experienced them all, which is absurd and impossible.[20]

He goes on to ask for Alphonse's advice. The letter is important because it negates the belief that from an early age he had a burning desire to be a poet. It may be that he was trying to soft-soap his lawyer half-brother by introducing him gradually to his plans, but it seems more likely that at this stage Baudelaire simply did not know what he wanted to be.

The plan he eventually announced to his parents, the plan to pursue a literary career, must be viewed with some reserve. It does not appear to be the fulfillment of a long-held and steadfast commitment to the Muses. In any event, deciding to become a writer was not that risky a financial step for Baudelaire, for he stood to take possession, on his majority, of a half share of his father's estate. It was a substantial inheritance, and enough to dispense him from working if he were to content himself with a relatively modest existence. In the second place, it was possible in the 1830s to live off the writing of "high literature"; Victor Hugo was the outstanding example of an author who had made a commercial success of literature—poetry still sold during that decade. Besides it was a period in which "low literature," popular novels and journalism, was expanding rapidly, offering at least the promise of a reasonable living to be made by the pen.

Baudelaire's family consented to his choice of profession although it caused his mother considerable initial distress—with more to come over the years. Aupick, on the other hand, was remarkably sensible. He regarded his stepson's decision as something he would grow out of; in the meantime he was prepared to let him try. "Let him be a poet if he wishes, as long as he does not draw his inspiration from the gutters," he said. This, his only known comment on literature, revealed great perspicacity about his stepson; he suspected that it was all too likely that this is just what Baudelaire would do—and he was right.

Most important was Baudelaire's unwillingness to commit himself to any profession. The late 1830s witnessed the birth of Baudelaire the indolent dandy, the elegant arbiter of taste and life-style: to adopt a profession, to work, was inconsistent with his idea of himself as an elegant, sophisticated young man of means who had just escaped the discipline of family life. In the next few years he was to embark upon a quest for identity and self-affirmation through stylishness and conspicuous elegance of both being and appearance. He at last had the opportunity to be himself: a self he would create through a blend of charm, wit, insolence, irony, talent, and a fastidious elegance of dress. What could be a more suitable activity for him than the part of a man of letters?

ETWEEN 1839 AND 1841 the would-be writer lived the life of a
nonstudying student in the Latin Quarter. Rather than embark
at once upon a serious literary career, Baudelaire used his time
to sow wild oats. He made friends with a number of young men
in the Pension Bailly, a high-class student lodging in the Place de
l'Estrapade, in the heart of the student quarter. There he met Ernest
Prarond, Gustave Le Vavasseur, Philippe de Chennevières, and Jules
Buisson, minor men of letters in-the-making, none of whom would be
remembered today where it not for their recollections of Baudelaire.
Together they formed the so-called Ecole Normande, the Norman
school, and produced a number of unremarkable poems. Baudelaire
was to publish some work in an anthology they had planned, but withdrew his poems just before the collection went to press.

Le Vavasseur recalls Baudelaire at the Pension Bailly, telling us
how much he felt drawn to him:

> He had dark hair, I was blond; he was of average height, I was
> short; thin as an ascetic, I was fat as a prelate; clean as a stoat
> where I was as scruffy as a poodle; he dressed like the secretary
> of an English embassy, I dressed like a box-office clerk; reserved
> where I was noisy; a libertine out of curiosity where I was virtu-
> ous out of laziness; a pagan out of rebelliousness, where I was a
> Christian out of conformity; caustic where I was kind; wracking
> his brains to mock his feelings, where I let the two trot along
> side by side as if in harness.[1]

Baudelaire's association with the students of the Pension Bailly
marked the beginning of his dandyism. The elegant, exquisitely
dressed youth would pick his way through crowds of bearded, pipe-
smoking, beer-drinking students, with their exotic cloaks, their velvet

hats, or artists' smocks. Like Le Vavasseur, Ernest Prarond describes him, placing great emphasis on his delicacy, elegance, and aloofness:

> I can still see him today, coming down a staircase in the Bailly house, slim, a low collar, an extremely long waistcoat, detached cuffs, carrying a light cane with a small gold head, walking with a supple, almost rhythmic step . . . at twenty Baudelaire had a somewhat yellow and even complexion, which had a little color on the cheekbones; a delicate beard which he didn't clip, and which did not smother his face.
>
> His expression, sharpened sometimes by genuine malice, sometimes by irony, would relax when he stopped talking or listening to withdraw into himself. It would become very calm, without going slack. I cannot remember him ever losing his temper. By gosh, though, he would not suffer fools, or cliché-mongers, or boring *poseurs*.[2]

The elegance, poise, and pose, the hint of aggressive irony, the aloofness, are basic ingredients of Baudelaire's dandyism. In one respect this dandyism was unusual: it was quite unrelated to the activity which absorbed the time and energy of most would-be elegant young Frenchmen of that, and later, ages—compulsive social climbing.

The burning urge to go up and up in the world until finally penetrating the rarified and exclusive milieu of a decaying nobility was for a hundred years the ambition of virtually every young hero of French literature trying to make his mark. In the nineteenth century we find ambitious young men of this kind in the works of Stendhal, Balzac, and Flaubert; Proust, in the twentieth, was to create the definitive version of the type. The conventional would-be dandy would not feel that he had achieved that perfection of the self to which all dandies aspire until he was a welcome guest in the pathetically exclusive *salons* of the Faubourg St.-Germain. It is true that heroes of French literature tended eventually to discover that the acquaintance of duchesses was a dead sea fruit, but it was a lesson that they learned the hard way.

Baudelaire was free of such ambitions and aspirations. His dandyism was not a means to an end, it was an end in itself. From the days of the Pension Bailly onwards, he would always be quite happy to be "all dressed up with nowhere to go." He dressed for himself, not for society. As E. Crépet writes:

> Despite his cult of dress Baudelaire was not a socialite. It was for his own personal satisfaction that he sought elegance. He only moved among his own set, for he had bravely dedicated himself to a long apprenticeship, which, in poetry as in any other art or

trade, is the necessary condition of mastery. His incipient originality took on a fiercely aloof and truculent form.[3]

Although some of the poets of the Ecole Normande were to remain close friends, he also made more important literary contacts at this time. He met the poet and man of letters Gérard de Nerval, whose suicide some years later was to haunt him for the rest of his own life. Nerval wrote some of the most remarkable sonnets in the language, but he is better remembered by some for his eccentricities—such as the lobster he used to take for long slow walks on a leash in the Bois de Boulogne. Baudelaire also made contact with Victor Hugo. He wrote him an adulatory letter thanking him for the pleasure caused by his play *Marion Delorme*. He eventually summoned up enough courage to call on the great man, almost running away when the door was opened. Hugo received the timid young Baudelaire with great kindness.

He also met Honoré de Balzac—in rather different circumstances. Ernest Prarond describes their meeting:

> Balzac and Baudelaire were walking towards one another along a *quai* on the Left Bank. Baudelaire stopped in front of Balzac and started to laugh, as if he had known him for ten years. Balzac also stopped, and replied with a great guffaw, as if meeting a long-lost friend. And after having *recognized* and greeted one another, they set off together, talking, charming one another, each finding it impossible to astonish the other.[4]

The Pension Bailly has been portrayed as a hotbed of frivolity and vice. Yet this is not entirely so. Most of the young men there were engaged in academic study and were basically perfectly serious. Baudelaire himself enrolled in law school, although he did not spend much time there. For all the studying done, however, this was also a time of wild parties and the assertion of eccentricities, a time for practical joking, student pranks, and the sowing of wild oats.

Students of the age made a habit of taking *grisettes*, or working-class girls, who were on the whole commercially disinterested, for their mistresses. Baudelaire was no exception; but he was to continue reaping his particular harvest of oats for the rest of his life.

He acquired a mistress, a certain "Squinting Sarah," who was apparently Jewish. Judging by a line he once wrote—"One night as I lay beside a hideous Jewess"—she was far from lovely. That is all we know of her appearance. Yet there is a very faint possibility that her portrait is today hanging in the Louvre. One of Baudelaire's earliest poems is entitled "A une mendiante rousse" ["To a red-headed beggar girl"], a delightful evocation of a red-haired, ragged, yet beautiful beggar. Now the painter Emile Deroy, a close friend of the poet who painted the finest portrait of him, also painted around this time the portrait of a red-headed beggar girl—which now hangs in the Louvre. On close inspection she can be seen to be cross-eyed. If she is Baudelaire's Sarah, she was far from ugly.

Ugly or not, his association had disastrous consequences that first appear as early as 1839. He writes to Alphonse, thanking him for the money sent to buy medicines. He goes on:

> No pains in my joints anymore, and the headaches have almost gone, I am sleeping better, but my digestion is terrible and I have a continual slight discharge which does not hurt; my complexion is splendid so that no one suspects a thing.[5]

Baudelaire has had his first experience of the disease that was delicately termed *le mal du siècle*. The nineteenth century in France might indeed be termed the age of venereal disease, syphilis was almost as common then as nonspecific urethritis is today, and it was even harder to cure. On this occasion, however, Baudelaire seems to have suffered no more than a severe attack of gonorrhorea from which he made a partial recovery. But by 1841 it is certain that he already had syphilis.

In the meantime his relationship with his family was beginning to disintegrate. He had been obliged to turn to his brother for extra money to obtain the drugs he needed. The request inaugurates the long and wretched series of begging letters which he was to continue writing for the rest of his life. As usual he says that he is begging for the last time:

> I say *one last time*, not in order to make you worried about your generosity, but in order to force myself not to rely continuously upon someone else's money, for my brother will not be there for ever.[6]

He was perfectly correct; his half-brother was not prepared to continue bailing him out for ever. Baudelaire would soon be obliged to look to other pockets.

Alphonse lent a little money to his half-brother, on the assumption that boys will be boys. But Alphonse, who had become a careful and hard-headed lawyer, soon understood that Baudelaire was no ordinary boy. The youth continued to run up debts. He requested more and more money, always including with his plea acknowledgments of his present idleness:

> I imagine you would like to know how I spend my days in Paris.

Since I left you, I have not been near the Law School or the lawyer—in fact there were complaints that I attended so rarely. But I have postponed a general reform of my behavior to 1841.[7]

What Alphonse really wanted to know, however, was where his money was going. Accordingly Baudelaire sent his half-brother an account of his debts—which he found to his surprise were far greater than he had supposed. They include items such as 200 francs spent on clothes for a prostitute kidnapped out of a BROTHEL (his capitals). Of the 2,185 francs he owed, 1,395 were spent on clothes. It is significant that the long list of itemized debts should finish with the statement that "all these figures are approximate."[8] One may be tempted to dismiss this as an idle young man's inability to keep accounts. But future events suggest that there is more here than incompetent bookkeeping.

As he grew older Baudelaire would suffer more and more from an inability to face the facts of his situation. This manifested itself in a refusal to keep an accurate record of his expenditures—he could not bear to see his extravagance clearly spelt out. Anyone who finds checking his bank statements so painful that he destroys them after a single furtive glance at the size of his overdraft—or who finds it impossible to open the envelope at all—will understand something of what Baudelaire felt, with ever-increasing pain, whenever he could no longer avoid facing his financial situation. Eventually his phobia would become so bad that he was obliged to ask his friends to write their names on the envelopes of their letters; otherwise he would not open them in case they turned out to be requests for payment. The roots of this fear, which will develop into an inability to face reality of any kind, is already present in Baudelaire's reluctance to admit to Alphonse, or to himself, precisely how much he owes.

Alphonse, the kind of man who would positively look forward to receiving bank statements, finds his vagueness intolerable:

My dear brother,
You must realize that I was most upset the other day when you told me that you needed money, because that in itself suggests that you are leading a disorderly life. I asked you then to describe your situation in writing, to place in my brotherly hand the overall balance sheet of your debts, and to tell me the names and addresses of your creditors, and the reasons for your debts. I hoped for a letter from a serious man, not a scrap of paper covered with ink stains, an apothecary's account of the sort presented to stage-comedy relatives who pay all debts in their totality without checking them.[9]

He then proceeds to go through the account, asking, ironically, for more details, for names and addresses. The steady Alphonse has advice to give the young dandy about his mode of dress:

> 120 francs. 3 waistcoats. That means 40 francs a waistcoat. Waistcoats only cost me 18–20 francs, and I am huge![10]

He goes on to say how much he respects Aupick, who had brought Baudelaire up as his own son. (Baudelaire had been refused money by a number of persons reluctant to upset a man so widely esteemed as General Aupick.) Alphonse, however, was ready to help. If his half-brother was really prepared to reform his behavior, Alphonse would tell Aupick the whole sorry story, thereby saving Baudelaire the humiliation of telling it himself. He also offered to settle the debts—by borrowing against Baudelaire's inheritance. Warning him that he had already alienated much of the general's affection, "which I consider to be very bad of you," he urged the youth to give up his disreputable liaisons and mend his ways.[11]

Baudelaire's response to the admonition was pure rage. He replied, describing it as a "harsh and humiliating letter," and then begged Alphonse at least to settle the two most pressing debts—a tailor and a shirtmaker.

THE BEGINNING OF 1840 was a busy time for the Aupicks. Baudelaire's stepfather had received two promotions within three months: in mid-January he was made commandant of the Second Infantry Brigade of the Paris garrison, and in early March he became head of the Staff College. His career was clearly advancing apace, and it is understandable that he failed to observe his difficult stepson, still living in the Latin Quarter, as closely as he would have liked.

It was at this time, however, that the Aupicks—thanks to Alphonse, no doubt—began to get an inkling of the extent of Baudelaire's misconduct. The youth was about to come into his money, and his family clearly had misgivings about the boy, his future, and the future of his capital. Then as now, "raiding capital" was the most serious offense a sensible French family could imagine. Something had to be done to straighten out the dissolute young spendthrift. Accordingly, Aupick wrote Alphonse the following letter, which reveals so much about the officer and his incisive, well-intentioned, though exceedingly conventional personality. It also indicates why his stepson would come to hate him:

Dear M. Baudelaire,
The time has come when something must be done to prevent the absolute ruin of your brother. I am at least more or less aware of his situation, his behavior, his habits. The danger is great; perhaps a remedy may still be found; but I must see you and discuss what I propose, tell you the point of mental and physical degeneracy which Charles has reached. I should like a meeting with you [and other members of Charles' *conseil de famille*], without Charles knowing—we will all tell what we know, to get things perfectly clear, and discuss what is to be done. I don't

want Charles to know in case he gets suspicious. . . . [Charles will then be summoned before the meeting, and his devoted friends] will reveal to him the shortcomings of his behavior, the error of his ways, and persuade him to agree to our proposals.

It is essential in my . . . opinion to take him away from the slippery path of Paris. It has been suggested to me that he be obliged to take a long sea voyage to India and the East Indies, in the hope that, away from home and his abominable friends, confronted by so much to be observed, he might come good and return to us still a poet perhaps, but a poet with better sources of inspiration than the sewers of Paris. Think about it; if we agree I can arrange matters. Taking the debts Charles has admitted, together with those which each of us reveals, we shall be in a position to get . . . a *conseil judiciaire*, an essential measure if he is to be [stopped].

My wife is most unhappy. . . .

General Aupick[1]

The general was both shocked and concerned by Baudelaire's behavior. He felt that desperate remedies were called for, and that Charles had to be forced back onto the path of righteousness. He was prepared to use his stepson's record to secure a *conseil judiciare*—a legal measure which would provide the subject with a guardian who had absolute control over his finances—in effect, making him a legal minor for an indefinite period. Yet for all his readiness to wield parental authority, Aupick was not against the idea of Baudelaire's continuing his literary career.

Despite this genuine concern, a long sea voyage was no way to make Baudelaire mend his ways, although it would inspire him as a poet. Aupick had always sought to make his stepson comply with authority—witness his choice of schools—and now that his stepson was becoming increasingly wild and assertive, Aupick sought to rein him in. He never learned that you cannot stop a young horse from pulling by riding him on a tight rein: he just pulls more and more until his mouth goes so hard that he can no longer feel the bit—and you have lost all possibility of control.

Baudelaire's mother was also deeply upset by his behavior although she was less concerned by his debts than by the transformation of his personality. She saw him turning into a cynical, immoral, and godless "*enfant du siècle*," and could no longer recognize her once affectionate son.

The family lawyer, Narcisse Ancelle, was asked to try to talk some sense into the young man. Baudelaire reacted to this new source of admonition by setting out to shock the worthy lawyer for all he was

36

worth, taking his independent and unconventional attitudes to hysterical extremes. His mother comments on Ancelle's report:

> . . . this sovereign disdain for humanity, not believing in virtue, not believing in anything, all that terrifies me and distresses me. It gives me food for thought and makes me afraid; for it seems to me that when you do not believe in any decent feeling, an evil action is but a step away, and the very thought of that makes me shudder; and here was I happy to think that, for all his disorder and his extravagant thoughts, my son was imbued with honor, and that I need never fear that he might commit a base action; I also had as a guarantee his pride and a certain dignity of spirit, while I believed, into the bargain, that he was essentially religious—not practicing, but still a believer.
> . . . It's no use pretending that the situation is not getting worse, and it continues and the years go by. Though it is not as if I have not prayed to God fervently for him to change.
> If I am resigned to this separation, which I find so cruel, and which may have been the reason for Charles's dissolute life, it is because I wished to spare my husband the sight of a young man whose ideas and habits were so unlike his own.[2]

Baudelaire was trapped in a vicious circle. His outrageous behavior was an assertion of his independence and resentment of Aupick. The behavior was so outrageous that his mother discouraged his visits to the house, for fear of distressing Aupick. Baudelaire, jealous and rejected, reacted by being more outrageous still and scandalizing poor Ancelle.

Aupick completed his plans for the trip to India, and wrote to Alphonse again, providing financial details: he has already borrowed three thousand francs to pay off Charles's debts; the four thousand francs, which was the estimated cost of a round trip to Calcutta, would have to be met by the boy's estate. Aupick ends the letter with the following frank observation: "That is the situation at the moment. Our two personalities have clashed."[3] He admits that stepfather and stepson find one another impossible. One can quite see why. Although there can be no doubt that in dispatching Baudelaire to India Aupick felt that he was acting in the best interests of his stepson, we can be sure that when the latter reluctantly consented to go and sailed from Bordeaux on June 9, 1841, General Aupick must have heaved a sigh of relief.

Baudelaire set off in fairly high spirits. En route he wrote his parents a pleasant letter which they interpreted as a good sign. However, Baudelaire, who would always need the stimulus of city life to relieve his remarkable capacity for instant and overpowering boredom, was singularly ill-equipped to endure the monotony of a long sea voyage. Years later his mother recalled his shipboard behavior:

> Charles had been entrusted to the care of Captain Saliz, a decent man, jovial and witty, whom Charles ought to have liked and did in fact like. He sailed for Calcutta, and was to go further; the trip was to have lasted eighteen months, Charles was twenty years old. Very soon he became very depressed, and alarmed the captain, who did what he could to cheer him up, without success; he lived in complete isolation, avoiding the other passengers—mostly merchants—and the officers. If he spoke at all, it was to express a desire to return to France.[4]

Saliz himself wrote to Aupick to confess that the experiment had failed:

> . . . From the moment we sailed from France it was clear to us on board that it was too late to hope that we might cure M. Beaudelaire [sic] either of his exclusive love of what passes today for literature, or of his resolve not to pursue any other kind of career. This determination prevented him from entering into any other kind of conversation, particularly those which usually occur between us sailors and the other passengers, mostly merchants or soldiers. I must also say, although I fear I will upset you, that his cutting, dogmatic ideas and sentiments about all forms of social bond, which are quite contrary to the ideas we have been accustomed to respect since childhood, were distressing in a young man of twenty and dangerous to the other young people on board, and thus restricted his contacts with the rest of us. . . .
>   I was myself . . . the more upset by his misguided attitudes, since his education, the ability I thought I detected in him, and the gentle, friendly way in which he behaved with me, made me really concerned for him. I was obliged to abandon the hope I had conceived of playing my part, by winning him over, in making him adopt a career which would permit him to make an honorable use of the abilities with which nature had endowed him.[5]

The letter shows several sides of Baudelaire's character: first, that as a young man he had a very high opinion of himself and, second, that he adhered to the "new" ideas, attitudes, and values. It shows how Baudelaire—and indeed his generation—felt estranged from the culture they had inherited. His was a young man's estrangement which asserted itself with a jejune violence and desire to shock. It is a mode of behavior which has come to be familiar enough, but a mode which was inaugurated by Baudelaire's generation. He himself was the first poet to express with any clarity the neurotic, aggressive, desperate quality of the modern consciousness, with its sense of estrangement and insecurity in the hostile environment of nineteenth-century reality. What begins on board as the rebelliousness of an affected, exasperating, and self-consciously stylish twenty-year-old, would mature, to create, in his poetry and his prose, the first clear artistic expression of the exasperated consciousness of modern man.

The letter reveals yet another side of Baudelaire. As a dandy he owed it to himself not to suffer fools, not to compromise himself by adapting his conversation and his views to the restricted and limited temperament of his fellow passengers. He would rather be miserable and lonely than compromise. But the considerable if idiosyncratic effort of will that this demanded did not prevent him from appreciating the decency of Captain Saliz. He responded to the captain's kindness, without going so far as to reward him by mending his ways. Much of Baudelaire's character can be seen in that strange blend: his desire to shock and insult coupled with a certain essential gentleness and kindness.

Upon his return, Baudelaire was to shroud his sea voyage in a cocoon of myth, legend, and rumor. However, it seems quite believable that he horrified his fellow passengers by his immoral and cynical conversation; slightly less possible that he had an affair with a Negro maid so ardent in her pursuit of him that the captain ordered her to be locked in her cabin. There is no doubt that the ship had to weather a terrible storm off the Cape of Good Hope, in the course of which it nearly sank; but the suggestion that it was only the courage and resourcefulness of young passenger Baudelaire that saved her does not ring true. (Indeed, his mother suggests that it was the "demoralizing" effect of that storm which made him very much want to leave the ship when it finally docked at Mauritius, in the Indian Ocean. The same slightly suspect source shows us Baudelaire trying to cure a stomach ache by spending hours in a lifeboat, with the tropical sun beating down on his naked torso and getting dreadfully sunburnt as a result.[6]

For all his desire to remain in Mauritius, the captain persuaded him to rejoin his ship. But at the next port of call, L'Ile Bourbon, or Réunion as it is known today, nothing could induce him to continue traveling. He disembarked in a way which captures to perfection the dignified and slightly ridiculous quality of the twenty-year-old dandy and man of letters:

. . . at Saint-Denis de Bourbon the sea is usually so rough that landing used to require climbing a rope ladder, hanging at the end of a jetty on piles. The ladder was kept straight by two huge cannon balls attached to the bottom end. To disembark it was necessary to grab the rungs at the very crest of the wave.

Although he had been warned what to do, Baudelaire insisted on climbing the ladder with some books under his arm, original but awkward, and he climbed the ladder slowly, gravely, pursued by the next rising wave. It reached and engulfed him beneath twelve to fifteen feet of water and tore him off the ladder. He was fished out with some difficulty but, amazingly still had the books under one arm. It was only then that he consented to leave them in the boat at the foot of the ladder; but on his way up he was again overtaken by a wave, kept hold, arrived on top and set off for the town, calm and cool without appearing to notice the emotions of the onlookers. All the sharks got was his hat.[7]

In later years the poet would maintain that he went on to India, where he enjoyed all kinds of exotic adventures: going on trading expeditions to the interior, buying cattle for the Indian Army, joining a pirate ship, living in the jungle with a beautiful Negress who cooked strange dishes for him. There is no limit to what his friends would believe—simply because they wanted to believe in the legendary figure that he made himself out to be.

While the ship was refitting in Mauritius, Baudelaire stayed with a delightful Creole couple, Autard de Bragard and Emmelina, his wife. He was a lawyer in Port-Louis; Emmelina was extraordinarily beautiful. When in Réunion, Baudelaire sent her a sonnet he had written in her honor, "A une dame créole" ["To a Creole Lady"], by means of a polite and respectful letter to her husband. It is one of his first pieces to strike that note of rich and rhythmic sensuousness which was one of the characteristics of his best work. It begins with a lovely evocation of the tropics:

> In the perfumed land caressed by the sun,
> I have known, beneath a canopy of purple trees
> And palms from whence idleness rains upon the eyes,
> A Creole lady whose charms remain unknown.

> *Au pays parfumé que le soleil caresse,*
> *J'ai connu, sous un dais d'arbres tout empourprés*
> *Et de palmiers d'où pleut sur les yeux la paresse,*
> *Une dame créole aux charmes ignorés.*

The poem urges Mme Autard de Bragard to come to France, where alone her beauty would be properly appreciated. Ironically, she eventually seems to have taken his advice, with fatal consequences: she was to die, at sea, on her way to France on June 22, 1857, within a week of the publication of *Les Fleurs du Mal*.

Having failed to follow his family's instruction to press on to India, and having exhausted the money provided for a much longer voyage, Baudelaire docked at Bordeaux on February 15, 1842. He had been away for eight, not eighteen, months. He wrote to the Aupicks:

> I am back from my jaunt. I arrived yesterday and left Bourbon on November the fourth. I have come back without a sou, *and I often lacked the bare necessities.*
>
> You know what happened on the way out. The return voyage was less remarkable, but more tiring, always either high seas or dead calm.
>
> Were I to write down all I thought and imagined, far away from you, a whole ream of paper would not be enough; so I shall tell you in person.
>
> I believe I have returned bearing virtue in my heart.
>
> I will probably set off tomorrow. So I'll be able to embrace you in two or three days.[8]

Charles returns optimistic as ever. In the meantime Alphonse curries favor with Aupick by "sharing his concern." He suggests that they wait and see if Charles has improved:

> Let us now try to receive Charles as the prodigal son returning to his family; either he has seen the extent of his wrongs and it is the fear of confessing them which stops him from writing about them, or he is unaltered. In that case we shall have to observe him, see whether he has gone wrong by virtue of an abuse of his knowledge, or because of something wrong with his constitution.[9]

The letter goes on to remind the general that Charles is about to draw lots for military service. If he gets conscripted—he will not—this will give them the chance either to make a soldier of him or to gain control over his capital. Alphonse proposes to ensure that if he tries to use his capital to purchase a substitute they take care that the sale of capital is made to them. He finishes with the hope that they can secure Charles' future without having recourse to more extreme measures.

The abominable Alphonse is kowtowing to Aupick, who is fast becoming a person of real authority and influence. He is even prepared to consider having his half-brother certified insane in order to ensure that his capital remains intact. In due course they would indeed resort to "more extreme measures," but too late to preserve the capital, for within three weeks of his return to France, Baudelaire attained his majority.

He had indeed been affected by his voyage to the East, though not as his family had hoped. Aupick's expectations were fulfilled in one respect only: the Orient would provide the poet with an alternative source of inspiration to the sewers of Paris.

Baudelaire would always remain a poet of city life. He was the first major poet to make the modern city the central theme of his art. Unlike earlier romantics who were drawn to nature and the countryside, Baudelaire would declare himself "incapable of getting sentimental over vegetables." Throughout his life he was to remain strangely insensitive to the watery landscapes of Corot, Rousseau, Daubigny, and the rest of the Barbizon school. With the exception of this sea voyage, and a few months in the seaside town of Honfleur at his mother's cottage retreat, Baudelaire was to spend his entire adult life in cities. He neither knew nor liked the countryside—perhaps because he had had no experience of it. His poetry, however, makes an exception for the sea. Not only does it feature prominently in his imagery, but its rhythms, the movement of a ship on the waves, play a subtle part in creating those soothing, rocking patterns which inform so many of his finest and most serenely sensuous poems. From the East itself he also brought back a feel for the exotic quality of the tropics. Warmth, indolence, relaxed sensuality, its smells, its tastes, would all play their part in creating those special, specific, and original patterns of spiced sensuality which his poetry would weave. Finally, he brought back a taste for the exotic quality of dark beauty, a taste which would prove, in the long run, to be a mixed blessing.

BAUDELAIRE WAS TWENTY-ONE on April 9, 1842. Five days later he made a formal request to take possession of his fortune. The fortune was fairly considerable, amounting to 100,000 francs. It is difficult to provide accurate equivalents to nineteenth-century fortunes, but it has been suggested that today the sum would be roughly equivalent to 500,000 new francs (about 100,000 dollars, or 50,000 pounds). Although Baudelaire's father had lived comfortably, he did not die a wealthy man; however, about 70 percent of his son's inheritance consisted of agricultural land which his father had bought at Neuilly and which had subsequently been built on, appreciating some six hundred percent in the process.

The sum of 100,000 francs was an awkward one for a twenty-one-year-old spendthrift to inherit. It is neither a modest nest egg which can be seen to be finite, nor a large enough fortune to guarantee a lifetime of conspicuous consumption. It looks like a lot of money, a bottomless cornucopia, large enough to make you feel a rich man and to enable you to live like one for a time. Yet it is not large enough to survive a young man's determined efforts to spend it. The consequence for Baudelaire was disastrous.

In the meantime the young dandy had fun. The twenty-one-year-old Baudelaire was good-looking, charming, and elegant, with a wispy, dark beard and an abundance of curly hair. He took tremendous care with his appearance and seems to have modeled himself on romantic images such as Delacroix's Romeo. There is a faint air of sixteenth-century doublet and hose about him. Contemporary accounts stress the almost feminine quality of his exquisitely manicured hands and call attention to his bright, dark eyes, like two coffee beans.

There is an outstanding portrait of the young Baudelaire by Deroy which stresses these characteristics; it was commissioned by Baudelaire himself, a close friend of the artist. Deroy's early death was a severe loss to French painting for he was one of the very few artists to have assimilated the technical achievements of Delacroix, displaying a comparable understanding of the virtues of loose brushwork and rich color. For proof of his talents one need look no further than his portrait of Baudelaire, with its emphasis on the poet's delicacy and dandyism and his vaguely archaic appearance.

The best pen portrait of Baudelaire is by the poet himself. Baudelaire would always prove adept at self-analysis, whether of his appearance or of his own weaknesses. In 1847 he would publish *La Fanfarlo*, an extended short story featuring as its hero Samuel Cramer, a slightly hysterical, oversensational poet and emotional poseur. From the following description, there is little doubt that the work is a satirical and distanced self-portrait:

> Samuel has a pure and noble forehead, eyes as brilliant as drops of coffee, a teasing mocking nose, impudent and sensual lips, a square domineering jaw, pretentiously Raphaelesque hair. At once a great idler, a sad ambitious man, and an unhappy celebrity; for all his ideas were always incomplete. The sun of idleness which always shines on him, evaporates and destroys that moiety of genius with which heaven had endowed him.[1]

The charge of being incomplete, flawed by fate—that flaw compounded by idleness—is true of the young and relatively happy Baudelaire; his talent would only mature beyond youthful hysteria once he had come to know the true taste of despair.

On his return to Paris, Baudelaire went to live on the Ile-Saint-Louis, the easterly of the two islands in the Seine which were the original cradle of Paris. His first address there was 10 Quai de Béthune (22 today). The Ile-Saint-Louis was an unusual place for Baudelaire to choose. His friends complained that it was miles from anywhere. Prarond describes it as seeming further away than the island of Mauritius. When he suggested to Baudelaire that he might get bored so far from the center of things, he replied, "No, the fox likes his earth." Not only was it a long way off and hard to get to, it was also expensive. He announced to his mother that he was moving to the Quai de Béthune and paying a high rent, "Because there is nothing else, and I have a furious need of solitude."[2]

One can understand this need, considering that he had spent much of the last year deprived of privacy and cooped up on board ship. He would indeed always cultivate solitude and isolation. His out-of-the-way choice throws an interesting light on his so-called dandyism, confirming it as a private affair which had nothing to do with the social swim. Baudelaire chooses not a fashionable address, but a poetic one—

in the inaccessible heart of old Paris. He is already developing that sense of a private self which is the basis of a high poetic vocation.

Nevertheless, he did not stay at his first address for long. He would never remain anywhere for long. A map has been made of Baudelaire's Parisian residences over the next twenty years, and they sprawl all over the city. He was never to have a permanent home and would live in lodgings or hotels for the whole of his adult life, with only a few brief exceptions. In later years he had to keep on the move to avoid creditors, but his frequent changes of address also suggest a fundamental restlessness. He would have undoubtedly agreed with Pascal that all man's problems derive from his inability to stay still and content within four bare walls. As a poet Baudelaire would be one of the great chroniclers of restlessness and of the savage lengths to which man would go to alleviate it. The fourteen or so Paris addresses he would have as temporary-permanent homes in the next sixteen years are enough to suggest that he knew what he was writing about.

His first move was to the Faubourg Saint-Germain, in the Rue Vanneau, where he sojourned for a few months before returning to the Ile-Saint-Louis to take up residence at what was to be his "best address," the Hôtel Pimodan—originally and again today known as the Hôtel Lauzun. In Baudelaire's day the superb seventeenth-century house by the architect Le Vau was broken up into separate apartments, but still preserved much of its original magnificence, with its sumptuous paneling and painted ceilings. It was a totally appropriate residence for Baudelaire, the high-romantic poet-dandy with a taste for old paintings, Renaissance furnishings, and bric-à-brac.

His apartment consisted of two huge rooms and a smaller one. Prarond recalls:

> I can still remember the main room, the bedroom, and the study, all decorated with a red and black wallpaper on wall and ceiling alike, lit by a single window, with all but the top row of panes in frosted glass "in order to see nothing but the sky," he said.[3]

Deroy's portrait hung beside the chimney breast and on another wall was a copy of Delacroix's *Femmes d'Alger*, also by Deroy. Baudelaire had an unfashionable love of antiques. His rooms were full of them—and they were to prove the immediate cause of his ruin. The apartment also contained a superb eighteenth-century walnut table, a number of rare old books (Renaissance and decadent Latin poets), thick rugs, low lights. It was, in fact, a reflection of the murky sensuality of Baudelaire's own verse.

The occupant was worthy of the setting he had arranged for himself.

This was the poet's golden age, the one period in his adult life when he was supremely happy. He could be—indeed, he could create—himself, making this also the time of Baudelaire the self-made dandy.

In *Le Peintre de la vie moderne* [*The Painter of Modern Life*; 1863], he produced a fascinating analysis of the sociology of the dandy. The dandy, as he saw it, was a historical phenomenon, the product of a particular kind of age, an age of decadence. Baudelaire understood that the aristocratic society of the *ancien régime*, with its values of honor, elegance, nobility of attitude and life, was gone forever. It had been replaced by the base world of capitalism and industrial progress, a world in which "Get rich" could be an electoral slogan. The dandy, however, still clings to the now-dead values of the by-gone age. Despairing in the face of naked materialism, he seeks to re-create those values, single-handed, for his own benefit. He does so through style. In contrast to the pennywise society in which he finds himself, he indulges in extravagance and conspicuous consumption. He dissociates himself from that society in other respects: through his impractical emphasis upon elegance and the poetry of appearance, through his cult of artificiality, and through his supreme and unshakeable impassivity.

Baudelaire's dandy was a kind of ascetic. Totally devoted to the construction of his own self through style, and the worship of that creation, he must never allow emotion, spontaneous or natural and hence vulgar behavior, to put that creation at risk. The dandy treads a narrow path in search of the sublime. He seeks to create himself through poise, a poise that is permanently at risk because the dandy is in permanent danger of making a fool of himself. In his attempt to be different from the bankers, notaries, and money grubbers that surround him, the dandy attempts to turn himself into a self-made aristocrat, if only an aristocrat of style. He aims at distinction:

> Dandyism is not, as is commonly supposed, simply an excessive love of clothes and material elegance. To the perfect dandy such matters are merely symbolic of his own spiritual perfection. To his eyes, valuing as he does *distinction* above all, perfect dress is founded in absolute simplicity—which in fact is the best way to distinguish yourself. . . . [Dandyism] is above all the urgent need to make oneself original, within the exterior limits of conventional behavior. It is a kind of cult of the self, which [goes beyond] the quest for happiness through women . . . which can even survive the loss of . . . illusions. It is the pleasure of astonishing and the proud satisfaction of never being astonished. . . .
>
> In truth, I am not altogether wrong to consider dandyism a form of religion.[4]

Style, self-creation, asceticism, mastery over one's emotions, self-discipline, the cult of the self—these are the essential ingredients of Baudelaire's dandyism. It is above all artificial, man-made, the result of a sustained effort of will. Baudelaire believed passionately in man's natural sinfulness, in his original sin. Consequently all that was natural was evil; all that was good, artificial, the result of an effort of will. It is in that sense that dandyism becomes a form of religion: a quest for spiritual perfection through style. Fundamentally an ascetic, the dandy triumphs above lust and appetite, and reaches for spiritual purity. Woman in this respect is diametrically opposed to the dandy in Baudelaire's view: a natural being, she is essentially impure. As he writes in some of his most savage lines:

Woman is the opposite of the dandy. Therefore she must repel us.
Woman is hungry and wishes to eat. Thirsty and wishes to drink.
She is in heat and wishes to be fucked.
Is that not splendid?
Woman is natural, that is to say abominable.
Consequently she is always vulgar, that is to say the opposite of the dandy.[5]

At twenty-one Baudelaire is not yet as lucid as this, but the basic elements of his dandyism are already there. His aspiration has nothing to do with social ambition, and although ideally it requires money to express it, we shall see that, even when reduced to abject poverty, even when struck dumb and virtually paralyzed by the disease that was to kill him, Baudelaire, in all other normal respects a weak-willed man, would still find the strength to spend two hours each morning upon his appearance.

As yet, however, he was more a charmer than an ascetic. His appearance corresponded to the Renaissance quality of Deroy's portrait, as an old school friend, Henri Mignard, fondly recalled:

Always handsome, charming, distinguished, a waisted velvet tunic made him look like those young Venetian patricians that Titian painted.
He was bare-headed. He explained to me that it was more than a habit, it was a deliberate decision. Bare-headed, in the remotest districts of Paris, however far from home, he liked to look as if he lived locally.[6]

Baudelaire would soon go beyond this romantic, backward-looking elegance of velvet and gold chains. Nineteenth-century attitudes to "modern dress" are fascinating. The early romantics—and the young

Baudelaire among them—had reacted against the sober livery of black frockcoat which had replaced the rich fabrics of the *ancien régime* and the uniforms of the Napoleonic age. For the first decade of the century France had been ablaze with uniforms. But Napoleon went, an age of boredom set in, and now everyone wore black. Alfred de Musset saw his age in terms of the black frockcoat worn by men and the virginal white dress worn by girls. The black coat had come to symbolize the drab new commercial reality.

Baudelaire saw beyond that obvious symbolism. Just as he prided himself on extracting beauty from the decadence of his age, so he was to don the black coat and find poetry in that nineteenth-century uniform. He longed, in his art criticism, for a painter who would portray the beauty and poetry of modern life, show how "grand and poetic we are, in our cravats and our patent leather boots," and bring out the secret poetry of frenzied modern man beneath the "funereal and convulsionary black coat that we all wear." He was the first poet of modernity, the first romantic not to take refuge in imaginary countries of the past. His developing sense of the poetry of modernity is evident in the changes that his dandyism underwent at this time. Dandyism was, in a sense, his first attempt at "modern art." As Mignard recalls him in the early 1840s:

> Every fold of his coat was the work of reason. What a marvel was that black outfit, always the same at all hours of the day, at all times of year, that graciously ample frockcoat, with a manicured hand teasing its lapels, that prettily knotted cravat, that long waistcoat . . . carelessly open over such a fine shirt with its pleated cuffs, those trousers "corkscrewing" over impeccably shining shoes. . . .[7]

Another eye witness described him as looking like Byron dressed by Brummel. He was trying to extract poetry and elegance from the most austere contemporary fashions, rather than seek an image of exotic escapism through his dress.

It was at this time that Baudelaire began to sport the ultimate mark of the dandy—pale pink gloves. Such gloves were symbolic—in the sense that the dandy would never dirty his hands. The fashion had been introduced by one of the great dandies and spenders of the age, the enormously successful popular novelist Eugène Sue, who would use several pairs of gloves in a day—and never wore the same pair twice.

Baudelaire did not confine himself to ascetic elegance. We have an account of his dealings with a tailor from whom he had ordered a special, exotic blue coat with brass buttons. He went through fitting after fitting, finding fault after fault until the luckless tailor finally produced the desired effect; whereupon the lordly young Baudelaire, having inspected himself carefully, turned to the tailor and said, "Make me a dozen just like it."

The young poet was a brilliant talker and a delightful companion. He could hold an audience for hours and was already beginning to gain a reputation both as a writer and an eccentric. He would spend much time in the company of friends such as Prarond and Le Vavasseur, wandering around Paris or eating at La Tour d'Argent on the Left Bank, just across the river from his apartment. It was at that time that he met Théodore de Banville, at twenty already a successful poet, and also the photographer-to-be Félix Tournachon, better known as Nadar. Nadar was the most famous of all nineteenth-century portrait photographers, and would also be one of the most famous balloonists of his age. When they met he was a minor man of letters. He would remain a lifelong friend of the poet, and has left us a series of remarkable photographic studies of him. Something of a jack-of-all-trades, he was a designer and a journalist before taking up photography, and he would remain at the center of artistic and journalistic Paris for a generation. A happy, jovial, and coarse-minded character, he was to be one of Baudelaire's first biographers, with his strangely titled book *Charles Baudelaire intime, le poète vierge* [*The Intimate Charles Baudelaire, the Virgin Poet*], written in 1867.

Nadar's title was intended to startle his readers by its incongruity, because to those who knew the legend but not the man, no one was less a virgin poet than Baudelaire. To them, he was the poet of corruption and exquisite vice, of immorality and violence, the author of the gamiest and most shocking verse of the age, a Satanist and lover of the flowers of evil. Conventional sensations were not enough for him; he had to go to the extreme of vice to find a stimulus for his precociously tired palate.

The Baudelaire legend is an important aspect of his life story and it was Baudelaire himself who was entirely responsible for setting this legend in motion. It did not start to roll despite him; he encouraged it. This was, in effect, a manifestation of his urge to provoke unfavorable reactions as a kind of defense. If people rejected him for the poses he struck, then they were not rejecting *him*, but simply the image he offered. Only someone stupid enough not to see through that image would recoil; others would realize that he was not actually like that and consent to become his accomplices in mystification.

But this only partly explains his provocative behavior; there is a more complicated answer, which is bound up with his conception of art. Baudelaire believed shock, surprise, the bizarre to be essential elements in the experience of beauty. There can be no beauty without surprise. It is reasonable that shock should play a particular part in the style and aesthetics of his own decadent age. Baudelaire will portray the attitudes of modern man, the city dweller, bending under the pressures of urban, materialistic culture; it is a culture which stretches the nerves too tight, making for savage and destructive personalities. Shock, violent response, was an essential characteristic of what Baudelaire described as "the age of the convulsionary frockcoat." It was a quality which he strove to achieve throughout his writing and his life. Add to these psychological and aesthetic motivations for shock the dandy's desire to astonish without being astonished, and we can begin to understand how the Baudelaire legend was born.

One of the lasting elements of this legend has been the belief that Baudelaire was a drug addict. If he had not taken hashish already, he most certainly did so at the Hôtel Pimodan. Its magnificent salon was the meeting place for the notorious Club des Haschischins, a gathering of distinguished men of letters and others who would meet regularly to partake of hashish. It appears, from the exotic account provided by the poet and journalist Théophile Gautier, that the salon was the scene of extraordinary orgies set in an elegant, incense-laden atmosphere, in the midst of which enormous quantities of hashish fudge were consumed. Baudelaire was a member of the club and has left us a charming portrait of himself under the influence of the substance.

Here the legend takes over, turning Baudelaire into a regular user if not an addict. In fact, he never took hashish regularly, and would come to disapprove of it for strictly moral reasons. It is true that his *Les Paradis Artificiels* [*Artificial Paradises*] was to give an accurate and exotic account of the experience, but the work would also condemn the drug precisely because the paradise it creates is artificial: it is an illusion, a cheap parody of spiritual fulfillment and ecstasy. Baudelaire never believed in narcotics as a way of expanding the consciousness; he disapproved of artificial aids. He would, it is true, become increasingly addicted first to laudanum and then to alcohol, but he never believed that such stimulants had any beneficial effect upon his art: they merely sapped the will. Despite the legend, Baudelaire is not the founding father of drug culture.

The more immediate elements of his legend were of his own, not posterity's, making. He loved to create scandal. Witness the following reminiscense of a close friend, which also demonstrates the fundamental misogyny of a shy young man who has conquered shyness:

One night we were sitting in some brasserie and Baudelaire was telling us something . . . monstrous. A blonde woman sitting at our table listened to it all, wide-eyed, her mouth gaping. Suddenly the narrator paused and said to her: "Mademoiselle, you who are crowned with golden corn, and who, so superbly blonde, listen to me with *such pretty teeth*, I am about to bite you, and, if you will permit me, I shall tell you how I should like to make love to you. Indeed, I must confess that to adore you in any other way would appear to me as something of a bore. —I would like to bind your hands and suspend you from the ceiling of my bedroom by your wrists. Then I would kneel and kiss your naked feet."

The poet was quite sincere . . . he could only imagine making love to her while she was hanging. He talked of nothing else till midnight. "Little idiot," he said as we left, "I would really have enjoyed it."[8]

Such public performances were ecstasy to the young Baudelaire. On another occasion he had ordered a steak with great care. When the proprietor asked him if it was all right, the following transpired:

"It is precisely the steak I wanted," he replied. "It is as tender as the brain of a baby."

"The brain of . . .?"

"Of a baby," pronounced the hoaxer, looking up with a steady stare. The restaurateur went down with all speed to protect his children from a customer who seemed to be a ferocious maniac.

Baudelaire did not care for children.[9]

Another time he was leaving a theater when he saw a drunken woman tottering along the pavement. He went up to her and gave her forty sous, saying, "You feel so good encouraging vice."[10]

The countless anecdotes of this kind have one thing in common: Baudelaire's deadpan expression. He utters monstrosities in order to test and assert his own impassivity and to demonstrate that he does not embarrass himself. The French expression for this kind of humor is *pince-sans-rire*—pinching without laughing. It was one of his favorite activities.

Baudelaire also loved baiting fools. He enjoyed irritating the wrong people quite as much as he loved to charm the right ones. He took enormous pleasure in making ludicrous observations for the sheer joy of watching solemn fools take him seriously—which they did. "How sweet it is to be hated by fools," he once said. But this love of provocation would regularly get out of hand. All too often he would find himself mocking people whose favor he was supposed to be seeking. He once attempted to get some free theater tickets from Verteuil, a theater manager, by using the peculiar method of describing some picture of Chinese tortures which he had just been to see. Verteuil found the description distressing:

But the terrible Baudelaire maintained his grip upon his victim and went into still further detail. "They scalp them, hair and all. They draw out all their nails."

"My God!" panted Verteuil.

"Is it not splendid, Monsieur Verteuil, to suffer for one's faith?"

"Oh yes, indeed, very fine, very fine, but, Monsieur Baudelaire, I do not believe that I could ever aspire to such a virtue."

"What, Monsieur Verteuil, would you not suffer gladly for your beliefs?"

Now and again a flirtatious little actress would slip into the office to ask for some favor. Verteuil would grab her like a savior, seize her tits or her bottom, as if to bring himself back to normal.

"One of the Chinese soldiers," continued the pitiless Baudelaire as the actress left, "opening his victim's chest with his dagger, cuts out the bleeding heart and swallows it. A pun in action. Do you seize my meaning, Monsieur Verteuil—to give himself heart."

Finally Verteuil asked for mercy, and absent-mindedly gave us some front row seats. Baudelaire left beaming. It had been such a splendid spectacle that he forgot to use the ticket. Complete triumph would have required Verteuil to die of heart failure that very night.[11]

Baudelaire's contemporaries make it all too clear that he did not take pleasure in the company of women. They were for him objects of adoration or sources of sensation; as companions they bored him:

He did not enjoy women's talk, and on visiting a recently married friend one evening he said, towards nine o'clock, "It is getting late, send the little woman off to bed; you can't talk properly with those pretty little birds."[12]

In later years he would describe the company of intelligent women as "the pleasure of a pederast."[13] Women were fundamentally evil. He considered them to be made up of the sum of their appetites, unable to separate soul from body, perhaps because they did not possess souls:

Eternal Venus, caprice, hysteria, fantasy, is one of the seductive forms [assumed] by the Devil.[14]

The greatest pleasure he derived from the sexual act was the certainty of committing evil. He offers the following image of love:

Were I invited to portray Love, I would paint it in the form of a crazed horse, devouring his master, or else as a demon, eyes ringed by debauchery and insomnia, dragging, like a ghost or a galley slave, burning chains at his ankles, and shaking in one hand a vial of poison, in the other the blood-stained dagger of crime.[15]

Pain, violence, enslavement, these were indeed basic elements in Baudelaire's experience of love, and yet the portrait he paints here remains one-sided. In love Baudelaire would also find ecstasy and a strange kind of calm, the calm of a sexual contemplative. More important still, Baudelaire would be able to weave all these contradictory emotions together in his art and make love the inspiration of some of his greatest poems.

Violence, calm, and poetry were to be the dominating themes of Baudelaire's relationship with the first and longest-lasting love of his life, the mulatto actress Jeanne Duval. Although at first sight a dark mistress might appear an appropriate companion for a young dandy recently returned from the East, Baudelaire's choice is, nevertheless, a perverse and surprising one, for in his *Advice to Young Writers* he properly warns would-be authors against three kinds of woman: actresses, honest women, and blue-stockings. Only whores or stupid women are suitable companions for men of letters.

Jeanne Duval was certainly no blue-stocking, but she was a sort of actress, a remarkably beautiful one, though without much stage talent. Nadar and Banville had seen her perform, and both seem to have known her rather well before she began to associate with Baudelaire. Nadar describes her as a sensuous, dusky, undulating beauty. Perhaps he exaggerates her appeal in light of hindsight, wishful thinking, and the utterly extraordinary poetry that Baudelaire composed to honor his "Black Venus."

From the outset Baudelaire elected to adore his Venus. Jeanne to him was the very incarnation of his idea of beauty, a combination of the exotic, the sensuous, the melancholic, and the bizarre all blended together. Years later he would write of his conception of beauty in his *Journaux intimes* [*Intimate Journals*] and the passage tells us much about his early vision of her:

I have found the definition of Beauty—of my Beauty. It is some thing ardent and sad, something a little vague, leaving room for conjecture.

. . . I shall, if I may, apply my ideas to a concrete object, why not the most interesting object of society, a woman's face. A beautiful seductive head, a woman's head that is, is a head that makes one dream, while confusing them, of pleasure and of sadness; which conveys an idea of melancholy, of fatigue, of satiety even—or else a contrary idea, that is to say ardor, an urge to live, coupled with surges of bitterness, which might derive from hardship or despair. Mystery and regret are also characteristics of Beauty.[16]

Jeanne must have embodied to perfection that strange blend of contrasting elements. Certainly, veneration for her appearance made him treat her in a manner which she found both flattering and confusing. Accustomed to somewhat more direct and cruder forms of courtship, she was puzzled by the exquisite young man who sent her flowers and called for her in a carriage, who treated her like a goddess. He eventually installed her in her own apartment, conferring upon her the coveted status of a kept woman. When she told Banville about her protector, the latter imagined from her description that "Monsieur Baudelaire" must be a white-haired old gentleman approaching his dotage. He was astounded when she finally introduced the young dandy to him. Banville has left the following account of the relationship:

She was a colored girl, very tall; who carried her . . . superb head covered with very fuzzy hair remarkably well; her regal walk, filled with savage grace, was both bestial and divine. As it happened . . . I knew her before I ever saw the poet who was to immortalize her, and who was then quite unknown. Wearing a little velvet cornet that suited her to perfection, and a thick dark-blue woolen dress with a band of gold, she talked at length of *Monsieur Baudelaire*, of his fine furniture, his collections, his *whims*; what a maniac he must have seemed to this beautiful idiot—a man taken with an absolute love of perfection, who devoted the same degree of care to everything he did; who was as meticulous about polishing his nails as he was about writing a sonnet.

Into the bargain this contemplative would make Jeanne sit before him in a large armchair, as he looked at her lovingly, admiring her, or reciting poetry written in a tongue she didn't know. Perhaps that was the best way of conversing with a woman whose speech would disrupt the intoxicating symphony of her beauty; but you must expect the woman in question to disagree, and to be surprised at her lover adoring her as he would a beautiful cat. Moreover, Baudelaire, who was very rich in those days and who had chosen to live in a small apartment, was in the habit of having his furniture removed whenever he saw better pieces at his dealers; he would have them replaced so that his porters were never surprised to find his staircase blocked by removers engaged in the perpetual process of moving furniture in and out. Nothing could be more understandable in an artist than this love of beauty and variety, but you can see that these comings and goings must have perplexed the beautiful black girl.[17]

Baudelaire had made Jeanne a sensual pet. The "beautiful black girl" both evoked his memories of the tropics and was good for his legend. He adored her beauty and his own role as the protector of a kept woman and beautiful object. It was a state of mind that he manufactured through his liaison, not carnal satisfaction, which was his chief source of pleasure. Some years later, reflecting on such relationships, he would write:

> The sensual joys of the protector partake of the angel and the owner of property. Charity and ferocity. They are even independent of sex, beauty, and animal genus.[18]

Baudelaire's sexuality was essentially contemplative. He was never much concerned with coupling. The mental excitement he derived from contemplating his woman and imagining he was making love to her was too intense to wish to destroy it, regularly, in the aftermath of postcoital sadness. He did not care for sexual fulfillment, which he considered destructive, and preferred more lasting sources of sensation, such as anticipation and imagination.

This accounts for his adoration of Jeanne—and for his perverse view of women and the demands of their appetites. He was not undersexed, not truly a virgin poet; he simply felt that there were greater pleasures to be derived from sex than the hiccup of orgasm. Yet he adored his Black Venus in his fashion, and lived with her intermittently for many years, good and bad, bad mostly, long after the charm of her beauty, and indeed that beauty itself, had worn away.

La Fanfarlo evokes the early phase of their relationship. The heroine is a high-class courtesan with whom Cramer has an affair. The episode shows us how Baudelaire conceived of Jeanne:

> Although or perhaps because Samuel had a depraved imagination, love, for him, was less an affair of the senses than of the intellect. It was above all admiration and thirst for beauty; he considered reproduction to be a vice of love, pregnancy to be the disease of a spider. He wrote somewhere: angels are sterile hermaphrodites. —He loved the human body as a material

harmony, like fine architecture, with movement, and this absolute materialism was not far removed from pure idealism.[19]

In an extraordinary poem to Jeanne, "Les Promesses d'un visage" ["The Promises of a Face"], he evokes her head and her tight, kinky hair which, in turn, promises or points to:

>A rich fleece, which is indeed sister
>   Of that fuzzy head of hair,
>Supple and kinky, and which equals you in density,
>   O night without stars, O night of darkness!

>*Une riche toison qui, vraiment, est la soeur*
>   *De cette énorme chevelure,*
>*Souple et frisée, et qui t'égale en épaisseur,*
>   *Nuit sans étoiles, Nuit obscure!* [20]

It would seem that Jeanne shared his view of pregnancy and the cult of sterility. Another, somewhat extraordinary poem in her honor suggests that she avoided pregnancy in order not to be disfigured by stretch marks:

>Priestess of debauchery and my sister in pleasure
>Who always disdained to bear and nourish
>   A man in your saintly cavities,
>So greatly did you fear and flee the disturbing stigmata,
>Which virtue ploughs with its infamous share
>   Across the flanks of pregnant matrons.

>*Prêtresse de débauche et ma soeur de plaisir*
>*Qui toujours dédaignas de porter et nourrir*
>   *Un homme en tes cavités saintes,*
>*Tant tu crains et tu fuis le stigmate alarmant*
>*Que la vertu creusa de son soc infamant*
>   *Au flanc des matrones enceintes.* [21]

La Fanfarlo describes the atmosphere of heavy, perfumed and soft-textured sensuality, the dream setting in which the poet's imagination places Jeanne, his sterile love object:

>Thus La Fanfarlo's bedroom was very small, with a very low ceiling cluttered with things that were soft, scented, and dangerous to touch; the air, heavy with strange perfumes, made one want to die there slowly as if in a hothouse. The lamplight filtered through a mass of lace and material of a violent

but ambiguous hue. In places, on the wall, it illuminated paintings full of Spanish sensuality; very white flesh against very dark backgrounds. It was in the heart of this ravishing hovel, which was like both a brothel and a sanctuary, that Samuel beheld advancing toward him the new goddess of his heart, in all the radiance and sensual splendor of her nakedness.[22]

Baudelaire's imagination creates an image of a temple-brothel with a prostitute goddess as its votary. He always enjoyed such combinations of opposites. He found pleasure in pain, and—more important—perhaps pain in pleasure. The paradoxical blend of the profane and sacred in the form of the prostitute-goddess points also to his own conception of art. Art had all the spiritual high seriousness of religion, indeed art *was* a religion which replaced the degraded Christianity of the age. But art was also prostitution, and the artist who sold his wares a kind of whore. As he wrote in his notebook some years later:

Love is the taste for prostitution. Indeed there is no noble plea-sure that cannot be boiled down to prostitution. At the theater, at the ball, everyone possesses everyone else. What is art? Prostitution.[23]

For Baudelaire sex was an essentially aesthetic experience. The paradoxical and misogynistic poet deliberately took as his lover some-one essentially beautiful yet remarkably limited. The blend appealed to him. At the time he appreciated nothing so much as Jeanne's blank incomprehension of his behavior. He would actually provoke that incomprehension, dictating his poems to her, and boasting to his friends that her spelling mistakes actually improved them.

The view we have of Jeanne is prejudiced in that it is the view of Baudelaire and of friends of his who disapproved of her. History has denied her a voice of her own. However, living as she did off her wits and her looks in a Paris in which it was all too easy to sink like a stone, she must have felt enormous relief when Baudelaire appeared to guarantee her financial security—enormous relief soon to be followed by enormous bitterness when she learned just how insecure her position really was. She could not even have consoled herself with Baudelaire the man, who was too remote from her in his tastes, and whose con-templative approach to sexuality must have been a distinctly one-sided, egotistical mode of pleasure.

There is no positive evidence to suggest that Jeanne ever felt any-thing for Baudelaire except, just possibly, a fleeting gratitude for his support through thick and thin. Only one of the innumerable letters that he wrote to her has survived, since she was unwilling, or quite possibly unable, to keep them. A later admirer of his work purchased a copy of *Les Paradis Artificiels* from one of the secondhand bookstalls that line the banks of the Seine. Judging by the inscription in Baudelaire's own hand, it was the copy he presented to Jeanne Duval.

From the very start their relationship was stormy—even when both lovers believed Baudelaire to be a rich man. His friends maintained that Jeanne was the ruin of his life. Not only did she impose a crushing financial burden, but her lack of understanding and her nagging made it almost impossible for Baudelaire to work. Certainly that despairing longing for calm and serenity which runs right through his work was derived, at least in part, from the querulous bickering of his shrewish companion.

She also betrayed him, indiscriminately. A friend recalls a moment when Baudelaire saw Jeanne walking arm in arm with another man. The poet remarked sadly that it was not so much her treacheries as her choice of partners that appalled him. Yet his poetry celebrates her as a traitress. It shows us an impassive, cold goddess, cruel, hard, and deceitful, so sensual yet so remote that one can only worship the image of her indifferent and destructive sexuality.

Baudelaire was beginning to gain a reputation as a poet, and a highly original poet at that. His earliest work is founded in his aesthetic of shock. One poem which contemporaries recall relates the experience of an unfortunate lady who had enjoyed the enforced attentions of a whole cavalry regiment. Another memoirist, member of a group of gentle young poets, recalls Baudelaire's presence at one of their readings:

> Baudelaire, having put up with the crystal flow of our poems, now took his turn. He began in a grave, slightly vibrant voice, with an aesthetic expression. He recited the poem "Manon the Streetwalker" ["Manon la Pierreuse"]; the first rhyme concerned her *chemise fangeuse* [filthy chemise], and the rest matched the opening. The most basic words, beautifully combined, the most daring descriptions, followed one on another, and we listened filled with stupor, blushing, putting away our seraphic verses and feeling the frightened wings of our scandalized guardian angels beating against our brows. Actually it was superb; but so removed from our literary principles that we felt, for this excellent and depraved poet, a nervous admiration. . . . Baudelaire did not return.[24]

The poems he wrote in Jeanne's honor were not like that. They were, like "Le Serpent qui danse" ["The Serpent that Dances"], erotic evocations of an impassive goddess, with eyes "where nothing sweet or bitter is revealed." They recall her polished body as she lay naked, except for her sonorous jewels. He adores her as he adores the sky at night. He plunges his head in her hair and is transported into a world of images, conjured up by its smell and texture. The poetry is dreamy, erotic, and exotic. Above all, it is the incarnation of a langorous rhythm which rises and falls gently as the sea. It can touch upon the most detailed aspects of their relationship. "Sed non Satiata" evokes a bizarre deity as brown as the nights, a Faust of the savannah. The elixir of her mouth is a greater drug than opium. The poem ends with the regret that he can never satisfy her demands. He begs his pitiless demon for less fire—for he is not able to "embrace her nine times" and lacks Proserpine's gift of eternal renewal, that gift which alone might wear her down in the "hell of her bed."

As we know them today, the poems of the so-called Black Venus cycle—pieces such as "Les Bijoux" ["The Jewels"], "La Chevelure" ["Hair"], and "Parfum exotique" ["Exotic Perfume"]—are among the finest that Baudelaire ever wrote, and among the richest poems in the French literary heritage. Here as so often we find paradox in the very heart of Baudelaire's being. As a woman Jeanne Duval seems to have tortured and betrayed him, stretching his nerves and making it almost impossible for him to work. Yet whatever kind of a companion she may have been, she was also his Black Venus, his finest inspiration—both torturer and Muse.

ONE HUNDRED THOUSAND francs do not last long when Baudelaire is managing them. He was living very high indeed in 1842, up to an image of elegance set by persons with much larger purses. He spent considerable sums of money on *objets de valeur* such as paintings and furniture, and would frequently dispose of recent acquisitions for a fraction of the original cost to make room for still finer and more expensive pieces. It was unfortunate that a tenant of the Hôtel Pimodan, one Arondel, should have been a somewhat shady dealer in such articles. A not altogether honest man, he took advantage of the innocent young dandy and would-be collector, selling him Italian paintings of the most dubious attributions, which Baudelaire believed he had "discovered." Arondel would obligingly buy back pieces of which the poet had tired and did not insist on payment in cash.

Baudelaire was not only royally swindled, but became enmeshed in a web of promissory notes which was to entangle him for the rest of his life—and would actually drive him from Paris some twenty years later. In due course he would face up to the extent of the swindle, admitting that he had signed notes to the total of some fifteen thousand francs, in return for the paltry four thousand francs which is all he received from Arondel.

In the meantime he remained content to live on credit, signing any scrap of paper to obtain the piece he wanted, or the cash to acquire it. He could think only of satisfying an immediate compulsive need and had no sense of the long-term cost of satisfaction. He placed Arondel in a position to squeeze him for the rest of his life. Indeed Arondel was the main claimant upon Baudelaire's estate after his death, but the illegitimate and excessive nature of his claim was confirmed by the courts, which dismissed it virtually in its entirety.

Baudelaire used to pride himself upon his business acumen, although he was quite disastrously inept. We saw how he went about trying to gain the goodwill of a theater manager—by terrorizing him. He was no more tactful with Arondel. The latter was a painter as well as a dealer. He sent some paintings to the Salons of 1845 and 1846, which Baudelaire reviewed. A circumspect reviewer of a creditor who was also an indifferent artist might have felt in an invidious situation, obliged to choose between hypocritical praise or tactful silence. Baudelaire was not circumspect. He said that the paintings were crude and amateur bits of work, striking combinations of incompetence and ability, clumsiness and skill. Despite the concessions, this was not the sort of notice to enchant a man with the power to make your life a misery.

It is hardly surprising that Baudelaire's extravagant way of life began to test his relationship with his family from the moment he returned. He would write affectionate yet frequently infuriating letters to his mother. In late 1842, for example, he begged her not to scold him for failing to attend law school; it was just that he lacked a hat and a pair of trousers. But to prove he is a good boy who thinks of his mother he has sent her some earrings.

In the meantime Baudelaire is growing further estranged from his stepfather. Aupick is no longer "papa," but "the general." The personality clash is stronger than ever, and his unfortunate mother is caught in the middle. She becomes worried and upset; mother and son now begin a long series of painful exchanges and misunderstandings. Just after New Year's Day 1844 Baudelaire writes to her:

> I suggested leaving my card at the general's because I thought that that was what one does, and because my good manners would please you— Since you think that he will take offense instead of understanding my actual motives, there is nothing to be done, it's beyond me. I find these dreams you have of reconciliation distressing. All I can do, as I said, is to promise you a year of work and good sense—nothing more.
>
> There is a kind of male pride which you, as a woman, and his woman, cannot understand; why do you oblige me to be so hard, and why do you have such illusions?[1]

Estrangement is now definitive. Baudelaire is naive enough to suppose that his plan of paying an official call on his stepfather and leaving his card would not be construed as a piece of cocky insolence. The gap continues to widen—to the point that Baudelaire cannot bear to visit his mother in the general's "cold, empty house," which creates a sad and violent impression upon him. Baudelaire felt himself not only a stranger in the house, but jealous and rejected, as the Aupick ménage functioned without him. Much of his extravagant and defiant behavior over these years derives from a sense of the loss of a family life he had never known.

Yet for all the impending financial disasters which his wildness and extravagance had prepared, the early years of his majority were of vital significance, a serene and happy time during which he had had the means to be what he wanted. He would never look back on them with either remorse or nostalgia. They were the foundation of his poetic career and went a long way towards making him the kind of artist that he became. He had had the time and the calm to find his creative center, to develop his sensibilities, and to turn himself into the dandy artist—indolent, insolent, provocative perhaps, but an artist who believed in perfection, who would never allow superficial posing to threaten his talent, who would never abuse the high seriousness of his vocation. The leisure and elegance he enjoyed between 1842 and 1844 would also give him a taste for that langorous luxury and sensuality which was to play such an important part in his poetic imagination for the rest of his wretched and impoverished existence. As he put it:

> It is through leisure that, in part, I developed. To my great detriment, for leisure without a fortune increases debts, and the humiliation that results from debts.
>
> But to my great profit, in what concerns sensibility, meditation, and the ability to be a dandy and a dilettante.
>
> Other men of letters are, on the whole, base and extremely ignorant hacks.[2]

The passage speaks for itself, but it can also be read between the lines. Baudelaire had a profound strain of masochism, a taste for self-destruction provoked in part by parental rejection. In passages such as this he virtually admits to courting debts and disaster—for the sweet sensation of loss and destitution which only disaster can provide. He did not "think" when racing through his capital any more than the compulsive gambler thinks as he stakes his last coin. Indeed there is a sense in which both the spendthrift and the gambler are not averse to losing; there is a certain savage exultation to be derived from having spent one's last coin. The exultation of the young Baudelaire at the spectacle of his financial ruin should not be exaggerated, but it should be remembered that self-destruction came easily to him and that an element of such exultation was always there.

In the meantime his mother was growing ever more alarmed by her son's extravagance. The sea voyage of 1841–42 had had no visible effect except to encourage him to take a dusky mistress—a fact so shocking that Mme Aupick chose to ignore it. She and Baudelaire together made a half-hearted attempt to control his expenditure. She took hold of the purse strings and doled out a fixed sum of money each month. However, she was weak enough, kind enough, to give in to his urgent and convincing requests for extra funds, and to her credit she would almost always remain so. Baudelaire, as usual, is not ashamed to beg:

> January 5, 1844
>
> You know that I have got a new tailor—I needed one—and that the first time you make use of those people you have to give them cash. —He'll get suspicious of me and pull a long face at a promissory note. You have to advance me three hundred francs at once, which is twenty-five francs more than the February installment. If you have any money at home, to spare, even if it is a great deal less, let me have it, it will always be that much less that I shall owe him. The money you sent me on New Year's Day went to settle a note of three hundred francs from last autumn—and on presents.[3]

Clearly matters were beyond Mme Aupick's control. Ancelle, who had administered Baudelaire's estate in his minority and who had subsequently negotiated his capital transactions, was getting alarmed. Eventually Mme Aupick, yielding to the urging of Ancelle and her husband, accepted that drastic measures were needed. The family discovered that over the past few years Baudelaire had managed, as the French have it, to "eat" half his capital, and he was deeply in debt into the bargain. They decided to seek a *conseil judiciaire*, a financial guardian approved by law at the request of a family. It would have the effect of turning Baudelaire back into a minor, no longer responsible for managing his own capital. Minority, in his case, was to last until his death twenty-three years later.

In August 1844 the family council, of which Alphonse was a member, submitted a report of Baudelaire's behavior to a tribunal in order to secure the appointment of a *conseil judiciaire*. The report reproached him for having, from an early age, "displayed extravagant tastes and a love of leisure, such that, in order to overcome them the plaintiffs felt obliged to dispatch him on a long sea voyage." On his majority he had sold his Neuilly property, partly in order to settle debts. He had borrowed eight thousand francs from his mother, who had also settled other debts of some five or six thousand. There was every reason to fear that he would have recourse to money lenders. As instances of his behavior Mme Aupick mentioned a debt of nine hundred francs to a restaurant and two pictures bought for four hundred francs and resold for eighteen. Baudelaire was reproached for the "most lunatic extravagance" and for having spent half his fortune in eighteen months. Without hesitation, the tribunal granted a *conseil judiciaire*.

Baudelaire had counted on his mother to prevent the appointment. Now he felt utterly betrayed: Alphonse and even his mother had yielded to Aupick, and agreed to stab him in the back. The plan threatened destruction to the whole edifice of dandyism which Baudelaire had erected since his majority. Betrayed by his family, made to look a fool to his friends, Baudelaire was left with nothing—save bitterness and resentment.

When begging his mother to prevent his humiliation, the only hope he could hold out to her was a lunatic confidence in his ability to repair the damage to his fortune by writing. He knew little enough about the world of journalism and literature to believe that it was easy to get rich quick by the pen. His letters from this period are full of wretched promises of instant success waiting just around the corner. The exquisite young spendthrift had no inkling of the kind of success that would await him, or of how hard the road to success would be. In the meantime he prayed to his mother, sending letters written from absolute need, pleading for love, understanding and financial independence:

I ask you to read this very carefully because it is very serious and is a last appeal to your good sense and the great tenderness you say you feel for me. . . .

I am writing this in a state of calm, and when I think how sick rage and astonishment have made me in the last few days, I ask myself how I shall be able to endure the thing when it is done. You keep trying to make me swallow the pill by repeating that it's all perfectly natural and not in the least dishonorable. That may be, I believe it, but in truth what does it matter what it is really like for most people, if it is *quite different* for me? You say that you regard my rage and my unhappiness as being purely temporary; you think that you are just giving me a maternal cuff for my own good. But understand one thing which you never seem to realize, that is that it is my real misfortune not to be made as other men—the thing you regard as a necessity or a passing source of pain is something I cannot, cannot endure. . . .

You have broken your word in two ways. When you were good enough to lend me eight thousand francs we agreed that in due course you would have the right to receive a proportion of the payments for any work I might do. I ran up a few more debts; and when I told you they were tiny you promised me to wait a little longer. Indeed a few paltry advances, combined with a little money earned, would eliminate them rapidly. Now your mind is savagely made up; you get to work so fast that I simply do not know what to do—and am obliged to give up my plans. I thought that my first work should practically be a piece of scholarship, and that coming to the notice of various persons you would receive certain compliments, and seeing the money come in you would not refuse me a few fresh advances, and in a few months I would be clear again—back to the point I was at just after you lent me the eight thousand. No: you did not want to wait, did not want to wait a fortnight.

Do you see the falsity of your reasoning, your illogical conduct? You cause me an infinite pain, and you take an altogether offensive step, perhaps on the very eve of the beginnings of success, the eve of the day that I have long promised you. That is just the moment you choose to break my limbs, for, as I told you I cannot accept a *conseil* as something ordinary and harmless, I can already feel its effect. And in this respect you made another mistake, more serious still, which consists in supposing that it will be a stimulant, you can have no idea of what I felt yesterday, the feeling of discouragement I felt in my legs when I saw that things were getting serious, something like a sudden urge to let it all go hang, not to take any part. . . . Saying to myself calmly: what is the point? All that remains is to be happy to accept like an idiot anything she deigns to give me.

You are making such a mistake that Monsieur Ancelle said to me at Neuilly, "I told your mother that if letting you spend it all were to make you work and get a proper job, I would advise her to allow you to do so; but that would never happen." I did not think it possible that anyone could say something ruder and stupider. Never did I dare go that far and tell myself, calmly, that I would spend the lot. I imagine you are not as permissive as he, and as for me, I love my independence too much to do anything so foolish—now although I am your only son, you must have enough respect for my person not to subject me to the judgment of strangers, when you know the pain it causes me, and to pay heed to the difficulties inherent in my enterprises. I promise you, mother, that this is not a threat to make you change your mind, but really is what I feel—the result will have the opposite of the desired effect—a total loss of morale.[4]

He reiterates the priceless observation that "I never meant to spend it all," surely the finest epitaph on a lost fortune. But despite his ranting against Ancelle's stupidity and rudeness, there is no doubt that the lawyer was right. Baudelaire would certainly have spent it all; and not even that would have made him take a job.

His commitment to literature was now total. From that moment on, the notion of taking regular employment never occurred to him again. He would remain ready to accumulate debt upon debt, even risking prison, and would endure very real hardship rather than take a job. Although paid employment would seem a ludicrous occupation for the first great "damned poet" of modernity, it is worth remembering that Baudelaire never had to be a poet in the first place. The choice was his, made freely and adhered to without wavering. Even though one may not altogether believe that Baudelaire derived satisfaction from the compounding of his financial plight, it is certainly true that he never made any serious effort to remedy it—except by means of a pen which drew its inspiration from his own despair.

The letter speaks of Ancelle, who was appointed his legal guardian. Eighteen years later Baudelaire would describe him as having been "the scourge of my life," the man responsible for two-thirds of his misfortunes.[5] Ancelle was in most respects a hopelessly inappropriate choice to watch over a young man like Baudelaire. True, no one could have made a complete success of the task, at least while Baudelaire still smarted with humiliation and betrayal. Yet by any standards the choice of Ancelle was disastrous. A steady, cautious lawyer, dreadfully limited, Ancelle had all the mentality of a small-town professional dignitary and was motivated largely by a perverse and bumbling curiosity. It is true that he succeeded in keeping the rest of Baudelaire's capital relatively intact, but he saved that capital at the expense of the man. Not only was he cautious and conventional to an excessive degree; his curiosity made him "take an interest." He would spy on Baudelaire to discover details of his way of life, have furtive talks with his concierge. Only in the very last years did he lose his talent for sending Baudelaire into paroxysms of hysterical fury.

Baudelaire had no illusions about him from the start. Immediately after his appointment he wrote to his mother: "Ancelle has administered the last rites. So all that remains is for me to withdraw into myself and wrack my brains."[6] In another letter written after a quarrel with his mother, he injects a note of real hysteria:

> What do you want me to write—That I suffer to see you suffering; what could be truer and more believable—but basically I think the whole thing has been greatly exaggerated.
>   One may love one's mother and still be rude and tactless, nothing could be more natural; but why upset and torture me for a fault that I feel and know well? *I am working*. Monsieur Ancelle —Monsieur Ancelle—Monsieur Ancelle.[7]

Baudelaire's exasperation derived from his guardian's good intentions. Ancelle took his duty seriously, but he was also fond of his charge and took an interest in him despite the latter's frequent explosions. Indeed, as the years passed, Ancelle, although he understood nothing of contemporary art, was to develop a great interest in the work of his ward. In 1868, on the eve of the publication of the posthumous edition of Baudelaire's works, he would regularly go to the bookshops and press his face to the window to see whether the edition was out yet.

Ancelle had to endure sallies such as the following, which Baudelaire had written from Dijon. He had sent Jeanne to call on Ancelle for funds, and not surprisingly the old lawyer had quibbled with her about the amount that her lover was entitled to receive. It would seem that Ancelle treated her less courteously than Baudelaire would have liked, and delivered her a lecture into the bargain. Baudelaire was not pleased:

> As you know I have been seriously ill. My stomach has been more or less ruined by laudanum, but it is not the first time and I will survive.
>
> Jeanne came this morning and talked to me at length about her meeting with you. Everything has been distressing and upsetting me for some time now. Consequently I was not surprised to hear things which prove that you understand not the first thing about my life. . . .[8]

The letter goes on to give a detailed account of Ancelle's stupidities: his slowness to pay Baudelaire's allowance, his refusal to provide advances, his incompetence in paying too little. Chief among all these faults was the fact that he took an interest:

> Apparently you do not wish to restrict your role with respect to me, with respect to anyone indeed, to that of unfeeling agent and business man . . . all the justification [for my complaints] is contained in something you said. *I would consent to the destruction of your entire fortune in a moral aim!*—Well, what do you think? . . . What is the meaning of your senile mutterings, your egotistical precepts, your brutalities, your rudeness? I know it's true that I paid you back in your own coin, but still it does not make sense. Our relationship must improve.[9]

Ancelle did everything he could for Baudelaire's good, while all the poet wanted was freedom. The lawyer made it difficult for him to collect the pittance now allotted to him. He made him tramp out to Neuilly to collect it, and, as Baudelaire said, he came to know every stone on the way. But for all his good intentions Ancelle never understood the kind of help that Baudelaire needed. So obsessed was he by the need to conserve the capital that he refused to help Baudelaire settle his debts. He had to borrow at high interest rates in order to meet long-standing obligations as they came due, although the old debts had commanded a lower rate of interest than his new ones. Moreover, the interest on his debts was higher than his actual income. Thanks at least in part to Ancelle, Baudelaire continued to sink ever deeper into the financial quicksand.

He did not just resent his guardian's lack of financial perspicacity. He was really enraged by Ancelle's attempts to play an active part in his life. He complained to his mother that Ancelle exhausted him with his detestable conversation. When the poet was longing for rest, Ancelle would force his way in. He would even join him in public and strike up literary conversations with his friends. Baudelaire would remain on the edge of his seat for fear that his guardian would make a fool of him. He would rather have fallen into the hands of loan sharks than into the tutelage of Ancelle. To a sensitive young writer and former young man of leisure his attentions were intolerable. It would not have been easy to endure the supervision of a man who could write so naively: "I envy you. Time never hangs heavy on your hands. When you feel boredom approaching you *seize* your pen and the hours slip by unnoticed."[10]

Baudelaire blamed his mother for Ancelle's tutelage, but even in its earliest and most humiliating phases, he was not too proud to beg from her. He wrote, and would continue to write, as a desperate and harrassed man. His despair, however, was tempered by a terrible optimism which, in retrospect, has a ring of gallows humor about it. He wrote his begging letters under pressure; the sheer burden of his situation put him under great strain and made him long for enough money in hand to buy even a few days' release from tension. Baudelaire would never count the cost of raising money to meet short-term needs; he required money and had to have it immediately, no matter what. In one letter he wrote to tell his mother that for the last twelve days he had scarcely had an hour's peace. He claimed to be preparing three works of art criticism (which would never, in fact, be published), and to complete them he must buy time:

I never have thirty francs in front of me—which represents eight days' work. When faced with such facts, no accusations are possible.

I need twelve days to finish something and sell it. If for a sacrifice of *sixty francs, which means a fortnight of calm*, you get from me the pleasure of seeing me at the end of the month, show you proof of *three books sold*, which means at least *fifteen hundred francs*, and thank you for them, will you regret the expense? You can be sure that I would not congratulate myself on such a feat were the said volumes not already begun so long ago that the paper has turned yellow. If tonight or tomorrow I have no furniture left, *the said sixty francs will still represent the same number of days, that is to say potential working hours*. As for the prospect of selling them, you may be surprised to learn that . . . I have made new contacts, namely the *Revue des Deux Mondes* and a bookseller; but those people believe much less in my industry than they do in my talent, and they will only pay me for a manuscript that is *completely finished*.

Sixty francs! Can it be possible, and must I despair of a last favor from my mother?

I cannot visit you at home anymore, it is too painful; but I would like to see you sometimes. Let me think of something in a day or two when I have finished these arduous tasks. . . .

He goes on to tell her to send the money through a mutual friend. Baudelaire's hysterical sense of need emerges in his saying that he will call for it three times, at three, five, and six o'clock! He then beseeches her not to humiliate him by writing one of her usual letters; he finds them too upsetting. He rounds off with some emotional blackmail and another promise:

I ask you this favor not only in order to carry out the work I spoke of, but in order to convince myself that I ought to continue to love you.

Needless to say I will return your sixty francs in a fortnight, upon my word of honor.[11]

It is unlikely that Baudelaire had even been considered by the prestigious *Revue des Deux Mondes*; equally unlikely that he actually had three major works in progress. Yet he is not exactly lying; he is about to start writing at any moment, and the books seem real enough to him. He will always believe in the reality of the good things about to happen which, for the moment, exist only in his imagination. He has all the confidence of the inveterate gambler, whose optimism can make each bet seem a certain investment. Moreover, like the gambler, Baudelaire never allows past failure to diminish the conviction that next time he can't lose.

It is clear that he now came under severe pressure. He had to endure the humiliation of being a legal minor, a fact known to his friends and to every moneylender in town. He had to tolerate Ancelle. He had to endure further humiliation, at the hands of Jeanne, when she discovered that he was not the rich protector she had assumed him to be. He was growing increasingly estranged from his family. The instant success to which he had looked as a brilliant talker and aspiring writer was slow in coming. The pain of having to ask his mother for a paltry sixty francs, after playing with his own thousands and knowing that half his capital still remained, was intolerable. Everything combined to make him desperate.

As an artist and a personality Baudelaire was formed by a combination of indolence and strain. Periods of physical idleness and emotional calm gave way to short bursts of work and savage emotional intensity. The excitement to be derived from despair, from destitution, from having to tolerate the intolerable, satisfied his craving for strong sensations—and inspired the artist in him. As a writer Baudelaire needed pressure, which is why the artist succeeded at the expense of the man: the man crumbled beneath the pressure that inspired the work.

The artist was lucky to survive at all. In June 1845 the pressures grew too severe and Baudelaire attempted suicide. The facts are somewhat obscured by legend, and by the would-be suicide's capacity for histrionic clowning *in extremis*. Baudelaire never took himself solemnly. As he wrote of Cramer in *La Fanfarlo*, it is impossible to tell where the man ends and the actor begins. Like his creation he got too much emotional satisfaction from playing parts ever to stop playing them.

He called on two friends in a highly agitated state, tempered by moments of owlish gravity. He asked them with some urgency for their views on the immortality of the soul. He was disappointed by their replies, since he needed to know the truth at once. He proceeded to discourse on the aridity of life, an aridity he considered increased by the introduction of large format newspapers. He then took one friend for a long walk—too long. The friend objected that his parents would begin to worry about him. Baudelaire was reproachful—they would never meet again, and he begrudged him a few measly hours . . .

He then wrote to Ancelle in more serious vein. His letter begins with the statement that when Jeanne places the letter in Ancelle's hands its author will be dead. He will have died a worried man, worried that his mother and half-brother will dispute the will that leaves everything to Jeanne. To prevent this he explains to Ancelle his love of Jeanne and his reasons for commiting suicide. Jeanne is the only person who ever gave him any serenity or pleasure. His half-brother, whom he scarcely knows, has no need of him. His mother, who "so often and always involuntarily poisoned" his life, does not need the money since she has a loving husband. Baudelaire had only Jeanne; she must be his sole heir. He begs Ancelle to see her right, help her with money, advise her. The request is made with an urgency which is witness to the quality of the poet's feelings for his Black Venus.

The reasons he cites for his suicide are fascinating. He is not driven by obvious unhappiness:

70

I *kill* myself without unhappiness. I feel none of those emotional disturbances which men call *unhappiness*. My debts have never been a source of *unhappiness*. Nothing is easier than keeping that sort of thing under control. I am killing myself because I cannot live anymore, because I find that the tedium of going to sleep and the tedium of waking up are intolerable. I am killing myself because I am useless to others—and *dangerous to myself*. I am *killing* myself because I believe I am immortal, and I *hope*.[12]

Baudelaire is anxious to convince that the balance of his mind is as it should be. He probably underplayed the pressure of his debts, since Jeanne might be held to be responsible for them. He was indeed being hard-pressed by creditors at that time, yet it was not banal financial ruin that made him want to die. It was an overpowering disgust at the thought of continuing to live. The price paid for the intense sensations which Baudelaire craved was long periods of emotional and creative sterility, during which nothing, no sensation, no inspiration, could alleviate the overpowering sense of emptiness. It was a sense of self-disgust beyond any alleviation that was the real motive for his attempt.

The suicide plan was not a momentary whim; it remained an enduring urge. Much later, in 1861, truly broken, he would write to his mother on Christmas Day. Years of despaire and failure had simply developed his disgust at living:

> . . . when I have the misfortune to neglect a duty, the duty becomes harder to carry out the next day, and then, daily it grows harder still, until it comes to seem something quite impossible. It derives from the state of anguish and nervous terror in which I live constantly, and it affects obligations of all kinds. I only get out of difficult situations by exploding; but what I endure in living, . . . is really impossible to describe. . . . I constantly see before me suicide as the sole, and above all the easiest, answer to all the horrible complications in the midst of which I have been condemned to live for so many, many years. Most of the time I say to myself if I live I shall always live in the same way, damned, and when natural death comes I shall be old, worn out, out of fashion, crippled by debts, and still dishonored by that infamous tutelage. While if I ended it all at once, after summing up enough energy to compose a strict account of my affairs, the ruins of my fortune really would have to be used to settle. Besides, life, in itself, even without debts, appears to me to be quite devoid of pleasure.[13]

Not much of a Christmas present, the letter has the same undertone of disgust as his suicide note. It is less dramatic and carries a note of almost serene acceptance, but the essential feeling is unaltered.

The actual suicide bid was peculiar, public, and ineffectual. Baudelaire attempted to stab himself in a restaurant, did not do too well, and was required by the police to convalesce in the care of his mother. To his friends he made light of the incident. A companion meets him shortly afterwards:

> "Well, how are you, your wound?"
> The poet interrupted him sharply.
> "You are questioning me? Privat, Banville, Vitu, Deroy were all magnificent, full of tact; they did not mention it. . . . But since you must know, you may as well hear it. You suggested using a dagger . . ."
> "No, a pistol."
> "You informed me that steel was more reliable than poison . . ."
> "I beg your pardon, lead, the pistol bullet."
> [Baudelaire continues] "I had just finished taking luncheon in a restaurant. I took my . . ."
> "Penknife!"
> "My weapon. I stick it in, . . . and feel nothing. Then I tighten my grasp on the handle, and turn the blade in the wound. There is a crack. I thought I had found a vital organ and I pass out."
> "Was it?"
> "No, listen. After I don't know how long, I hear, with increasing clarity an irritating buzz. I seem to be very close to a waterfall or a running tap. As it gets nearer I hear, "Young man . . . kill yourself! At your age! You belong to your family, your country, your *quartier*, your *commissaire de police*!" And then the voice of that splendid girl Jeanne interrupts the guardian of the law and his flow of tepid water.[14]

The episode blends farce and despair. Baudelaire is clowning. He will always enjoy putting on one-man shows, as dandy or as suicide. He did not, it is true, take every step to make sure he would die. He was certainly in part playing to the gallery, more particularly to his mother. But this does not make the affair a meaningless charade. The difference between meaning and not meaning to kill yourself is too clumsy and absolute a separation to be of much help when assessing that extraordinary complex of motives which can persuade a man like Baudelaire to fool with the idea of taking his own life.

His action had, at all events, the immediate effect of returning him to his family. There was a sincere and general attempt at a reconciliation. Baudelaire tried to lead a regular and punctual family life, but the attempt to become a steady *fils de famille* was bound to fail. In less than a month's time he walked out of the Aupick household leaving a note behind him, in which he declared that he was obliged to leave for various reasons, among them psychological ones. While staying with his mother, he had fallen victim to that paralyzing lethargy which he dreaded above all else. It sapped his will, making him incapable of any kind of action. It was a state from which he could only escape by "exploding." He was leaving to try to jerk himself out of it, and because he had to be alone. Moreover he felt he could not become the sort of man the general wanted him to be. He would rather leave and live in hardship than stay on in luxury under false pretences. Then, having taken rooms in a hotel, he asked his mother to forward his things, forbidding her to reproach him. She would be proud enough of him in due course.

Typically he gave a different reason for leaving to his friends: His stepfather served only claret and he was a Burgundy man.

POVERTY HAD ALTERED Baudelaire's appearance without destroying his dandyism. He no longer wore pale pink gloves. Instead he made a virtue of necessity by putting working-class clothes to good, and dandyish, use. Nadar describes him—part dandy, leather shoes, with a new carter's blouse, stiff and meticulously pressed. Hardship was not allowed to destroy his style. Baudelaire remained a dandy and a clown, an elegant, extravagant, and charming companion. He was a natural stylist, both as writer and human being. His dandyism was a mixture of art and life which did not need a hundred thousand francs to survive.

Baudelaire and a friend set off to pawn one of his coats. They need five francs to eat. It is raining, and Baudelaire suggests they take a cab. The friend timidly points out that they might, in the circumstances, be wiser to take a public coach. "I have never been on one of those things," Baudelaire replies haughtily.

He remained a *pince-sans-rire*, ever ready to sacrifice to a good joke. On one occasion he calmly suggested to Banville that they take a bath together. Banville refused to show surprise and agreed. They went to a bathhouse and installed themselves, whereupon Baudelaire announced with a whoop of triumph that he now proposed to read to his captive audience a tragedy in five acts.

On another occasion Baudelaire, immaculately turned out, visited an apothecary. In his politest manner he requested the unfortunate shopkeeper to be so good as to administer him an enema. He maintained that chemists of every class were obliged by law to provide this service. If, said Baudelaire, he was exposing himself to ridicule by demanding it, he was simply trying to keep an old custom alive.

He could also be a delightful, if demanding, companion, as his devoted friend Asselineau attests in this charming sketch:

Baudelaire was the most tyrannical of men in his living habits. Having neither set hours nor rules, living from day to day, from moment to moment, he did not imagine that others might live differently. He came to my place at noon, as I was finishing eating, and wanted me to eat at his time. I objected that not being hungry it was not possible for me to eat.

"Well, when will you be hungry?" he asked, looking me in the eye. "In half an hour perhaps?"

"No."

"In an hour then, eh?"

"No, I tell you, I finished eating a sit-down meal at noon. I shall dine at six, or half-past, like everybody else."

"Like everybody else. Do you regulate your stomach by public clocks?"

On another occasion he said:

"Look, it's 3:15; go and get dressed, it will be 3:30. Then we will proceed slowly along the boulevard. So it will be about 4:00 when we get to a restaurant. By the time we have ordered, been served, etc. . . . ."

The object was to get me to do his bidding, at once. Into the bargain he had an unfortunate taste for adventures. We had left Paris proper and were in an impossible area. Baudelaire wanted to dine, and dine at once. He knew of an eating house where we would do splendidly. . . .

"Why don't we eat here? It does look good."

Hating not to know where I am eating, I insisted on returning to Paris. He grew angry, called me a maniac, a glutton, finicky, a Sardanapalus. However I knew all about his marvelous eating houses, where the food was always frightful. One of his great pleasures was to argue with the owners and their staff. He subjected them to interrogations, exhausted them with questions, comments, instructions, had stand-up arguments with them, until they lost their tempers and made a scene.

"Monsieur, do you cook in fat or in butter? Is your butter fresh? Do you have *excellent* wine?"

"Do you," I asked, "expect him to answer: 'No sir, I have rancid butter and my wine has gone off'?"

But this argument left him unmoved. On the way out, if there had been a good row after eating some filthy stew, he would say, with conviction, "Well, we didn't do too badly."

He imagined himself to be economic and resourceful. One day when we had four francs between us he assured me that we could dine per-fec-tly at Katkomb's and that we should still have a franc each. The only trouble was that he ate three francs' worth of pears for dessert. . . .

[On one occasion] I had a cold in the head, and Baudelaire and I were strolling on the boulevard about five o'clock when he suddenly wanted to eat; it was too early; I agreed anyway, on condition I went home and got another handkerchief.

"All right, after dinner we'll go to your rooms . . ."

"No, this handkerchief is finished. I shall be uncomfortable; let's go to my house."

"But dirty as this handkerchief may be, it will get you through dinner."

"No, damn it, I know that it will not, let me have my way."

"But," insisted Baudelaire, "how long will dinner take? Three-quarters of an hour? During that time *how many times will you have to blow* your nose? Twice? Three times? eh? Now it is just possible that there are two or three spots left to blow on your handkerchief."

"You go too far."

"Let me see it!"

He stretched out a majestic hand. . . .

I have often said that Baudelaire was one of the rare men in whose company I never knew boredom. I seriously believe he was the only one. With him the conversation never flagged.[1]

For all his natural stylishness, this Baudelaire had come a long way from Hôtel Pimodan. He had joined the motley band of impoverished young artists which Henry Murger would portray in his *Scènes de la vie de bohème* [*Scenes from Bohemian Life*; 1848]. A far cry from the sowing of wild oats and the amateur poetry of the Ecole Normande, these artists knew real hunger and hardship, and many of them ended their days coughing up their lungs in a charity ward. History, and Puccini, have glamorized their world, but there was little glamor for writers living on and off the hunger line; so hungry indeed that, in the words of a contemporary, even "cats are wary of them."

If there was no glamor, though, there was a certain manic cheerfulness and sense of style among them. Take one of Baudelaire's earliest literary associates, Privat d'Anglemont. He came from a prosperous family in Guadeloupe. They sent him a regular remittance, which, according to Banville, he would spend at once on buying food for all the prostitutes of the quarter. He wrote a very remarkable book entitled *Paris inconnu* [*Unknown Paris*], published posthumously in 1861, two popular pieces of entertainment, a number of minor works, and probably gave his name to a number of poems that were actually composed by Baudelaire (scholars have amused themselves trying to find out). But regardless of whether or not he did so, Privat was one of the

76

more exotic figures of the 1840s. He was the supreme literary Bohemian, complete to his dying a pauper's consumptive death in a public ward at the age of forty-four. And yet he never let poverty destroy his sense of style. A friend describes him having a shoe shine. Privat sat in splendor upon the shoe shine boy's throne, while the little Savoyard went about the business of polishing what remained of the distinguished writer's boots. Looking up, he inquired with considerable politeness, "Shall I polish the toe nails?" It was in this comical and uneasy world that Baudelaire now moved.

The middle of May 1845 saw the publication of his extended review of that year's art exhibition at the Louvre. The Salon, an annual or biannual affair, was a great social occasion for the whole of Paris. Parisians of all classes, art lovers, and others would crowd through the Louvre, elbow to elbow, admiring some paintings, pouring conspicuous mockery upon others. The bourgeois at the Salon was a traditional butt of artists, art lovers, and caricaturists. But the Salon was not only a social occasion. Commercial art galleries were virtually nonexistent at that time, and the exhibit was the only showcase a painter could expect for his work. An aspiring artist would hope feverishly for acceptance by jury, subsequent public approval, and perhaps even a medal from the state. There was much to be said for the system in which the government provided a link between artists, public, and patron; the Salon served as a meeting place which could bring together the various interests and values held by those factions, forming an excellent foundation for that official Academic art, which was the major form of the age.

Baudelaire had long been obsessed with art. By the time he was twenty-four, he had evolved his own likes and dislikes and went his own way. He would, for example, spend hours in the Louvre looking at the El Grecos, at a time when the painter was quite out of fashion. His *Salon of 1845* is a remarkably original work. The young critic is sure of his likes and dislikes, shows a great sensitivity of response, and a no less great capacity for describing his response in words which re-create its quality for the reader. This capacity is the key to the quality and the nature of his art criticism. A painting inspires feelings in him, and rather than describe the painting he will put his feelings into words in order to re-create in the mind of the reader precisely what he *felt*. The result is a remarkable blend of poetry and criticism, combining the precision of a critic with the emotional resonance of a poet.

He opens his book with a short piece in defense of the bourgeois art lover. The invocation has little to do with the sociology of art; it is simply that Baudelaire is looking for a wide readership. Optimistic to the point of overconfidence, he believes that the bourgeoisie have long been mystified by Salon critics writing for the happy few. Baudelaire believes it possible to talk directly to an uneducated public that knows what it

likes; to help it understand and value its responses without the media-
tion of jargon. The enterprise will also help the public tell good painting
from bad. Baudelaire embarks on his literary career as an optimist; it
would take him twenty years to understand that he had devoted his life
to writing for a nation of Philistines who enjoyed only paintings and
poems with a military and/or Napoleonic content.

The *Salon of 1845* focuses on the paintings of Delacroix. It describes
the pictures he had sent to the exhibition, and seeks to convey both their
appearance and their feeling tone. The author writes with a conviction
and a sensuality of response to plastic values that already makes him
one of the most original critics and prose stylists in France.

Probably the most important and original feature of the work is
Baudelaire's magnificent plea for a painter who would portray the
heroism of modern life:

> The painter, the *real painter* will be the one to catch the epic
> side of contemporary life, and make us see and realize . . . how
> noble, how poetic we are in our cravats and patent leather
> boots.[2]

The arts had hitherto ignored contemporary urban life—escaping into
the past or into nature. Both as critic and poet Baudelaire wanted art
and literature to isolate the beauty that lay beneath the surface of
everyday and seemingly mundane reality and catch the epic side of
modern nineteenth-century civilization, with its new passions and
appetites.

Baudelaire's book was not a commercial success, yet it laid the
foundations of his reputation among the writers and journalists of the
age. It also gave him entrée to a journal with the sinister name of *Le
Corsaire-Satan*. Its elderly editor, Le Poitevin Säint-Alme, had grouped
around him a number of talented and underpaid young writers, including Baudelaire's friends from the Ecole Normande, Prarond and
Le Vavasseur. Baudelaire wrote short pieces of literary criticism for
the paper.

He was working remarkably hard and consistently, producing a
quantity of work, including the peculiar *Choix de maximes consolantes sur
l'amour* [*Choice of Consoling Maxims on Love*; 1846], a collection of blasé
aphorisms, which include little excursions into the shocking, bizarre,
paradoxical, and perverse:

> Your mistress has just recovered from a disastrous bout of small-
> pox, and her face is still encrusted with its scars. As you look
> sadly at her scarred body you hear a dying air played by
> Paganini, which recalls lost hopes and lost happiness. Smallpox

and music blend to become the very formula, the embodiment of your love, and a source of sexual pleasure! For certain still more curious and *blasé* characters, the enjoyment of ugliness derives from a yet more mysterious feeling—a thirst for the unknown, and a taste for the horrible. It is this feeling which we all have in embryo more or less, that sends certain poets to operating theaters and clinics, and women to public executions.[3]

Despite these sadistic and lyrical undertones, Baudelaire sent a copy of his work to a lady with whom he claimed once to have been in love. She is none other than the wife of his treacherous and careful half-brother Alphonse. The book is accompanied by a mildly flirtatious letter. He probably wrote it to spite Alphonse, also perhaps because he indeed once loved her a little in his strange cerebral manner. Baudelaire would never be averse to whistling up a small psychodrama by dint of wishful thinking. At all events Mme Alphonse Baudelaire plays no further part in the poet's emotional life.

A month later the twenty-five-year-old writer published his *Advice to Young Writers*. The piece has its ironies; it is full of counsel which the young Baudelaire would have been wise to take himself. He tells young men of letters that success can only be achieved through steady work and regular hours. More to the point is his observation that there is nothing glamorous about being in debt!

Such perceptions are strange enough; stranger still is his comment upon *"le guignon"*—a favorite expression, meaning an evil star, a permanent bad luck which pursues one for life. Both his poetry and his letters show us that he believed in his unlucky star. Yet here he suggests that belief in *le guignon* is simply evidence of one's own inadequacies.

Baudelaire was not actually a hypocrite. Congenital optimist that he was, he genuinely believed that he had freed himself of those financial and psychological burdens that were to continue to drag him down for twenty years. At all events he was at least preaching from experience.

These were relatively prolific years by Baudelaire's standards. He also produced a second piece of art criticism during this time: the *Salon of 1846*. This is a major work; much more than a critical tour of inspection. After an extended address to the bourgeoisie, the new patrons of art, Baudelaire launches into a justification of criticism, which, as he saw it, was an art form—a kind of poetry through which the critic seeks to convey sensations and judgments to his readers. Criticism, he wrote, must be "partisan, passionate, political, that is to say written from the point of view that opens up the most horizons." By this Baudelaire did not mean that the critic should be committed politically, but that he should be committed to his own opinions, fiercely one-sided; only then can he bring his temperament into play, and temperament is an essential ingredient of good criticism.

He then provides the best analysis we have of the essence of romanticism. Romantic art consists not in choice of subject matter, but in a certain way of feeling. It strives to capture the mood, the temperament of the mid-nineteenth century, to fix modern man's dreams, appetites, passions, and fantasies. Baudelaire penetrates beyond the trappings of the movement—its emphasis on local color and easy exoticism—to see that its essence consists of new modes of emotional experience: modern neurotic man reacting to a hostile world by withdrawing into his divided self. It is tone and not content that signs a work as being romantic. Terror, neurosis, violent feelings—these are its dominants.

The author completes his introduction with a magnificent essay on color. It has all the richness and talent of the mature writer, with Baudelaire using words, their feel, rhythm, and resonance, to evoke a magnificent symphony of rich and sensual colors. We *feel* the colors quite as much as we *see* them, and respond to the texture of the writing as much as to its meaning. The ability to build this kind of rich, strong, yet controlled environment out of words, stringing them together into tight-muscled sentences, will remain Baudelaire's greatest achievement as a prose writer.

The *Salon* proceeds with an extended essay on Delacroix. He begins by giving a brief history of the painter's life, emphasizing the impression that North Africa made upon the painter during his trip to Morocco, a trip which inspired his splendid lion hunts and canvasses such as *The Women of Algiers*. Baudelaire defends Delacroix against critics who steadfastly refused to recognize him as a genius. He presents him as the great romantic painter, a man who realized through tangible forms "the intimate thoughts of the artist." Although never neglectful of Delacroix's technique, it is the feeling tone of the pictures, above all, that fascinates Baudelaire—the pain, melancholy, and savage pleasure which he finds running through such paintings as *Dante and Virgil*, *The Massacre of Scio*, and *The Crusaders' Entry into Constantinople*. The artist's aesthetic principles also fascinated Baudelaire. For Delacroix, nature was "a vast dictionary" of signs and significant symbols; it was a notion strikingly similar to the aesthetic of "Correspondances" which Baudelaire was to formulate himself, as we will see shortly. He also stresses the fact that for Delacroix there is no random element in art. A picture is a machine in which every part plays a definite and determined role. Baudelaire will apply just this approach—careful calculation and the working out of effects—to his own poetry. A poem, too, will be a machine in which every image, every rhyme, is put there to make its own particular contribution to the effect.

Baudelaire understood that modern art was essentially an art of decadence. The Academic tradition was moribund; the painters of his day were all individuals, lacking the support of collectively endorsed heritages of values and traditions. For Baudelaire, the modern age was a time without values, a time of dispersal and fragmentation, of individualism and lack of faith. It is a view which accounts for the sterility of nineteenth-century Academic art, and it provides one of the underlying themes of *Les Fleurs du Mal*.

Baudelaire was not loathe to express his impatience with paintings he disliked, even when executed by artists such as Ingres or Horace Vernet, who were household names. He detested glossy, highly finished work which lacked texture, but which told a story and made the folds of a garment seem so real that you could touch them. For a critic who loved the texture and color harmonies of Delacroix, such cheap and pointless technical virtuosity was intolerable.

The *Salon* ends with a section entitled "On the Heroism of Modern Life." It is an extended defense of modern art in which he suggests that every age has its own particular brand of beauty, the modern age being no exception. High fashion and the sinister Parisian underworld of criminals and whores were just two possible sources of contemporary beauty:

> Parisian life is rich in miraculous and poetic subjects. The miraculous surrounds and feeds us like the air we breathe; but we do not notice it.[4]

Yet for all the originality of Baudelaire's criticism it is arguable that the most important page of the entire work is its back cover, announcing a forthcoming collection of poems. The announcement suggests that Baudelaire had already composed a considerable number of pieces, and that he had some conception of the work which, eleven years later, would become *Les Fleurs du Mal*. His choice of title, *Les Lesbiennes*, was important.

It was sensational and played upon that strange erotic curiosity which the image of lesbian love arouses. Erotic lesbianism had already been featured in romantic literature—in de la Touche's *Fragoletta* (1829), in Gautier's *Mademoiselle de Maupin* (1836), and above all in Balzac's masterpiece *La Fille aux yeux d'or* (1831), a superb study of exotic sensuality on the wilder shores of love. Baudelaire was himself drawn to this kind of forbidden subject, and the sensational ring of *Les Lesbiennes* was justification enough for his choice of title.

Yet there is more here than erotic sensationalism. Lesbians will play an important symbolic role in *Les Fleurs du Mal*. A poem "Delphine et Hippolyte" features a pair of lesbian lovers. The elder mocks the younger for worrying about the eventual fate of her immortal soul. The couple are irrevocably damned, and must live and love in the knowledge of that damnation. The lesbians are heroic and defiant, ignoring all conventions and breaking taboos all in a quest for fulfillment. Yet they are doomed to failure because they seek the infinite through sensation, which is fatally finite. Baudelaire chooses to render this, the essential theme of *Les Fleurs du Mal*, through the image of lesbian lovers not just because they defy convention and are unnatural, but because of the essential aridity of their physical relationship. The lesbians can only irritate one another's desires; they are doomed to an eternity of titillation and delicate stimulation which can go no further. He evokes their frustrated striving and craving in some of his finest and most unequivocal lines:

> The harsh sterility of your sexual pleasures
> Aggravates your thirst and stiffens your skin,
> And the furious wind of concupiscence
> Makes your flesh flap like an old flag.

> *L'âpre stérilité de votre jouissance*
> *Altère votre soif et roidit votre peau,*
> *Et le vent furibond de la concupiscence*
> *Fait claquer votre chair ainsi qu'un vieux drapeau.*

It is the aridity of this misguided quest for the infinite that inspires Baudelaire's first choice of title. Although the actual work would take much more time to mature—it would not reach its definitive form for another fourteen years—by 1846 it is evident that its basic conception has already been found.

Early in 1847 he published *La Fanfarlo*, and this ends the three-year burst of productivity. Never again would he find it so easy to write. His *guignon* was to play an ever more prominent role. Baudelaire would lapse into increasingly frequent bouts of moral paralysis and indolence, during which it was impossible to work. What, at school, had been no more than a faintly disturbing capacity for procrastination had now become a vice which had taken a terrible grip upon the young writer. It is hard enough for any writer to keep regular hours, to get up and turn out his daily quota, every day, regardless. For Baudelaire it now grew well nigh impossible. The prospect of what remained to be done would grow so oppressive and overpowering that he could not bear to make a start: "The only long work is the one you do not dare begin, it becomes a nightmare."[5]

Procrastination was bad enough in a writer; in a journalist it was disastrous. Baudelaire did not respond to the pressure of a deadline;

indeed he enjoyed the feeling that time was slipping away faster and faster, until, once again, he would derive a delightful sense of pain and remorse from having missed yet another boat. Asselineau recalls:

He used to go and ask his friends to put him up, for a night, a day, or longer. There were two reasons: first a hate of his own place, the unpleasantness he had to endure when not living alone, the annoyance of creditors, his constant craving for conversation. How many times used he to come round at four or five P.M. looking busy; "My dear fellow, I have come to ask a really tiresome favor; I know you disapprove but it is urgent. I've promised to let the *Revue de Paris* have sixteen pages by tomorrow noon. You know that that is no problem. You know how quickly I work" (on the contrary, he worked very slowly like all painstaking persons). "Sixteen pages in sixteen hours! That's nothing, but for various reasons I am unable to work at home. So you really must put me up till noon. I shall not disturb you. I will not make any noise. You can put me wherever you like. I'll be as good as gold . . ."

"That's no trouble at all. I have to go out and will only be back in time for bed. You will have the place to yourself."

"By the time you return I shall have broken the back of it. Let's see, five o'clock. Shall I dine first, or dine when I've finished?"

"It's up to you, in any case I'll make you up a bed."

"Oh, a bed—for later, yes please. I shall probably sleep an hour or so to recover."

I came in at midnight, expecting to see Baudelaire hard at work. [He was not in] . . . At one o'clock there was a ring at the door. It was Baudelaire. "My God!" he said, teeth clenched, rubbing his hands.

"What's the matter?"

"The matter, the matter is that as I told you I went and had some dinner. Only, after dinner, to stretch my legs, I went up to the boulevard where I met S . . . that indiscreet and idle chatterbox who kept me talking till midnight. We had to go and have a beer . . . anyway I was thinking up my piece as I talked and it's all written in my head."

He looks up at the clock.

"One o'clock. I have eleven hours. At four pages an hour, four hours is all I need. Ah! you have made up a bed. I scarcely need it, but I suppose I'll have an hour or two of sleep to recover from the sound of S's voice."

"Be careful!"

"Oh! So you think I am a soft liver like you! You don't know that I can awake when I please—in half an hour, if I want to. Yes, that's it, I shall just lie down for an hour, to be in better form, and I'll be done by four in the morning. Good night!"

On waking next morning at eight, I saw Baudelaire wrapped in blankets, head turned to the wall.

"I know, I know," he said after a moment in his clear voice. "I have been awake for some time."

On the table the paper had not been touched, the books not opened.

"What about the sixteen pages . . .?"

"Joking again, are you?"

"But you have not written a line!"

"All right, I yielded to idleness."

"But what will they say at the *revue*?"

"I shall explain."

"Anyway, it's only eight o'clock and that gives you your four hours. There is still time."

"Joking again!"

Of course, not only did Baudelaire not go to the *revue*, he had lunch with me and we talked all afternoon.[6]

Such scenes occurred regularly. Baudelaire loved his leisure too much to sacrifice it to regular work. Yet as he talked "all afternoon," the pleasure he derived from conversation was tempered by a nagging feeling of remorse at having missed another deadline. Although such behavior had a comic side, it also caused him real distress. There are few things as painful as the admission that time is slipping through one's fingers, that day after day has been wasted and nothing achieved. Yet every time one is about to settle down to work, there is another distraction—sufficient to stop one from working, but not sufficient to alleviate one's sense of guilt. Time and again Baudelaire would long for spiritual order and discipline, for the strength to force himself to settle down to steady concentrated work. His very view of good and evil is conceived in terms of concentration or waste. He writes: "Of the centralization and the vaporization of the self. All is there."[7] Centralization is achieved through the will which focuses all spiritual and mental energy upon the task in hand. Vaporization is its negation—the wasteful dissipating and frittering of energy. Baudelaire knew a lot about vaporization.

This period also saw a further deterioration in his relationship with his mother. He asked her to return to him all his letters written in 1847, since they were too dreadful to be preserved. Only four survive, but they are eloquent enough. The first is a brief note. Baudelaire had tried to extract more money from Ancelle, to cope with a period of real hardship. Ancelle required his mother's approval. Baudelaire had taken a cab to her door and sent her up a note:

It is only when I am reduced to the ultimate extremes, that is to say *when I am very hungry*, that I come to visit you, so much does it upset and disgust me. . . . [He asks for enough money to last a few days.] I am not coming up because I know what *insults*, what insulting humiliations, I shall have to endure to pay for what I want. I am going *straight* back to Neuilly with your authorization. I am waiting downstairs in the cab. Destroy this letter, *it would be shameful to you if it were ever found*.[8]

Among these 1847 letters is one of the most revealing the poet ever wrote. A devastating piece of self-analysis, it reveals his inability to work, his addiction to alcohol and drugs, his physical hardships, and his hopeless way with money; but we also see that he set himself the highest standards and had real faith in his genius. The letter combines desperate begging with occasional bursts of dreadful optimism, and suggests as well that his sanity is at risk. Despite the cruelty of his mother's last letter, he is turning to her one last time:

If you knew the effort it cost me to write to you again, despairing of making you understand, as your life is so easy and ordered, how I get into such predicaments. Imagine a perpetual idleness, the result of a constant ill-being, with a deep loathing of that idleness, and the absolute impossibility of getting out of it, owing to a constant shortage of money. . . . Here is what has just happened to me. Delighted to have a place to live and some furniture, but short of money, I had been looking for some for two or three days, when, last Monday, worn out with fatigue, *ennui*, and hunger, I put up at the first hotel I came to, and am still there, *for good reason*. I had just given the address to a friend to whom I had lent money four years ago, in the days when I had money, but he has let me down. Anyway I have not spent a lot, thirty or thirty-five francs in a week; but that is not the worst. For supposing, by dint of your, alas, always insufficient generosity, you were good enough to get me out of this wretched scrape, what would I do *tomorrow*? For idleness kills, devours, consumes me. I really do not know how I have the strength to cope with the disastrous consequences of that idleness, and still retain total intellectual lucidity, and a perpetual hope for wealth, happiness and peace. Now, I beseech you with *hands joined in prayer*, so strongly do I feel that I am nearing the limit not just of other people's patience but of my own. Send me, *if it costs you a thousand efforts, and even though you may not believe in the actual usefulness of this final favor, not just the sum in question but enough to live on for three weeks.* . . . I believe so firmly in the value of time and in my strength of will that *I know for certain,* that if I could live an ordered life for two or three weeks, *my sanity will be saved.* It's a last attempt, *it's a gamble.* Bet on the unknown, dear mother, please. The explanation for these six years which would have been so strangely and disastrously spent, had I not a mental and physical health which nothing could destroy, is a simple one; it is summed up as follows: thoughtlessness, procrastination of the most mundane and sensible projects, and therefore poverty, and more poverty still. Do you want an instance: it often happens that I am obliged to remain in bed for three days, sometimes for lack of clean clothes, sometimes for lack of wood. Frankly, laudanum and wine are poor ways to fight unhappiness. They pass the time but do not rebuild your life. Besides it takes money to stupefy oneself. The last time you were so good as to give me fifteen francs I had not eaten for *two days,* forty-eight hours. I spent all my time going to Neuilly, I did not dare confess to Ancelle what I had done, and I kept awake and on my feet thanks to the brandy I had been given, and I detest spirits, they ruin my stomach. I hope these confessions . . . are never made known to a living soul, or to posterity! For I still believe that posterity matters to me . . . I have just reread these two pages and even I find them strange. I have never dared complain so vocally. Please understand that I am excited by sufferings of a kind *of which you have no conception.* The absolute idleness of my life, on the surface, contrasts with the constant turmoil of my ideas and sends me into incredible rages. I detest my faults, and detest you for not believing in the sincerity of my intentions. The fact is that for the last few months I have been living in an unnatural condition. . . . In general then my absurd way of life is to be explained as follows: thoughtless spending of money intended for work. Time flies, the necessities remain. *For the last time* wanting to get out of it and believing in my willpower, I have turned to you.

Baudelaire goes on to assure his mother that it really *is* the last time, that he finds his situation too painful not to wish to extricate himself once and for all. He plans to go back to the tropics, where he has been offered a job. If he goes it will be to punish himself for having failed to live up to his dreams. He then talks of some distinctly imaginary literary plans, including a novel. He assures her again that he will make a fresh start. He knows that he is starting late, but his mother must understand that some people mature more slowly than others. As for him, a few more days of idleness could prove fatal:

> I told you that I have abused my strength so much that I have reached the limits of my own patience, and that I am incapable of a last supreme effort without a little help.[9]

His recriminations and sense of humiliated disgust are not to be dismissed as attempts to convince his mother that he has changed. He both understands and detests his weakness. He sees it with a terrible lucidity, and on this occasion consciousness of evil is no consolation. He understands that he is destroying himself and that he has gone too far along the path of self-destruction to be able to stop. Although the protestation that he was a late starter may invite a cynical smile, Baudelaire was absolutely right. The dandy-wastrel could not write real poetry until he had known real despair. The dreadful and destructive idleness that crippled Baudelaire, the thoughtlessness that ruined and pauperized him, were both part of his spiritual and artistic maturing. It was thanks to them that he would be able to portray with such understanding, scenes of self-destruction, dissipation, and waste set against an awareness that time was running out.

The mention of wine and laudanum introduces another aspect of his self-destruction. From this stage on he would be a heavy drinker. He drank partly out of ostentation but chiefly out of need, and by the end of his life he would have quite a severe problem. Yet he never became an alcoholic. He saw drinking as an attempt to find satisfaction through short-lived sensation, and hence as symptomatic of a sensation-craving age. He planned to write a play about drunkenness for that very reason. Drunkenness, he believed, was a special characteristic of the modern artist: a despairing personality who receives inspiration from self-destruction and is one of nature's losers. He saw Edgar Allan Poe as the saddest and greatest alcoholic of the age, and he identified with him profoundly, as will later be seen. In an essay on Poe he describes the bitter and wretched drinking man of letters as an essentially nineteenth-century phenomenon; he hopes "to rediscover in drink the calm or terrifying visions with which he is already old friends."[10] The new man of letters, in Baudelaire's analysis, is an outcast, a pariah, a professional loser, which is why he both smokes and drinks to excess.

Baudelaire was not only becoming a heavy drinker, but an opium addict as well. Laudanum, or tincture of opium, was a perfectly reputable medicine in the nineteenth century, and Baudelaire had excessive recourse to it. By the end of his life he was taking up to 150 drops a day—75 drops would have been fatal to a non-user. But this was a relatively modest habit, since the consumption of 1,500 drops a day was not unknown. He initially took laudanum as a pain killer, and seems to have used it to alleviate the side effects of his syphilitic infection. However, he also complained frequently that laudanum had ruined his digestion at times. He constantly asserted that he was strong as an ox and would recover; but he overestimated his strength.

His reliance upon alcohol and laudanum, and the intoxication they produced, sapped a willpower which had never been strong. Moreover, his disease was beginning to reassert itself. In later years the condition he now described as a state of idleness and procrastination would develop into a dreadful physical and mental torpor, which made him feel heavy as lead and was the first really clear sign that syphilis was attacking his brain. However, it appears in retrospect that these bouts of so-called idleness were the earliest symptoms of this degeneration.

A whole series of factors conspired at this time to make Baudelaire find work impossible. His financial circumstances and the shrewish Jeanne Duval made it impossible for him to work at home—when he had a home. He was naturally lazy and reluctant to face reality, preferring to put things off as he had been doing since his school days. His craving for sensation and his misery made him a heavy drinker, often making it impossible to think or to write clearly on mornings after, and the effects of his disease had encouraged him to resort to laudanum, —which further sapped his will. Finally the disease itself was beginning to threaten his mind. His *guignon* had combined so many and various forces to sap his modest store of energy that it is finally a miracle that Baudelaire could ever write at all.

Contemporaries describe him apparently playing to the gallery by suddenly deciding to shave off his flowing curls and dye his hair green. The action is very much part of the legend, and at one with his perpetual and often childish desire to shock. Yet shock apart, secondary syphilis may already have been causing his hair to fall out, causing Baudelaire to make a virtue of necessity by cropping it short and turn virtue into a sad and dandyish gesture by dying it green into the bargain. With the loss of that hair so well painted by Deroy only four years before, the poet's last link with the elegant young man of the Hôtel Pimodan was severed. The new, shorn Baudelaire had a grim, skull-like look about him. The loss of his romantic appearance was a suitable preparation for the future.

BAUDELAIRE'S POLITICAL VIEWS and activities—more specifically the part he played in the revolution of February 1848, which brought in the Second Republic, and in the June Days, the savage street fighting which took place in Paris later that year—have puzzled his biographers. His attitudes were ambiguous and appropriate to a lover of contradiction and paradox. Contemporary fashion finds political ambiguity hard to understand, preferring to distinguish between the radicals, who are "the good guys," and the rest, deemed less good. Since Baudelaire is a great writer and analyst of the modern consciousness, his modern admirers wish to see him as a good guy. Yet it is less simple than that.

Strangely enough, the dandy of the Hôtel Pimodan had, by the late 1840s, acquired pronounced socialist sympathies. Half of him looked socialist: his working man's blouse was a kind of political statement. But in analyzing his political views one must remember that he wore that blouse on top of immaculate black trousers and patent leather shoes.

Dandyism and socialism were more compatible than one might suppose. The dandy rejects materialistic and finally capitalistic society; his image is founded in a gesture of defiance and refusal. The step from aesthetic rejection to political activism was not enormous, and was a step actually taken by Eugène Sue, who became a socialist deputy in 1848, elected by a massive working-class vote.

In the late 1840s Baudelaire moved in socialist artistic circles. Very much a part of the *Lumpenproletariat* of journalism, far removed from its prosperous and successful practitioners, he gravitated towards the so-called realists—the writer Champfleury and the painter Courbet. Champfleury was the first author to be known as a realist. His mediocre works were documentary novels, painstakingly observed re-creations of slices of provincial and peasant life. He was a humanitarian with a great concern for *les humbles*. This concern was shared by Courbet, who tried in his art to combine the grand manner of Academic painting with the portrayal of crude life in his native Franche-Comté—peasants, navvies, a provincial funeral, drunken clerics, and the like. His work had a massive and disturbing power, making a virtue of monumental and rugged provincial realities. He was a close friend of the poet for some years; indeed he painted his portrait at this time. A radical all his life, he was held responsible for the demolition of the column in the Place Vendôme during the Commune and made to pay for its restoration.

The realists were part of Bohemia. They affected large beards and a certain crudeness of manner and dress. They went in for hard drinking and noisy assemblies, frequenting the brasseries, or German beer palaces, that had sprung up in Paris in recent years. The most famous of these, the Brasserie Andler, was Courbet's headquarters. There he and his set would meet, drink, sing working-class and revolutionary songs, and have fierce discussions about the meaning of art, life, and property. The main room had a large stove in the middle, Bavarian oak tables, and benches. Courbet himself was a dominating figure, with his great frame, his large black beard; his appearance was described as "Assyrian." Another haunt was the Brasserie des Martyrs, a more luxurious establishment with splendid mirrors, an abundance of gold leaf, and paintings. Said to be so dazzling that it made the eyes ache, it was a model brasserie, with "serious" sofas, oak tables (both "pleasing and comfortable"), caryatids, artificial flowers, and much German beer.

The brasseries were centers for artists developing a new concern for details of everyday life and the problems of ordinary people—an aesthetic concern with realism that went hand in hand with political radicalism.

It is important to understand the close relationship which existed then between art and politics. Baudelaire is the product of an age which had witnessed the collapse of established guidelines to truth and morality. It was a period when the leadership traditionally provided by monarchy, aristocracy, and church was spiritually bankrupt. Art had begun to take over the functions these elements had once fulfilled; it became both religion and political creed. Discussions about the nature of art became discussions about its legitimate aims. Some poets had come to see poetry as something much more than the creation of beauty. Victor Hugo believed that the artist had a political and social mission; indeed in his later years he considered himself the founder of a new religion. The poet Alphonse de Lamartine went further still, becoming the first president of the Second Republic. In other words, a commitment to a certain aesthetic meant commitment to a corresponding political attitude. Art and politics were much of a piece and not, as yet, easily divorced. To be a convinced realist at this time meant that one was also a committed socialist, and Art itself could readily assume a political function.

Such commitment might seem foreign to Baudelaire, yet this is not so. He was intermittently moved by compassion for the victims of urban society—beggars, derelicts, broken old men and women all excite his sympathy, even though it may sometimes be tinged with sadism. He knew hardship at close enough quarters to have feeling for the human debris of his world, a world which did not look after its weaker members and in which it was all too easy for the weakest to sink like stones.

It was compassion of this kind combined with sheer propinquity that made him associate with Courbet, Champfleury, and the working-class poet Pierre Dupont. Feeling cast out of the world which should by rights have been his, Baudelaire joined forces with other outcasts. Yet his radical political convictions developed beyond compassion. One of his most famous sonnets, "Correspondances," was composed at about this time. It is an account of the universe, and men in it, as a unified whole, in which earthly realities reflect the reality beyond. On earth all sensations, colors, sounds "correspond" to one another, echo one another to achieve a "shadowy and profound unity." It is his affirmation that the world, which appears to the casual eye random, haphazard, unstructured, and meaningless, is in fact part of a unified and interlocking cosmic whole.

The views expounded in this poem are almost certainly derived from the thought of the radical utopian socialist Charles Fourier. His system sought to restructure human society according to certain ordering principles which underlie human behavior. Instead of a society which fails to meet the needs of human temperament, he would substitute a society based upon those needs, to re-create the world of Harmony.

This places Baudelaire's socialism in a very special light. His own work describes the plight of modern man adrift in a world devoid of certainties, who destroys himself by turning to sensation as a substitute. It is very plausible that in the late 1840s Baudelaire sympathized with the Fourierists because he believed that Fourier's system might provide just those certainties which traditional culture lacked. If Baudelaire was ever a convinced socialist, it was the possibility of order and meaning that socialism offered, rather than any humanitarian feelings, that made him one.

But not even Fourier was sacred to Baudelaire. On one occasion he and Champfleury heard of a Fourierist meeting to be held in the studio of a friend. They crept upstairs, locked speaker and audience in, and threw the key down the lavatory!

Even at this time Baudelaire had an uneasy relationship with serious socialists. The dandy derived too much pleasure from posing and shocking, too much pleasure from sheer sensation ever to take his politics seriously. Baudelaire would always enjoy going against the light, making outrageous observations for the joy of seeing his outraged hearers protest. It was to indulge that somewhat sadistic urge of his that, in the *Salon of 1846*, he had talked of the joys of beating a republican with a rifle butt:

> Have you ever felt, you who have all been drawn by your *flâneur*'s curiosity to the heart of a riot, the pleasure that I feel when I see a guardian of the public sleep—a policeman or municipal guard . . . beat a republican? Like myself you said in your heart: beat him, beat him a little harder, O policeman of my heart . . . the man you beat is against roses, perfume, is a lover of domestic utensils; he is against Watteau, against Raphael, passionately against luxury, fine arts, and literature, a sworn iconoclast, the executioner of Venus and Apollo. The humble and anonymous worker no longer wishes to produce roses and public perfumes; he wants to be free, the ignoramus, and is incapable of founding a workshop for new flowers and perfumes. Beat the shoulder blades of the anarchist religiously.[1]

For all his humanitarianism and his socialist associates, these lines describe the most consistent element in Baudelaire's shifting and often burlesque political convictions. He always detested vulgarity a little more than he could love the vulgar.

Nevertheless Baudelaire in 1848 was a republican in appearance, at least to the extent of his wearing red cravats:

> At that time he wore . . . red cravats, with a sack-like overcoat colored black, in which his extremely thin and lanky body danced about. The head was large compared to the body, with a big curved forehead. His eye was bright and lively, the mouth large, and often deliberately grimacing when he wished to express his loathing for the commonplace and conventional. It was a sensual mouth.[2]

The revolution which brought down the July Monarchy of Louis-Philippe after some fighting found Baudelaire in the streets, first as spectator then as participant. Parisians were used to street fighting. They had had ample opportunity to enjoy it over the last eighteen years. Contemporary chroniclers of the events of 1848 frequently describe taking a stroll from barricade to barricade, as they took in the scene.

Baudelaire also exposed himself, as a friend vividly recalls:

On February 22, 1848, I went, like crowds of others, to see what was happening towards the Champs-Elysées. I was with Promayet the musician, Courbet, and Baudelaire. A detachment of mounted municipal guards charged at a slow trot, simply to stop crowds from forming, and forced us to take cover behind the parapet of the little gardens that used to go round the edge of the Place de la Concorde. It was just before nightfall. There we were surrounded by soldiers, and looking for an opportunity to withdraw, when some firemen went by in the direction of the Avenue de Beaugeon, where it seemed that a handful of rioters had taken a small garrison by surprise and set it on fire. A few moments later the same firemen came back, pursued by a volley of stones from the rioters, who had forced them to retreat. Suddenly the scene changed. Down the Champs-Elysées came some municipal infantry with bayonets fixed and at the ready, and now the rioters began to run. One of them, unarmed and pursued by two soldiers, dodged round a tree, slipped and fell, and there, in front of us, one of the municipals bayoneted him in the chest. We all cried out in horror, and a worker who had also taken cover on the edge of a garden had such a violent attack of nerves that Promayet and I had to take him home, while Courbet and Baudelaire went to *La Presse* to denounce this act of terrible ferocity. . . .

The next day about one P.M. we set off for the Café de la Rotonde, Champfleury, Baudelaire, Promayet, and I, to see what was going on. We met Abrantès who told us that there was some fighting in the Quartier St.-Denis. . . . We could hear firing from the Place du Châtelet, and we carried on. All the shops had their shutters up. We went from street to street not knowing where we were going, turning back the two or three times we came to barricades. . . . All of a sudden . . . about a hundred meters away, we heard the sound of running—like charging soldiers—then a terrible fusillade, cries of "My God," and the screams of wounded and dying men. It was a company of the 17th Light, the Duc d'Aumale's regiment, which had just taken a barricade, not without leaving some of its blood on the pavements.

[They visit the soldiers, who are cursing about their casualties.] Three months later, in June, the rebels would have made us join them behind their barricades, and the soldiers would have shot at us for joining. In February it was just the municipals and the people who hated one another; the people yelling insults at the soldiers, and the soldiers bayoneting innocent bystanders.

Baudelaire's friend goes on to describe the celebrations that night when the fighting ends and a republic is established. Soldiers and workers crowd the streets, arms linked, singing republican songs.

> It was nearly nine o'clock when we went back to the Left Bank. Baudelaire, with his favorite expression, offered to "keep me company" during dinner; he was delighted with what he had seen in the last two days; he had been really interested by the opening of the drama, it was just the conclusion that was not to his taste, and he felt that the curtain had come down a little soon. I had never known him so gay, so cheerful, so tireless. . . . He who was not used to walking. His eyes sparkled. After dinner we went to the Rotonde, and in that café which had been so lively on the preceding evenings we found Courbet, entirely alone in front of a beer and in the company of his pipe. It was a dreadfully dark night and a mournful silence shrouded the area. Suddenly the tocsin rang out . . . and someone ran past crying in a voice that froze us with terror:
> "To arms, they're slaughtering our brothers."
> [They run out to a square near the river.]
> A hail of bullets struck the house above our heads, and we ran back even faster. Hearing the tocsin, the municipals had run up and bayoneted the bell ringer. Taking up a position in the porch of the church, they opened fire whenever they heard footsteps coming towards them. . . . They were no longer men, they were veritable wild beasts.
> [The next morning] I discovered a barricade on my doorstep, the district was thick with them. At the Buci crossroads I came across Baudelaire and Barthet, armed with shotguns, and ready to open fire behind a barricade that covered them, as yet, only to the waist.[3]

Baudelaire sided with the revolutionaries; he stood behind a barricade, thereby proving to later admirers that he was a committed radical. Yet he was not necessarily inspired to risk his neck because of any political conviction. Once again Baudelaire is clowning. He had been highly stimulated by the fighting; it had provided him with the kind of excitement which set his adrenaline coursing and enabled him to explode out of his habitual condition of lethargy. He thrived on the stimulus of his actions, and was less concerned by their political significance. This emerges from another eye-witness report of Baudelaire at the Buci crossroads, slightly drunk, in the midst of a crowd which had just looted a gunsmith's:

> He was carrying a beautiful brand-new double-barreled gun
> and a superb and no less immaculate yellow leather cartridge
> case. I hailed him and he came up in great excitement.
> "I've just fired a shot," he said. . . .
> He was shouting a lot, always the same refrain, they must go
> and gun down General Aupick.[4]

Baudelaire the revolutionary clown is all there. By looting and carrying arms he was in real danger of getting shot. But he courts that danger not for the republic, but for the excitement, and the exhilarating idea of bagging his stepfather who was commandant of the Polytechnic School at the time. There is no doubt that Baudelaire enjoyed bringing down the established order because Aupick was part of it, and stood totally behind its values. At all events, the Baudelaire of February 1848 had his own motives for manning the barricades, and they were not necessarily the motives of a revolutionary. He enjoyed the disruption, and also a certain ignoble quality in which he could wallow:

> There is in every change something both infamous and agree-
> able, something that resembles both infidelity and moving
> house. That is sufficient to explain the French Revolution.[5]

One immediate consequence of the revolution was a relaxation of controls over the press. This created numerous openings for would-be journalists such as Baudelaire; indeed, he briefly collaborated with Courbet and Champfleury to found a socialist sheet entitled *Le Salut Public*. The name was suggested by Baudelaire, and it recalled the Committee of Public Safety which was responsible for the Terror of 1793. The paper did not have a tremendous working capital—eighty or ninety francs. The first number, written in two hours, may or may not have sold well: the vendors hired to distribute it disappeared with the take. The second was sold by the publishers themselves. There was not enough money left for a third.

The republican clubs that sprang up at this time were a perpetual source of entertainment to the bohemians. Witness this account about the king of Bohemia, Henry Murger:

> I never saw Murger in a merrier mood than one evening in
> March 1848. He had wanted to see what a club was like. Some of
> his bohemian friends had taken him to one of the vaults of Saint-
> Sulpice where a [republican] club had been established. There,

a bourgeois seeking the votes of the great working class of Paris was fulminating against the infamous aristocrats, accusing them above all of waging furious war on the innocence of the pure young girls of the noble proletariat.

Thereupon a worker had jumped onto the platform and shouted:

"It's not true . . . the aristos get nothing but our leftovers. And they take them to their beds when we've had enough of them."

"There's the working class for you," Murger concluded. "A lot of conceited brutes. Their vanity is stronger than their hatred. They boast of the dishonor of their sisters and daughters simply to impress the bourgeois."[6]

Baudelaire himself soon lost any political high seriousness he may once have possessed. He attended an electoral meeting addressed by a socialist candidate who painted a moving and sensational picture of the plight of the working class under Louis-Philippe. Such trite humanitarian talk enraged Baudelaire. The invitation to applaud noble sentiments was too obvious, a cheap way of feeling good. The opportunity was too good to miss, and Baudelaire heckled the luckless speaker without mercy. He had never been a joiner, and he found the widespread and unreflecting endorsement of republican values intolerable. Republicanism had become an instantly received idea. Baudelaire could never stand conformism, which he considered to be particularly characteristic of the French. As he saw it, the French only enjoyed politics:

Not only because France was created by providence to search for the true rather than the beautiful, but because the utopian, communist, alchemical quality of all French minds admits only one single exclusive passion—social theorizing. Here everyone wishes to be like everybody else—provided that everyone is like him . . . whence the ruination and oppression of all originality.[7]

This sheep-like conformity encouraged Baudelaire to move away from socialism, but even more important was the sheer pleasure of heckling the republicans—beating up the good guys, and changing sides:

I understand that one should desert a cause in order to know what it feels like serving another. It might be nice to take it in turns to be victim and executioner.[8]

However, for all his misgivings and his clowning, Baudelaire did not desert socialism entirely; that would be too simple. The so-called June Days saw some of the most violent street fighting ever, with terrible casualties on both sides. The insurgents were repressed with a violence only surpassed by that exerted by the Versailles government in winding up the Commune. The April elections had returned an essentially conservative Chamber of Deputies—not at all to the liking of radical Paris. There was one attempt at a socialist rising in May. Then, in June, the decision was made to shut down the public workshops that had been opened earlier in the year to provide work for the otherwise unemployed. Fighting broke out in the streets. Fifty thousand workers took up arms. In three days of bitter hand-to-hand combat some ten thousand of them were killed, and it has been claimed that more officers were lost in the fighting than in all of Napoleon's campaigns. No prisoners were taken. Subsequently another eleven thousand men were deported.

Once again Baudelaire was exhilarated by the fighting—although it was very different from the events of February. Both sides were guilty of atrocious and idiotic violence on a terrible scale, a scale which excited Baudelaire to real hysteria and paradisiac emotional fulfillment. Le Vavasseur met him in the thick of it:

> Baudelaire took part in the June Days of 1848 as a rebel. Chennevières and I had been on guard duty at the Louvre during the days. As soon as the Faubourg Saint-Antoine surrendered, we set off to find out what we could. In the garden of the Palais Royal we met a national guardsman from home and took him off for a drink. . . . Cutting across towards the Café Foy we saw coming towards us two people with very different appearances: one was nervous, excited, feverish, agitated; the other calm, carefree almost—Charles Baudelaire and Pierre Dupont. We went into the café. I have never seen Baudelaire in such a state. He held forth, shouted, boasted, was longing to become a martyr.
>
> "They've just arrested de Flotte. Is it because his hands reeked of powder? Smell mine!"
>
> Then there were socialist pyrotechnics: "The apotheosis of social bankruptcy" and so on. [His companions have good reason to feel that his wild talk was endangering all their lives, and are relieved to get away.] . . . Whatever may have been thought of Baudelaire's courage, he was brave on that day, and would have gone to his death.[9]

By October Baudelaire changed his spots again. He became the editor of a conservative daily paper, the *Représentant de l'Indre*, at Châteauroux. He may have prided himself on being enough of a professional to do the job, however distasteful; but he discovered at once that his distaste was too much for him. On arrival the local dignitaries had arranged a banquet in his honor. The conversation of these provincial worthies, now recovered from their dose of red terror, did not inspire Baudelaire to break his silence. However, his first piece, a plea for law and order, opened with a eulogy of the "gentle Marat" and "Robespierre who was a real man," with his request for three hundred thousand heads. He did not increase his popularity by arriving with a mistress whom he tried to pass off as his wife. Baudelaire's perversity proved too much for Châteauroux, and he returned to Paris.

He retained his socialist affiliations. Baudelaire had long been in the habit of writing fan letters to the famous. The strangest of all such letters were sent to the working-class socialist leader and thinker Pierre Joseph Proudhon, the author of *Qu'est-ce que la propriété?* [*What Is Property?*], the father of anarchism and trade unionism in France, and the most prestigious radical of 1848. Baudelaire had admired him greatly. In August 1848 he wrote to Citizen Proudhon begging to see him. The letter was deferential—Baudelaire knows that Proudhon is very busy, but will wait indefinitely to meet him. He followed his first letter, which failed to secure a meeting, with a second informing Proudhon that his life is in danger: there is a plot to have him assassinated. The letter goes on to profess the poet's profound and continuing confidence in his leadership.

There is no reason to doubt Baudelaire's sincerity, nor is there reason to pretend that he did not enjoy writing letters which assured celebrities of his devoted admiration. Besides, writing to a radical leader about a government plot on his life was to place oneself in the very center of political intrigue—or thereabouts. The enjoyment Baudelaire derived from such a letter was altogether compatible with that derived from the beating of a republican. Both activities provided their own kind of drama and enjoyment.

In the meantime the incorrigible Baudelaire made use of the revolution in a different way—as a pretext for cadging money. He writes to his mother:

Another reason I would like you to comply with my request is that I really fear an insurrection here, and nothing is worse than being without money at such times.[10]

We know little of his activities in 1849. At the end of that year he spent some time in Dijon. He seems to have gone there to work on another newspaper, a socialist one this time. However, this did not prevent him from putting a would-be radical firmly in his place, one Madier de Montjau—an aspiring "eagle of democracy," full of revolutionary fervor. Baudelaire found his enthusiastic ignorance pitiful, and in a letter to Ancelle he spelled out what socialism meant in Dijon:

> So I talked to him of peasants' socialism—unavoidable, violent, stupid and bestial as socialism by firebrand or sickle. It frightened him, and cooled his ardor. He retreated in the face of logic. He is a fool, or rather an exceptionally vulgar climber.[11]

Any active interest Baudelaire took in politics came to an end with the coup d'état of December 2, by which the president of the Second Republic, who had sworn to uphold its constitution, took illegal possession of the state and proclaimed himself Emperor Napoleon the Third. The coup d'état was a traumatic experience for republicans of all complexions. It was not just the dawn arrests and mass deportations that seemed to inaugurate a new style in politics, nor was it the fact that this illegal act on the part of a head of state had put an end to the republic after less than four years. It was rather that the coup d'état enjoyed widespread popular acclaim. The people of France were only too pleased to be ruled by another Napoleon illegally come to power. It was the massive endorsement of Louis Napoleon's theft of a nation that sickened Baudelaire's generation of politics once and for all.

It is from that moment that the divorce between art and politics begins. Writers such as Flaubert, and indeed Baudelaire, shed any political awareness and took refuge in pure creative activity, an ivory tower. The shift away from political concern was not a conscious one— it was a consequence of the fact that for a decade or more there would be no politics in France.

Baudelaire greets the December coup d'état with profound disgust, as an utterly ignoble event, the antithesis of revolution. He refers to the "shattering effect" of events upon him. They have destroyed his taste for politics, and left him sick and indifferent. He did not even bother to vote against the official candidate in the rigged elections that followed. He wrote to Ancelle:

> You didn't see me vote; it was a deliberate decision on my part. *The second of December physically depoliticized me. There are no general ideas left* . . . if I'd voted I could vote only for myself. Perhaps the future belongs to the *déclassés*.[12]

Baudelaire was right; voting was indeed pointless in elections so designed to favor the official candidates that the opposition was reduced to a parliamentary party three strong.

By the early 1850s Baudelaire is not only depoliticized, he is also totally opposed to socialism. The socialism of the 1840s had had a

Fourierist basis, a tinge of almost mystic utopianism. The socialism of the 1850s was very different: utilitarian, practical, and boringly anticlerical; it reduced man to the sum of his physical needs, and upheld the virtues of science and its capacity to perfect the human race. For Baudelaire, with his profound belief in the intrinsic evil of natural man, such attitudes were anathema. He came to consider socialism as part and parcel of the "Americanization" of his culture—the subordination of all spiritual considerations to crass materialism. Socialism encouraged natural man to be himself.

Rejection of socialism also meant rejection of realism. Art which aspires simply to reproduce nature is not worthy of its name; art must improve upon nature, triumph over it. Consequently Baudelaire lost touch with Courbet and Champfleury, whom he came to regard if not as enemies, then at least as misguided simpletons. When Courbet wished to include a portrait of Baudelaire in his vast allegorical painting *L'Atelier*, he was obliged to base it on the study he had done six years before.

Marxists would regard Baudelaire's new state as one of bourgeois alienation. Certainly he withdrew from barricades of every affiliation. His poem "Paysage," which describes him drawing inspiration from the city, shows him tucked away in an attic:

> Riot storming vainly at my window
> Does not make me raise my head from my desk.

> *L'Emeute, tempêtant vainement à ma vitre,*
> *Ne fera pas lever mon front de mon pupitre.*

The poet is totally immersed in the world of his imagination.

Baudelaire's rejection goes beyond mere withdrawal: it becomes a positive loathing for democracy and mob rule. Looking back upon his work, he finds himself guilty of "certain base flatteries addressed to democracy."[13] He felt he had been a fool to seek popular success of any kind. Although his views are tempered by bitterness they are in sympathy with the early desire to beat up republicans. He comes to regard the "Marseillaise" as the "anthem of the *canaille*."[14] The explanation of his behavior in 1848 lies in the revelation that he considers revolution to be essentially evil: a mass yielding to a natural love of destruction. Making revolution offered Baudelaire the same pleasure as making love: the certainty of doing wrong. Accordingly, a revolutionary should go the whole way:

> When one talks of *real* revolution one horrifies them. Old maids!
> I know that when I consent to be a republican *I do evil, consciously,*

yes! Long live revolution! Always! Whatever! But I know what I'm doing! I always did! I say "Long live revolution!" as I would say "Long live destruction! Long live expiation! Long live punishment! Long live death!" We all have republicanism in our veins. As we have the pox in our bones. We are democratized and syphilitic.[15]

Although he wrote that as an older and bitter man, it was an observation that he might have made at any time in his life.

The enjoyment he derived from street fighting never blinded him to its futility:

The cannon fires, limbs fly. . . . You hear the groans of the victims and the shouts of the executioners. . . . It is humanity in search of happiness.[16]

Looking back upon his behavior in 1848 a decade later, he sees it as sensation seeking, a kind of drunkenness. It is part of his enduring quest for intense experience:

My intoxication in 1848.
What kind of intoxication was it?
A taste for vengeance. *Natural* love of destruction.
Literary intoxication. The memory of books read.
The 15th of May—a taste for destruction as ever.
Legitimate taste if everything natural were legitimate.
The horrors of June. Madness of the people and madness of the bourgeoisie. Natural love of crime.
My rage at the coup d'état. How many times I was shot at. Another Bonaparte, how disgraceful! . . .
To be a useful man always struck me as being something distinctly ugly.
1848 was only amusing because everybody constructed utopias like castles in the air.
1848 was only charming through its excessive ridiculousness.[17]

It might be argued that Baudelaire's definitive political statement is a prose poem in which he thrashes a beggar to teach him a lesson—in human dignity! Its title has a splendid humanitarian ring:

"Let's Beat Up the Poor!"

THE YEAR 1848 witnessed Baudelaire's final burst of youthful extravagance. Pressures, anxieties, tensions, and a steady reliance on "explosion" to snap him out of lethargy all contributed to making him age before his time. The 1850s, the years in which he perfected his mature work, were years of quiet despair. He lived in a state of perpetual insecurity and anguish—changing addresses compulsively, finding it harder and harder to meet deadlines or open letters: living on the metaphysical run. His life became a single sustained and precarious balancing act, without a safety net, so uniform in its cliff-hanging that it was strangely uneventful. In the 1840s he had dramatized his horror at getting up in the morning and going to bed at night—to the point of a half-hearted attempt at suicide. The next decade saw him facing the dull agony of carrying on without any dramatization to alleviate the terrible monotony of constant pressure. His conception of his art, its value and its nature, matured greatly as a result of those very pressures and burdens. It achieved a degree of spirituality and other-worldliness that is unique in modern literature, and peculiarly consistent with Baudelaire's profound understanding of the essentially arid but all-powerful appetites that regulated man's existence. Thus the 1850s saw his transition from a talented and dandyish eccentric into an embittered and lucid chronicler of human frailty, his own frailty in particular; such was the understanding he achieved that it reminded his friends of the sad and suspect insights of an unfrocked priest who has heard too many confessions to live comfortably with his own sins.

His real hardship was compounded by a further estrangement from his mother. In the past she had responded quite generously to his requests for money. He was her only child, and, distressing though his behavior may have been to her, she displayed a mother's readiness to believe in a wayward son's promises to change. If a mother loses that faith, she has precious little left to hope for from her child.

Lose it she did. Ancelle and Aupick combined to convince her that if she continued to assist her son, he would never learn to stand on his own feet. In a limited sense they were right. Baudelaire would always mismanage his affairs and look to others to bail him out. The combination of his personality and his debts was such that he could not do otherwise. Withdrawal of his mother's support did not induce him to look for work, it simply aggravated his hardship and made it more difficult for him to face the continuing need to live from hand to mouth.

Aupick had survived the revolution without losing his position— indeed he had improved it. The Second Republic was the fourth of the five regimes he was to serve loyally and with increasing success. In 1848 he had been appointed the republic's representative in Constantinople, where he and Mme Aupick stayed for three years. In 1851 he had been offered the post of ambassador to London, but he refused it out of delicacy. The exiled Orleanist princes were in England, and he felt that to represent the new government, having once sworn to serve the house of Orléans faithfully, would expose him to the charge of "high espionage." Aupick was man enough to sacrifice ambition to honor—or to delicacy of feeling. He did not harm his career in the process, for five months later he was appointed ambassador to Madrid, a post which he kept until 1853, surviving the transition from republic to empire without difficulty.

During most of this period there was no direct contact between Baudelaire and his mother. Although this was in part the consequence of her taking advice, she was so distressed by her son's often violent and ill-mannered behavior that she preferred to have no dealings with him. She was unable to understand or accept his rages, and felt simply that properly brought up persons did not behave in that way. She was as much distressed by his bad manners as she was by his self-destructive behavior—Mme Aupick was never good at distinguishing form from content. Nevertheless, she remained in her peculiar way a concerned and generous soul, and continued to take a mother's interest in her son's welfare and reputation. When in November 1850 Maxime du Camp dined at the embassy in Constantinople as a man of letters on his travels, Aupick asked him for news of the Paris literary scene. Du Camp, anxious to entertain, spoke at length, and ignorantly, of the sensational young poet dandy and debauchee Charles Baudelaire, who was making a reputation for himself. He was later informed by an official of the nature of his gaffe—he had no idea that the Aupicks were related to the poet, still less that Aupick had forbidden Baudelaire's name to be mentioned in his presence. Mme Aupick, however, was only too pleased to hear that du Camp thought her son had real talent.

Despite her interest, relations remained strained. Just how strained we may judge from the following of Baudelaire's letters to her:

I have been meaning to write to you for some months. I tried several times, and each time I was obliged to abandon the task. My unceasing pains and the loneliness of my thoughts have made me a little mad, and doubtless also very clumsy. I would like to be able to soften my language, but even if your pride were to find it inappropriate, I hope that your reason will appreciate the goodness of my intentions, and the credit I deserve for making an approach which would once have been so pleasant for me, but which, in the situation you have made for me in my relationship with you, must without question be the last of its kind.

It is a matter for your conscience and also perhaps for your husband's, that you have deprived me of your friendship, and all the contact which anyone is entitled to expect of his mother. I shall no doubt know about that in due course.

But there is a certain delicacy which warns one not to pretend to wish to oblige persons one insults or who, at the least, mean nothing to one. For that is yet another insult. You will understand that I refer to some money which M. Ancelle received. What! He receives money, without a letter for me, without a word which admonishes or advises me as to its use. You must realize that you have lost any right to be *philanthropic* towards me, for I do not even talk of maternal feeling. So, you feel remorseful. I certainly have no desire to accept the expression of your repentance, unless it takes a different form, and is more clearly expressed. *Unless you become once more, and altogether a mother*, I shall be obliged, by means of a lawyer, to provide Ancelle with my formal refusal to accept money coming from you, and I shall ensure that the refusal will be strictly observed.

I do not believe I need insist upon the importance of this letter, and of your answer, which must be sent *to me, to me*, do you hear? Upon this answer, or your silence depend both my future behavior towards you and my future behavior towards myself. In exactly three months I will be thirty. This gives me much to think about, as you can imagine. Thus, *morally* a part of my future life is in your hands. I hope you will write what I want to hear! If you deign to understand the importance of this letter, you will no doubt add to your reply very precise details of your health.

Since you have such an influence over M. Ancelle, you should tell him, when you write, to make my life less hard and more tolerable.

I desire, I *wish* him to take no part in the matter I discuss with you today. I shall accept no answer from his mouth.[1]

Baudelaire felt desperately humiliated and cut off. His mother was the only person he had left to insult, and who would feel anything as he did so. Neither Ancelle nor Jeanne could fit that bill. He resented her rejection as a blow to his pride and his feelings, and as confirmation that he was alone in a hostile world with which he could not cope.

Ancelle had become a serious problem. He held the purse strings cautiously and stupidly. He had grown so alarmed at Baudelaire's financial mismanagement that he could scarcely do otherwise. Baudelaire spent with the unreflecting compulsion that drove all his actions; small wonder that the notary questioned his requests for more funds.

Such questioning drove Baudelaire into a frenzy. Besides, he felt that for all Ancelle's caution he was guilty of financial mismanagement himself. Baudelaire constantly queried the details of Ancelle's accounts, insisting that he had been underpaid, or gulled by creditors. Ancelle, in turn, was quite prepared to humiliate his ward, who found this perpetual bickering unbearably tiring. He needed all the energy he could muster simply to live; the additional burden of Ancelle was almost too much. Furthermore, Ancelle was his parents' confidant; they trusted the lawyer and did not trust him—a value judgment which a less vain man than the poet would have cringed beneath.

When the Aupicks left Constantinople and returned to Paris in 1851, Ancelle arranged a meeting. With characteristic lack of understanding he had undertaken to arrange that Baudelaire dine with them at their hotel, but Baudelaire was unable to face Aupick—and for good reason. He had visibly failed to make good in the last three years and hardship had already marked him. Mother and son met eventually on neutral ground, and the meeting went well. Yet she was dreadfully shocked by his situation. Twenty years later she could still remember:

> When I came to spend two months in Paris between our two ambassadorial posts, Constantinople and Madrid, what a cruel situation did I find him in! What destitution! And I, his mother, with so much love in my heart, wanting so much to help him, I could not get him out of it![2]

Whatever hopes Mme Aupick had for her son after their meeting were soon shattered. Baudelaire had promised to write to her frequently in Madrid, but he remained silent for weeks, hoping to send her good news. Alas, when he did write he could offer her none. In anticipation of a publisher's advance he had spent his allowance. He was penniless and in a state of disorder which made him unable to work. Could she send him some money, anything would help? He then proceeded to unburden himself, talking of the dreadful difficulty he felt at working and of his basic, enduring mood of anxiety and sadness. He was writing in a state of terrible doubt not just about his ability to work, but about his very talent. All his confidence in the present was gone; he could only look to the future; things might get better:

There's no turning back. In the course of 1852 I must recover from my infirmity, *and before New Year's Day I must already have paid off some debts, and published my poems.* I shall end up by learning that sentence by heart.[3]

Inevitably things got worse, so much worse that Baudelaire could not bring himself to write again for a whole year, a year of further hardship and disappointment:

I know that I am going to hurt you a lot, it is impossible to conceal my miserable state of mind in my letter, let alone the confessions I have to make. But I have no choice. Despite the multitude of letters I have written to you in my imagination, since for a whole year I thought, every month, that I would write to you —my letter will be short. I am in such a predicament, with such complications that I can spend no more than an hour on this letter, which ought to be a pleasure to write, but which is the contrary. For ages I have made such a mess of my life that I cannot even find time to work.

I'll begin with the hardest and the most painful—I am writing with my last two logs on the fire and my fingers are frozen. I shall be prosecuted for a payment that fell due yesterday —for a second due at the end of the month. This year, that is to say from last April to now, has been truly disastrous for me, although I had the chance to make it quite different. I have the utmost confidence in you, the marvelous kindness you showed me on your way through Paris enables me to tell you all, and I hope you won't believe me to be totally mad, since I know my madness. Anyway, why pretend and compose a cheerful letter full of lying confidences, at a time when my mind is so burdened with anxieties that I scarcely sleep anymore, often have dreadful dreams and fever.

Why did I not write earlier you may ask? But *you* do not know about shame. Besides there was my promise to myself to send only good news. Also the undertaking never again to ask you for money. Today that is not possible.

After receiving your money *a year ago* . . . I used it as I promised. I made up the annual deficit and lived alone. Here the trouble begins. I lived in a house where the landlady made me suffer so much by her guile, her complaining, her deceit, and I was so uncomfortable, that I left, as I usually do, without saying anything. *I owed her nothing*, but I was stupid enough to let the rent run on without living there, so that I owe her rent for lodgings I did not occupy. I discovered that the wretch presumed to write to you. Now I left with her, in the assumption that I could send for them soon, *all my books, all my manuscripts some finished, others started, boxes of papers, letters, drawings, in fact everything—all my most precious things. . . .*

As a result, he had to try to complete work on the first commission he had received for years, a translation of Edgar Allan Poe, without his precious papers. He sent the printer such a hopeless manuscript that, after seeing it in proof, he realized that he would have to scrap the type —and pay for it himself. But, of course, he had no money, having already spent the publisher's advance. In the meantime, he was so paralyzed by the feeling that he had disappointed his publisher that he could not face doing any more work on the project. The manuscript just sat there on his table, and the publisher assumed that he was either dishonest or quite mad.

In the meantime he had lost another opportunity. The director of the Opéra had asked him for a libretto—a tremendous accolade: "But poverty and disorder make me so apathetic, so depressed, that I failed to turn up to any of the meetings." He had, moreover, failed to write a play he had promised the Théâtre du Boulevard. He had borrowed three hundred francs on the strength of the assignment, but could neither write the play nor repay the loan. The letter continues:

. . . What will become of me, what will happen to me?

There are times when I am overcome with the urge to sleep for ever; but I cannot sleep because I keep thinking.

I have no need to tell you that I have passed the winter without fire, but that is nothing. . . .

I owed it to you to give you for your old age the happiness which my talent might have led you to expect.—I did not—I am guilty towards myself; —this imbalance between the will and my talent is something I don't understand. Why with such a precise, clear idea of duty and utility do I always do the opposite?

That idiot Ancelle told me he had written to say I was well. The imbecile sees nothing, understands nothing, about one thing any more than another. Anyway my health is so good that

it can cope with anything. But this miserable life and the brandy
—which I am going to give up—have ruined my stomach for a
few months, and besides I have intolerably painful nerves—just
like a woman—anyway it can't be helped. Do you now understand why in the midst of the dreadful solitude which surrounds
me, I understand Poe's genius so well, and why I write so well
about his abominable life?[4]

Baudelaire has revealed himself in this "abominable" letter. He is
not quite mad, since he knows his madness—just as he feels that knowing his sinfulness mitigates its evil. He longs for oblivion, however, for
the abandonment of consciousness. Another revealing point is his behavior about his lodgings. When most people would have cancelled
their tenancy, Baudelaire walked out and could not bring himself to
give notice. He simply let it run, and run up rent; and every day it grew
harder to do anything about it. All his paralysis, his deadly inertia is
here, manifested in his inability to complete the Poe translation because of a minor setback, which in turn resulted in his growing so depressed that he missed several other opportunities. Above all he saw he
had failed everybody including himself, and recognized that it was his
own miserable life and self-destructive tendencies that made him
identify with Poe.
    In the wake of such abominable letters, relations with his mother
deteriorated to the point that she became for him a kind of *moral* creditor, whose letters, like those from his creditors, he could not bear to
open:

Do not be angry if I tell you that your letter stayed on my table
for two days, unopened; in my state of despondency I am sometimes unable to open letters for three months, and your handwriting is beginning to cause me the same fear as does that of
people who are my enemies by virtue of their claims upon me.[5]

Yet, for all his despair and self-pity, the writer retained a certain,
strange kind of self-discipline and, more important, self-respect. When
his mother expresses fear that poverty might be causing him to neglect
himself, he is still able to pour scorn on her suggestion:

As for your fears that poverty is making me slovenly, you had
better know that throughout my life, in rags or living decently, I
have always spent two hours a day on my appearance. Do not
sully your letters with such stupidities again.[6]

Even with frayed cuffs in an unheated room, he remains the dandy.

If things with his mother were bad, his relationship with Jeanne Duval was even worse. His letters of 1852 reflect his growing realization that he would now have to face real solitude. He broke with Jeanne reluctantly. Even though she felt she had nothing to offer him but her physical presence, it was a presence that he could not abandon without a real sense of loss. To abandon her was to abandon a vital part of his past. To make matters worse, he felt responsible for her, and felt guilty about leaving her, feeling that he needed to make some act of "expiation." She had betrayed him often enough, yet he was still grateful for the occasional flashes of devotion and kindness she had displayed in the past. By 1852, however, he had become increasingly exasperated by the ordeal of living with someone whom he knew to be totally out of sympathy with him. He now found it necessary to work at night to avoid her nagging. He also found it necessary to ask his mother to write to him via a friend, since Jeanne knew her hand and he could lock nothing away from her. He was in a perpetual state of bad temper, harrassed and harried out of his own home. He would stay away for a fortnight at a time, moving from friend to friend in search of peace.

It is clear that at this time Baudelaire had outlived his sensual infatuation. She was no longer his Black Venus, but a bickering, demanding, thankless woman:

> She *used to have a few good points* but she *has lost* them, and I can see more clearly. *Living with someone* who gives you no thanks for your efforts, who thwarts them out of clumsiness or constant malice, who simply thinks of you as her servant and property, with whom you cannot exchange a word about politics or literature, a creature *who does not want to learn anything*, anything you offer to teach her yourself, *a creature who does not admire me*, who takes no interest in my work, who would toss my manuscripts on the fire if that would bring in more money than publishing them, who gets rid of my cat which was my only consolation in my lodgings, and who brings in dogs, *because* the sight of dogs makes me ill, who does not know or will not understand that *being very very miserly just for one month*, would enable me, thanks to the temporary peace, to finish a sizable book—well, is it possible, is it possible?[7]

One feels that Baudelaire might have been able to tolerate mere malice. Masochist that he was, he could have seen it as a necessary punishment for his sins if only Jeanne had appreciated his art and his ambitions. But the ultimate crime, the only crime that he could not forgive, was that she neither understood nor admired him. Given this, the prospect of continuing to live with her proved intolerable.

Jeanne and Baudelaire part early in 1852, although he continues to support her. He had been with her for ten years, and, as he put it, exhausted ten years and his youthful illusions in the struggle, gaining nothing but bitterness. For all his sensuality, Baudelaire did not need a "constant companion," did not need sex at all. His sexuality was cerebral, though not intellectual. He had no need to relieve himself of pent-up frustration through frequent recourse to the sexual act—frustration was what he enjoyed, which may have helped explain Jeanne's disappointment.

Baudelaire appreciated the hollowness of pleasure. There was a notorious rendezvous for prostitutes and persons anxious to make their acquaintance known as the Casino de la Rue Cadet, which was frequented by Baudelaire and his friends. The latter used to leave in the company of the girls, but Baudelaire never did. He would walk past the diners and dancers, haughty and detached from the cheap pleasure world of the cancan and consumptive prostitutes. Once a friend actually asked him what he was doing there. "My dear fellow," he replied, "I am watching the deaths' heads go by."

Baudelaire was no more amenable to admirers. A friend introduced him to a beautiful blonde who had expressed a desire to meet him. She persuaded him to take her home. The friend went too. The lady grew more and more lascivious and finally began to strip. She had beautiful hair that reached to her feet and a superb body. The friend was tactfully on his way out the door when he heard Baudelaire, tired and worn out, say, "Get dressed."

Yet Baudelaire the dandy, the weary observer of deaths' heads and women stripping for his benefit was also dreadfully lonely. The break with Jeanne had left a terrible void. Now he had no one for whom he could feel anything at all, neither woman nor family. At least Jeanne had provoked irritation in him, hate even, but now there was nothing. It is perhaps the need to feel something, to make some kind of contact, that accounts for the strangest and most puzzling of all his letters. It is addressed to a "Madame Marie," a woman whose identity remains obscure. (There have been efforts to identify her as the actress Marie Daubrun, Baudelaire's "Green-eyed Venus," but they are unconvincing.) The letter is not unlike some of his fan letters, but it displays a lover's orientation, or rather the orientation of a worshipper from afar:

> Madame,
>
> Can it be that I shall not see you again? That, for me, is the important question for I have reached the point where your absence is already an enormous loss. When I learnt that you were giving up modeling, and that, involuntarily, I was the cause, I felt a strange sadness. I wanted to write to you, although I do

not really believe in writing letters. One always regrets them. But I risk nothing since I have decided to give myself to you for ever.

Do you know, our conversation on Thursday was very strange. It is that same conversation which left me in a new mood and which is the reason for this letter.

A man who says "I love you," and begs, and a woman who says "Love you! Me! Never! One man has my love. Pity anyone who comes after. He will only get my indifference and my disdain!" And that same man, to have the pleasure of looking longer into your eyes, lets you talk of another, talk only of him, and burn for him and think of him. From all these confessions there emerged something very strange, namely that for me you are no longer simply a woman one desires, but a woman one loves for her frankness, for her passion, for her vigor, for her youth and her folly! I have lost a lot through these explanations, since you were so explicit that I had to give way at once; but you, Madame, have gained a lot. You have won my respect and my profound esteem. Stay as you are always and preserve that which makes you so happy and beautiful.

Come back, I beseech you, and I shall be gentle and undemanding in my desires. I deserved your scorn when I replied that I would be content with crumbs. I lied. Oh, if you only knew how beautiful you were that evening! It's so banal! But your eyes, your mouth, all your lively animated form now moves before my closed eyes, and I feel that it is for ever. Come back, I implore you, on my knees, I do not say that you will find me without love. Yet you cannot prevent me from straying with my mind's eye over your arms, your extraordinarily beautiful hands, your eyes where all your animation resides, over all your adorable physical person. No, I know you cannot; but do not be alarmed, you are for me an object of worship and it is not possible for me to sully you. I shall see you as radiant as ever . . . your eyes could only inspire immense love in a poet.

. . . I love you, Marie, it is true, but the love I feel for you is that of a Christian for his God. So never apply a terrestrial name so often shameful to this incorporeal and mysterious worship, this soft and chaste feeling which unites my soul to yours despite your wishes, it would be sacrilege.[8]

He then describes her as the spiritual part of himself. She will be as Petrarch's Laura to him, acting as inspiration and guardian angel. Her rejection of him will not prevent him from admiring her.

This sentimental language comes strangely from the pen of a

thirty-year-old who had seen it all. But he would never be averse to manufacturing idealized situations. It suited him to place Marie upon a pedestal—and her obvious rejection made it that much easier. Baudelaire thrived upon distance, wanting not the woman but the idea of her.

His strange, nonsexual behavior is usually attributed to perversity, shyness, and his love of overdramatized situations. All this is true, yet there is perhaps another reason for the bent of his sexuality: the apparent chastity which made Nadar christen him "the virgin poet." In his letter he says that it is impossible for him to "sully" her—he prefers to worship platonically. Throughout his work he considers the sexual act to be a kind of pollution—which does not always stop the poet from imagining polluting his lover and taking pleasure in the process—and it seems likely that this attitude was compounded, if not created, by his venereal disease. He had for a long time supposed himself to be cured. There are no references to his infection in his letters of these years, although he does allude to the disease reasserting itself while he was in Dijon in 1849. It is thus unlikely that he held back from sullying Madame Marie because he thought himself actively infected. Nevertheless, the knowledge that he had once been so infected, that he had carried poison in his veins, might have been quite enough in a man as sensitive as Baudelaire to inspire an enduring sense of sexual self-disgust. The feeling that one's system is polluted, invaded by a secret poison, the wages of sin, which might course forever through one's blood and sperm, becoming part of one's physical being, is quite enough to make one detest one's sexuality. The moral impact of syphilis and gonorrhea can be quite as telling as the physical impact—and quite as difficult to cure. Baudelaire could never again altogether escape the possibility that he would spread infection through making love—a possibility sufficient to ensure that he remained sexually, if not emotionally, distant and inactive.

10

FOR ALL THE disasters and the failures of these years, Baudelaire was beginning to find his feet as a man of letters. He had become known in literary circles extending well beyond journalistic Bohemia. He had made the acquaintance of Théophile Gautier, the leader of the second wave of romanticism in the late 1830s and now a distinguished writer, journalist, and art critic, one of the most widely read poets of the age and the future dedicatee of *Les Fleurs du Mal*. He also knew Gérard de Nerval, in the eyes of posterity a much greater poet, although his contemporaries thought more of his journalism and his pet lobster. He also made friends with two men who would remain close to him for the rest of his life: the bibliophile Charles Asselineau and Auguste Poulet-Malassis.

A kind, gentle, and delightful man, Asselineau had known Baudelaire for some years, but they only grew close in 1850. He would remain a staunch friend, to the point of getting painfully involved in Baudelaire's precarious financial arrangements, and would write the first book about Baudelaire, published a year after the poet's death: *Charles Baudelaire: Sa Vie et son oeuvre* [*...His Life and Work*]. He also worked on the first posthumous edition of the complete works. Asselineau had acquired an extraordinary collection of the first editions of early nineteenth-century writers, simply by ferreting out bargains among the booksellers on the banks of the Seine. He lived for his collection alone—until he fell in love. He sold it all to raise money enough to do justice to his lady—then she abandoned him. Thereupon he started to collect again, and soon amassed a second collection even finer than the first. He was a great lover of modern poetry; Banville, one of the great poetic technicians of the age, said that Asselineau knew more about poetic technique than anybody else in France. His love of books was suitably rewarded when he was appointed chief librarian of the famous Mazarine Library. During the Commune in 1871 he stuck to his post and managed to discourage the communards from sacking the library and using its catalogues as sandbags to build their defenses. When order was restored, however, he was suspected of collaborating with the revolutionaries and lost his post. The dismissal deeply wounded him, and he never recovered.

Asselineau, together with most of literary Paris, used to frequent the famous café Le Divan le Pelletier, opposite the old Opéra just off the Boulevard des Italiens. For twenty years it was an overcrowded "bureau of wit" where there was more talking than drinking. Banville has caught Asselineau and Baudelaire sitting there in a poem entitled "Le Divan":

> One sees farouche Baudelaire
> Next to gentle Asselineau.

> *On voit le farouche Baudelaire*
> *Près du doux Asselineau.*

The second friend that Baudelaire made during this period, sometime between 1849 and 1852, was Auguste Poulet-Malassis, who came from a long line of printers in Alençon. He had been mildly involved in the June Days and spent six months in prison, after which he went back to his home town to take over the family firm, in partnership with his brother-in-law de Broise. It was a steady, lucrative, but unexciting business, relying upon the printing of the *Journal d'Alençon*. Poulet-Malassis was not content with this humdrum trade. He longed to become a publisher, which he did. He published the work of Banville, Gautier, the poet Leconte de Lisle, and Baudelaire. His association with Baudelaire, and with the latter's financial difficulties and professional disasters, combined with certain politically injudicious publications, would later be responsible for his financial ruin, causing him to spend several months in a debtors' prison. Yet, although the association with Baudelaire was ultimately ruinous, Poulet-Malassis has earned a place in literary history for the undying glory of having published the first edition of *Les Fleurs du Mal*.

It was during these years, the late 1840s and early 1850s, that Baudelaire acquired an enthusiasm that would stay with him for the rest of his life and earn him the only money he ever made—the works of Edgar Allan Poe.

Poe's work had first appeared in French in 1846, in an unsigned translation of the *Murders in the Rue Morgue*. *The Black Cat* came out the next year, and it was through this that Baudelaire was introduced to his writing.

The effect was astonishing. There has seldom been an example of such a profound impact of one author upon another. From the start Baudelaire found in Poe not a kindred spirit but a twin. As he read him he was amazed to discover that Poe had put into words, ideas and attitudes which Baudelaire had thought of himself years before, but had never expressed on paper. There can be no question of the American influencing Baudelaire: it is more a case of two parallel and identical processes of development. Poe may have confirmed Baudelaire in his ideas, but he did not inspire them. It was the discovery of his own ideas already expressed by Poe which made the American's work such a revelation, as he wrote, years later, to the art critic Thoré:

> . . . I can tell you something almost incredible. In 1846 or 1847 I came across some fragments of Poe; I experienced an extraordinary turmoil. As his complete works were only collected after his death, in a sole edition, I was patient enough to make the acquaintance of Americans living in Paris, to borrow from them collections of magazines which published Edgar Poe, and then I discovered, believe me, if you will, poems and stories that I had thought of, only vaguely, confusedly, in a disordered fashion, and which Poe had managed to put together and perfect.[1]

In another letter he wrote:

> People accuse *me* of imitating Edgar Poe! Do you know why I translated Poe so patiently? Because he was like me. The first time I opened a book of his I saw, with horror and delight, not just subjects I had dreamt of, but *sentences* I had thought of, and written by him twenty years before.[2]

Baudelaire began to take an obsessive interest in the works of the American. Asselineau recalls how Poe "possessed" him; he could talk of nothing else and was more anxious about Poe's literary reputation than about his own. He was profoundly grateful to the few people who had ever been kind to Poe and still, at the end of his own life, would pray to the spirit of Poe to intercede on his behalf.

On one occasion he learned of an American man of letters who was staying in Paris. He took Asselineau round to see him. They found the American half-dressed in the process of trying on some shoes. Between fittings, Baudelaire interrogated him urgently about Poe. When the writer revealed himself to be less than enthusiastic about the Southerner's works, referring to him as a peculiar person whose conversation was not always consequent, Baudelaire left in a huff commenting that the man was only a "wretched Yankee."

To do justice to his idol Baudelaire set to work on his English. He knew a little already probably from his mother, and now worked really hard; to the point of frequenting the English tavern in the Rue de Rivoli, where he drank whiskey, kept company with English lads, grooms, and jockeys, and even read *Punch*.

Baudelaire published his first translation of Poe, his *Mesmeric Revelation*, in the journal *La Liberté de Penser* in 1848. It was not until 1852, however, that he started to work on Poe in earnest. In March and April of that year *La Revue de Paris* published his study of the American entitled *Edgar Allan Poe, sa vie et ses ouvrages*, the earliest version of what would become the preface to his first book of translations, *Histoires extraordinaires*, published by Michel Lévy in 1856. The latter was a selection from Poe's *Tales of the Grotesque and Arabesque* (1840) and *Tales* (1845).

His first translations were somewhat shaky, but as time went on they improved beyond measure and stand today among the finest literary translations in any language. It may even be argued that Baudelaire, the greater writer of the pair, actually improved upon the originals. But it is not the quality of the translations which surprises— Baudelaire was a great stylist and a perfectionist—it is their quantity. When translating, Baudelaire found a capacity for sustained and concentrated work which he never otherwise approached. His friends were amazed to discover that nothing could distract him. He would often write for twelve hours at a stretch. Perhaps it was the existence of a text to be worked on that enabled him to concentrate in this way. For once he was not faced with the task that daunts all creative writers—the dreadful business of looking to oneself alone to extract every word from one's being and spin a book out of oneself. The release from this crushing self-reliance may explain why Baudelaire could work on Poe as he had never worked before, or would work since.

As a thinker Poe appealed to Baudelaire and later cerebral poets such as Mallarmé and Valéry for the emphasis he placed on the role of conscious calculation in poetic creation—and for a certain heroically extravagant intellectual rigor which he displayed. For Poe, as for Baudelaire, a work of art was not the product of what Poe termed "the fine frenzy of inspiration," but of conscious and deliberate calculation and control. Moreover, Poe's metaphysics, in works such as the *Dialogue of Monos and Una*, aspired towards synthesis, the unity of all creation in the face of apparent division; it was an aspiration that appealed profoundly to Baudelaire.

There were other reasons why Baudelaire should admire his work. The stories combine cold and lunatic cerebration with extravagant imagination—just the balance that Baudelaire sought in his own poetry. Moreover, Poe had succeeded in blending the Gothic with contemporary, high romantic exoticism in the "Masque of the Red

Death," and with detective fiction and studies in psychological decay and disintegration, as in "William Wilson" and "Berenice."

Perhaps more importantly, Baudelaire identified with the man. Poe was the first modern writer: a desperate loser, haunted by his own *guignon*, a man who lived a life of misery and drink, and died in suspect and ignoble circumstances. As such, he was supremely equipped to create a literature of decadence. Baudelaire makes the point in one of his studies, *Notes nouvelles sur Edgar Poe* (1857). By decadence Baudelaire meant an age on which the sun is setting, an era of decline when values and beliefs are dissolving. It is his contention, as true of his own work as of Poe's, that such a sunset age has its own splendid darkening beauty —the beauty of fading light and a crimson horizon, with all the richness and magnificence of a hashish or opium dream.

Although Baudelaire would achieve some commercial success with his translations, he got off to a slow start. The article he finally wrote for *La Revue de Paris* in 1852, *Edgar Allan Poe, sa vie et ses ouvrages*, was the first piece written about the writer in a foreign language. Part biography, part criticism, the piece is essentially a reworking of American material, but Baudelaire has added his own comments on *guignon* and literary drunkenness among the moderns.

As well as writing on Poe, Baudelaire attempted, with less success, to write on his own account. He worked briefly on a literary paper, but it went bankrupt. He then attempted to make his fortune by starting another but the banker withdrew at the last minute.

When Gautier, du Camp, and other friends took over the *Revue de Paris* in 1851, Baudelaire hoped they would publish his poems. He sent them a dozen, but they only published two: "Le Reniement de Saint-Pierre" and "L'homme et la mer." Du Camp did not appreciate Baudelaire; he was a vile little man who probably helped to ensure that the work of his so-called friend was not published.

Baudelaire had sent the batch of poems with a note stating that they were part of a book to be published shortly by Michel Lévy under the title *Les Limbes*. *Les Lesbiennes* had acquired a less sensational title, but one no less revealing. The expression derives from the jargon of Fourierism, which describes the age of the industrial revolution as a *"période lymbique,"* suggesting once again that Baudelaire had Fourierist leanings in these years.

The *Revue de Paris* at least published Baudelaire's piece on Poe and later "The Pit and the Pendulum." "Berenice," "Philosophy of Furniture," and "A Tale of the Ragged Mountain" (published under the French title "Les Souvenirs de M. Auguste Bedloe") also emerged in various publications in the same year. Baudelaire had experienced considerable difficulty in getting them accepted. He published Poe's "Philosophy of Composition" and "The Raven" in 1853 in *L'Artiste*;

117

in 1854 he tried to get a regular contract from *Le Moniteur*. The critic Saint-Beuve, a cautious man who believed much in his own merit, and also purported to be Baudelaire's friend, worked on *Le Moniteur*. For the first, but not the last time, he felt unable to use his influence to help the virtually destitute Baudelaire. He was kept waiting by another paper, *Le Pays*, which finally gave him a contract in 1854. He stayed with them for almost a year, publishing *Histoires extraordinaires*, which Michel Lévy would issue in book form in 1856. This was his first semipermanent berth—after more than ten years of writing.

In 1855 he fell out both with *Le Pays* and with a publisher who wished to do the tales in book form. The reason for his quarrel with the paper was his excessive attention to Delacroix in his art criticism— Delacroix was out of fashion. Eventually translations of Poe started to appear in book form: *Les Histoires extraordinaires* (1856), *Les Nouvelles Histoires extraordinaires* (1857), *Les Aventures de Gordon Pym* (1858), *Eureka* (1863), *Histoires grotesques et sérieuses* (1865). Poe was in vogue in the fifties, and the early translations sold well. However, Baudelaire's obsession with the American continued long after public interest had begun to wane. Nevertheless, he sold more copies of his translations than of anything else that he wrote, and they would provide him with a small but regular income—until he sold all his rights to Michel Lévy for a laughable sum in 1863, at a time of great financial pressure.

These were also years during which Baudelaire evolved his own aesthetics. He had long sought for an art which would capture the heroism, the pain, the exhilaration, and the neurotic quality of modern life. Now he added an element of aesthetic mysticism. The sonnet "Correspondances" had expressed a view of the cosmos as a single complex interlocking whole, based on what Fourier had termed the "principle of analogy": the cosmos is built upon a series of analogous patterns; perception of those patterns means perception of its hidden ordering principle. This was an attitude which played an important part in the early nineteenth-century literary imagination; beyond perceived reality lies true reality and its nature may be divined by detecting the analogous patterns which inform this world and tell us of the world beyond. Since everything is part of the great chain of being, a study of our microcosm can reveal the nature of the macrocosm.

The immediate sources of these views were Fourier, Balzac, and the Swedish mystic and scientist Swedenborg. The conception itself, the essential basis of the occult tradition, was anything but new; found in alchemy, masonic ritual, Rosicrucianism, it reached to the sixteenth- and seventeenth-century Neoplatonists and back to ancient Greece and Alexandria. It opposed, in its view of the cosmos as an essential harmony, the empirical attitudes of Renaissance man and later practical philosophers such as Locke and the utilitarian tradition. In Baudelaire's day it was practically a dead letter as a public philosophy, although it has continued as a system of thought among adepts up to the present day.

Baudelaire was no adept. He appreciated the system without elaborating it—from a mystical and philosophical point of view—for precisely the same reason that he had been attracted by Fourierism proper. Swedenborg provided a view of the world expressed in terms of cosmic order, ultimate truths, a framework of transcendental and spiritual meaning. It appealed to Baudelaire's own inherent and highly evolved sense of spirituality, living as he did in a crassly materialistic world. Moreover, the notion that the reality of the world contained hidden clues to the world beyond fitted his artistic temperament.

As an artist Baudelaire had always wanted to be able to write about modern city life and to create works of absolute spirituality and beauty. The loose corpus of ideas centered around "Correspondances" enabled him to do both simultaneously: to write about the ugly, the corrupt, and the sordid, not simply to dwell upon them as a realist might, but to go beneath the surface of his seemingly repellent subject matter and extract from it the spiritual beauty which lay within—just as he was to create beautiful poetry from the hopeless wreck of his own existence.

Baudelaire believed in the spirituality of high art: the creation of beauty was a form of religious practice, capable of securing the salvation of its creator. It was this faith in the redemptive power of beauty that enabled him to continue over the years.

What makes Baudelaire such an original poet is that the cult of beauty did not lead him, as it had so many others, to worship Raphael's Madonnas, or the plastic perfection of the art of antiquity. It took him onto the streets of Paris, and the peculiar beauty he found there and captured in his poems has lasted incomparably better than any of the countless poems to Grecian urns written by his contemporaries. He does not allow his inherent spirituality or belief in universal analogy to inspire poems of a doctrinaire mysticism. Indeed they seldom expound his theories. Rather his belief in universal harmony creates the way that poems such as "Harmonie du soir" or "Recueillement" are assembled, as tightly interlocking, controlled, sensuous, and melodious wholes. It is in their organic wholeness, in the resonances he sets up within them that his theories are reflected, not in their ideas. He assimilates theories like a poet, rather than regurgitating them like a trained brain. They form the substance of his poetry, not its subject matter. Thus he turns his back on facile nature mysticism, indeed on all theories, in favor of a poetry of rêverie and city life. As he wrote to Desnoyers:

You ask me for some poetry for your slim volume, poetry about *Nature*, eh? Woods, huge oak trees, greenery, insects, and no doubt the sun. But you do know that I cannot get sentimental over vegetables, and that my soul rejects that strange new religion which will always have, for a spiritual being, something *shocking* [English in the text]. I shall never believe *the soul of the gods lives in plants,* and even if it did, it would not matter much to me, since I would feel my own soul to be something much more precious than that of canonized vegetables. Indeed I have always thought that in flowering rejuvenated nature there was something impudent and unsettling.

As it is impossible to satisfy you completely according to the strict terms of the program, I am sending you two pieces of poetry which roughly represent the sum of the daydreams which assail me at twilight. In the heart of the woods, enclosed beneath those vaults that seem like sacristies and cathedrals, I think of our astonishing cities, and the prodigious music that rolls across the treetops sounds to me like the translation of human grief.[3]

He encloses two poems on evening and morning twilight in the city: "Crépuscule du matin" and "Crépuscule du soir." Prostitution, strange desires, theaters, restaurants, and orchestras on the one hand; the poor, the sick, prostitutes, and revellers coming home at cock crow on the other. Even in the heart of the woods, the poet of modern life dreams of townscape as the sun rises, shivering over the city, and Paris prepares for another day.

> Dawn shivering in a rose and green dress
> Passed slowly down the deserted Seine,
> And somber Paris, rubbing his eyes,
> Grasped hold of his tools, hard-working old man.
>
> *L'aurore grelottante en robe rose et verte*
> *S'avançait lentement sur la Seine déserte,*
> *Et le sombre Paris, en se frottant les yeux*
> *Empoignait ses outils, vieillard laboureux.*

II

THE MOST REMARKABLE example of Baudelaire's sexual platonism is his long drawn-out and long-distance relationship with Mme Sabatier, his "White Venus."

Mme Sabatier was the daughter of a seamstress who had been seduced and made pregnant by a prefect who became a viscount almost immediately afterwards. He provided the seamstress with a substantial dowery and arranged her marriage with a sergeant named Savatier, who gave the daughter she bore his name. Born Aglaé José Hine Savatier, she later took the name Apollonie, by which she was always known, and changed her surname to Sabatier—for reasons not unconnected with the fact that *savate* was a kind of slipper.

Mme Sabatier grew up to become a *demi-mondaine*—not a courtesan, she rather moved from protector to protector. She was strikingly beautiful, as attested to by this contemporary description, a portrait all the more flattering since the author is a woman:

> [She] came in from the back of the apartment, announcing her arrival with a ripple of pearly laughter. . . . She was quite big, and well proportioned, with very fine wrists and charming hands. Her hair, very silky, and golden chestnut, was amassed as if naturally in rich shiny waves. She had a clear, even complexion, regular features with something teasing and witty about them, a small laughing mouth. Her triumphant air spread light and happiness around her.[1]

Mme Sabatier moved in that peculiar no man's land of writers, artists, kept women and their keepers. She ran a salon where many of the most famous artists and writers of the age would congregate: a salon where it was possible to relax and liberate oneself from the constraints and conventions of polite society; where men could smoke cigars and talk freely in mixed company; and where a woman's wit was appreciated as much as her looks. She was a kind, good-natured, easy-going hostess, who did not object to a certain looseness of atmosphere, and whose hospitality was appreciated all the more for it; by most people if not by all. The Goncourt brothers, whose journal is such a fascinating record of the literary Paris of the age, reveal in their account of her that streak of snobbish small-minded meanness for which they are justly famous:

> Spent the evening at Mme Sabatier's. The famous Présidente with the marvelous body modeled by Clésinger for his Bacchante. A coarse nature with trivial lower-class vulgar bounce. One might define this slightly vulgar and raffish beauty as a "Fauns' camp follower"![2]

The reference to the fashionable academic sculptor Clésinger recalls a piece of his entitled *Woman Stung by a Serpent*, which created an uproar when it was shown at the Salon of 1847. It was felt that the lady in question, judging by her pose, had not been stung by a serpent at all, and that she was enjoying a spasm of a very different kind. The easy-going Mme Sabatier had had no objections to modeling for this notorious piece, but Clésinger's other sculpture of her, a bust, perhaps does her more justice. It gives the impression that she was a slightly plump woman with pale skin, possessing that happy-go-lucky, good-tempered, and sensual character that is so often found in that physical type.

Mme Sabatier became one of the most famous figures on the artistic fringe of the Second Empire. Gautier wrote poems in her honor, and letters to her—letters of such remarkable obscenity that even Baudelaire's greatest biographer, the late Enid Starkie, anything but a prude, could not bring herself to quote them. When Baudelaire knew her she was being kept by the Belgian financier Mosselman. He abandoned her in 1861 and for some time she was obliged to live very modestly—which she did with great cheerfulness. At the age of forty-four, she found a second protector, a wealthy man who settled a large sum of money on her. She outlived many of her friends, and died in 1889 at the age of sixty-seven.

Baudelaire frequented her salon in the early 1850s. He found her kind, warm, and charming, displaying neither the prudery of virtue nor the ugliness of vice; she represented to him the very image of balance, good order, and psychic health. The poet could relax and be himself at her receptions, too much so perhaps. He always enjoyed shocking fools who took his extravagances seriously. One of these fools has described him at Mme Sabatier's:

> La Présidente invited me to her Sunday dinners where she pre-

sided with as much urbanity as kindness. When I remember the *truculent* stories, to use an expression dear to Théophile Gautier, the abacadabrous paradoxes and subversive discussions which succeeded one another at her table, I never cease to wonder at the way that some of the guests would let themselves go, and at the exquisite tolerance of the mistress of the house. You really had to have the strongest of natures to stomach all Baudelaire's sallies. [He] perpetually wracked his brains in the attempt to make himself quite insufferable, and he succeeded. Baudelaire had insinuated himself into the small literary set to which I had the honor to belong, thanks partly to his real poetic talent; but he shocked almost all of us, let's be honest, he oppressed us with his intolerable vanity, his compulsive posing, the imperturbable aplomb with which he professed, without believing a word of it, the least amusing stupidities. . . .

One of his favorite jokes which did not really make great demands on his wit, consisted in reviling and knocking from their pedestals, men of the finest genius, those whose glory is consecrated by the plaudits of generations.

For example, he said with a deadpan face that Homer was almost as talented as M. Barbey d'Aurevilly; he compared Leonardo da Vinci to some English caricaturist he had discovered, who did quite decent pen and ink drawings. If he didn't treat Michelangelo as a complete rascal it was out of sheer good nature. Sometimes these impertinences of Baudelaire's earned him severe lessons. For a weakling like him it was not always wise to take on wits of the caliber of Sainte-Beuve, Théophile Gautier, Paul de Saint-Victor, Louis Bouilhet, and Jules de Goncourt. It was presumptuous to treat them like fools by setting off pathetic firework displays before them, which would not even scandalize the bourgeois.

I remember one day he decided *to bring down* Shakespeare, and maintain that the dramatist had been *invented* by the critics. Sainte-Beuve, who in those days was not exactly a passionate lover of romanticism, took up the challenge nevertheless. The fight did not last long and the issue was never in doubt. Baudelaire was squashed in no time.[3]

The speaker has missed the point completely. To be squashed is precisely what he wanted: the pleasure of seeing someone take his foolishness seriously and thereby declare himself the greater fool may be a childish one, but the pleasure is no less real, Sainte-Beuve's foolishness no less great for that.

In this atmosphere Baudelaire conceived or manufactured an

intense and protracted platonic love for the splendid Présidente. Although by no stretch of the imagination could one call her unapproachable, Baudelaire preferred not to approach. He contented himself with sending her, over five years, a series of anonymous letters in a concealed hand, accompanied by love poems which were early versions of one of the finest cycles of *Les Fleurs du Mal*.

He sent a series of touching, slightly aloof and timid letters—a form of courtship to which La Présidente was scarcely accustomed. The first was posted in December 1852:

> The person for whom these lines have been written, whether they please or displease, even if they appear the height of ridicule, is humbly *implored* to show them to no one. *Profound feelings* have a modesty that wishes to remain inviolate. Is not absence of signature a symptom of that invincible modesty? He who has written these lines in one of those moods of *rêverie* into which he is so often led by the image of she who is their subject, has loved her very dearly without ever saying so, and will *always* preserve the most tender feeling for her.[4]

The tone is less rhetorical than that of the letter to Mme Marie. It has a peace and conviction which the previous letter lacked. Peace above all was what Baudelaire sought in his anonymous courtship. He looked to Mme Sabatier for the calm and harmony missing from his own life. Just as his art would seek to make up what he lacked in life, so here, he set out to create peace for himself, through words—at least some of the time.

Yet the verse that accompanied this letter is anything but peaceful. "A celle qui est trop gaie" ["To she who is too gay"] is a deeply disturbing poem, one of the six which would eventually be banned from *Les Fleurs du Mal*. It opens with a celebration of Mme Sabatier, her health, her joyfulness, her bright colors. It then describes their impact upon the violent and broken personality of the poet, who finds such beauty and health arouse a sadistic thirst for destruction. He finds her perfection intolerable. He dreams of creeping through the night to punish her "joyous flesh," to bruise her bosom, to open a large wound in her belly. Then, in a vertigo of sadistic imagination, he dreams of penetrating her through her wound and pumping his poison into her.

The poem is both disturbing and beautiful in the sheer intensity and control of its vertigo, its rendering of a heady and sick imagination through the tight forms of the verse. It is a study in the psychology of a perverse and despairing man who yields to a surge of temptation and is momentarily carried away on a high tide of excitement. Yet none of this explains why Baudelaire should have sent it to inaugurate his courtship of Mme Sabatier. The piece is in fact an amazingly accurate poetic self-portrait. Baudelaire, shy and emotionally withdrawn, might very well continue to hide behind his clowning, but this did not prevent him from appreciating the beauty and good health radiating from his hostess, a radiance which only compounded his despair at his own flawed nature. The poem describes a yielding to the dark and destructive aspect of one's response to perfection; by sending such a poem to La Présidente, Baudelaire was once more giving in to that very side—in effect, imaginatively enacting the experience described within the poem in the very act of posting it. Both letter and poem become a destructive act, something like a rude telephone call from a timid and respectable person.

The correspondence does not sustain this note, for violence gives way to simple and touching adoration and envy. The next two letters are sent in May 1853. The first contains one of his finest poems, "Réversibilité." It addresses his "angel" of health and beauty, asking her how she could know the anguish, the despair, the sheer fear of life itself to which he is permanently subject. All he asks is that she pray for him. The second poem, "L'Aube spirituelle" ["The Spiritual Dawn"], describes a debauchee greeting the rising sun with a rising sense of self-disgust as he looks back upon a night of waste and vice. In the same way Mme Sabatier functions as an ideal and a sun for the poet.

The third poem, "Confessions," is a study in the psychology of a beautiful woman. It steps behind the idealized picture of her that Baudelaire had built, to imagine what her own attitude to her role might be. She "confesses" to the poet that being a beautiful woman is a hard profession: she has to keep smiling, keep going relentlessly, while her perpetual dependence upon the human heart means that she always builds on sand, as oblivion and eternity wait to receive her. It is a fine poem, but even more a fine and sympathetic study of a woman in Mme Sabatier's position—to whom people turn for beauty, support and comfort. It has none of the savagery which Baudelaire can display, none of the self-hate, and only a faint hint of that metaphysical vertigo which was an enduring projection of his own terror at being alive and his no less great fear of death.

The poem is accompanied by a letter. The poet apologizes for his anonymous scribbling, but says he cannot help it. He thinks of her when he is suffering, thinks in verse, cannot resist sending her the verse when it is written. He is the first to see the ludicrous side of it, but then love usually is ludicrous.

What adds a comic quality to this set of three poems is the circumstance of their composition. Baudelaire was suffering all right: from a combination of sexual guilt and financial worry.

The letters and poems were composed in Versailles, where Baudelaire spent a month in the company of the writer Philoxène Boyer. They had stayed at a hotel and run up a bill which they were unable to pay. They were ejected without their luggage and took refuge in a nearby brothel. From there Baudelaire wrote a letter to Asselineau which is so frank that it was not even published in the complete correspondence. He also wrote to Mme Sabatier. The poem about the debauchee seeing in the dawn is preceded by an epigraph in English: "After a night of pleasure and desolation, all my soul belongs to you."[5] The line echoes a sentence from Griswold's description of Poe's death: "After a night of insanity and exposure . . ."

It is typical that Baudelaire should have addressed his platonic mistress from a brothel. The extreme of vice encourages the extreme of idealism. He indulges his revulsion at a night of pleasure by turning to its opposite, making the most of both vice and virtue within a concentrated time span. The idea of looking up to Mme Sabatier upon her pedestal, from the lower depths of a cheap bordello, appealed to Baudelaire. The lower he sank, the higher he situated his idol, the more extreme his adoration became. It is precisely *because* he is stuck in a brothel that his thoughts turn to her—and inspire him to write poetry.

He next writes in the February of 1854. Again the letters come in spurts after a silence. This time he sends two within ten days of one another. The first mentions once more that he thinks of her when unhappy—the thoughts become a poem which he cannot resist sending. The letter is less a profession of love than an apology for being importunate. The second tells of his religious adoration of her, and speaks of his disinterested, ideal, respectful, and secret love. The poem accompanying it, "Hymne," is the early version of another of the finest pieces of *Les Fleurs du Mal*. With one exception there are no more letters for three years. Then, in 1857 Baudelaire writes openly to her, enclosing a copy of *Les Fleurs du Mal*, which had just been published. He no longer conceals his identity, but concedes that his disguise may have been ineffective:

This is the first time that I write to you in my real handwriting. If I were not overwhelmed with business and letters . . . I'd use this occasion to ask you to forgive so much idiocy and childishness. But anyway, have you not had revenge enough, above all with your little sister. Oh! The little monster! She made my blood run cold, one day when she met me and she started to roar with laughter, saying: *Are you still in love with my sister and do you still write her superb letters?* —I first realized that when I wanted to hide I hid myself very poorly, and then that underneath your charming face, you conceal an uncharitable character. Rogues fall *in love*, but poets are *idolaters*, and your sister is not, I think, made to understand eternal matters.

Allow me then, at the risk of amusing you too, to renew those protestations which so amused the little idiot. Imagine a blend of *rêverie*, feeling, respect, and a thousand childish follies, . . . and you will get an approximate idea of that very sincere something which I am not capable of defining more clearly.

It is not possible to forget you . . . the last time I had the good fortune not of my doing, to meet you! I said: "How strange it would be if that carriage were to be waiting for her, perhaps I should turn down another street." And then: "Good evening, Monsieur!" with that beautiful voice I love with its enchanting, devastating tone. I went off, saying to myself the whole way, "Good evening, Monsieur!", trying to imitate your voice.

. . . Remember that someone is thinking of you, that his thoughts are never trivial, and that he is a little resentful of your malicious gaiety. *I ask you urgently to keep to yourself henceforward anything I might confide in you.* You are my regular companion, and my secret. It is this intimacy, in which I have for so long been holding imaginary conversations with you, that is responsible for the audacity of this distinctly familiar tone.

Good-bye, dear Madame, I kiss your hand with all devotion.

Charles Baudelaire

All the poems between pages 84 and 105 inclusive belong to you.[6]

Mme Sabatier had long recognized Baudelaire as the author of those letters and poems. She may have talked about him to her sister, but at least she had the tact not to expose him to further ridicule by telling his friends or, worse, approaching him.

Baudelaire's own approach complicated the relationship. Accustomed to more forthright and less considerate treatment, Apollonie Sabatier was deeply moved by a delicacy and constancy which Baudelaire had sustained for nearly five years. The worst happened, and Baudelaire found himself in the unwelcome situation of having his idol reciprocate his emotions. Mme Sabatier fell in love, and Baudelaire was cornered.

She wrote him a love letter which was to prove disastrous to the relationship:

Today I am calmer. The influence of the evening we spent on Thursday is clearer. I can tell you without you accusing me of exaggeration that I am the happiest of women, that I never felt more clearly that I loved you, that I never saw you more beautiful, more adorable, quite simply my divine friend. You can preen yourself if you feel flattered, but do not look at yourself; for whatever you may do, you will never manage to give yourself the expression I saw on your face for a second. Now, whatever happens I shall always see you like that, that is the Charles I love; you can purse your lips and frown all you want, I shan't worry, I'll close my eyes and see the other.[7]

Virgin poet or not, this reads like a letter from a lady who has just spent a first night with a new lover. She suggests that the experience has only increased her love; there has been no disappointment. "Happy" in this context, in the language of French sexual relations, usually means sexual fulfillment. She notes his expression—at odds with his usually ironic appearance—which he only held for a second, suggesting that he may have been carried away at the time.

Baudelaire's reaction will surprise nobody with the slightest understanding of his personality. Mme Sabatier was in love, giving herself to him without reservation, and uncomprehending enough to recollect for him, in cold handwriting, a moment of self-abandon. Baudelaire's response was immediate: he ran away. He told her in person that henceforward there could be nothing between them; he followed this blow with a letter:

I have destroyed the childish torrent of babbling piled up on my table. It was not serious enough for you, my dear one—I look at your . . . letters again and answer anew.

I need a little courage, for my nerves are so painful I want to scream. And I wake up with the strange sense of moral unease which I had when I left you yesterday evening.

. . . *Absolute lack of morality!*

It is for that that you are so dear to me. *It is as if I have been young since the first day I saw you. Do what you will with me, but I am yours in body, mind and soul.* Please hide that letter, you poor thing! *Do you really know what you are saying?* There are people whose job it is to to imprison those who fail to pay promissory notes, but no one punishes the violation of oaths of friendship and love. So I said to you yesterday: you will forget me, you will betray me, he who amuses you will bore you; and today I add: he alone suffers who, like an imbecile, takes the things of the heart seriously. —You can see, my dear beauty, that I have *odious* prejudices about women, in short I have not *the faith.* You have a beautiful soul, but after all, it's a female one.

Do you see how in a few days our relationship has been devastated? In the first place we are both terrified of upsetting a good man who is fortunate enough to be still in love [Mosselman, her protector]. Then we are afraid of our own frenzy, for we know (I in particular) that there are liaisons which are difficult to break.

And besides, besides, a few days ago you were a divinity, which is so convenient, so beautiful, so inviolable. Now you are a woman—and suppose I were, to my misfortune, to acquire the right to be jealous! The horror! Even thinking about it! But with someone like yourself, those eyes are always smiling, looking graciously on everyone, it must be like enduring a martyrdom. The second letter bears a seal of solemnity which would appeal to me were I sure that you understood. *"Never meet or never part!"* [English in the text] That definitely means that it would be better never to have known one another, but that having done so, one must not separate. On a farewell letter that seal would be really funny. Anyway, let things take their course. I am a bit of a fatalist. But I do know that I have a horror of passion, because I know it, with all its ignominies. . . .

I don't really dare to reread this letter; I might have to alter it; because I really am afraid of hurting you; I may have let something of my vile side come through. . . . Good-bye, my love; I hold it against you that you are a little too attractive, remember that when I take away the scent of your arms and hair I also take with me my desire to return. So that the obsession becomes intolerable![8]

Mme Sabatier, who had never known such delicate courtship, was dreadfully upset by an equally unfamiliar and unexpected rejection. Baudelaire had written a cruel letter made worse by expressions of tenderness: it was the work of a weak man pretending he is still in love with the woman he is leaving, because he is too cowardly to admit that he feels nothing. La Présidente was too emotionally mature and straightforward to understand the perverse Baudelaire. She wrote to him twice, badly hurt and bewildered. She was generous enough to ignore the streak of insulting meanness in his letter, and her own love made her concentrate on the one thing that mattered: Baudelaire did not love her. Still she insisted that they meet, the next day, as she had to see him again. Oh, why did he take up the relationship again after his long silence?

Baudelaire did not appear. But she did not allow rejection to silence her. She had seen his face when he was not posing, believed enough in what she had seen, in the letters she had received, to write yet again. Her honest generous emotions did not permit wounded *amour-propre* to drive her into a corner to lick her wounds. All her magnanimity of spirit can be seen in her persistent efforts to make contact with him.

She simply could not understand the elaborate emotional games which Baudelaire had been playing, the psychodramas that he could drum up at his own, and others', emotional expense.

She writes to him asking him what kind of a comedy or tragedy they are playing:

> Your behavior is so strange that I can understand nothing. It is too subtle for a simpleton like myself. Please explain, my friend, all I want is to understand. What deadly cold wind has extinguished this beautiful fire? . . .
>
> I cannot resist saying a few words to you about our quarrel. And yet I had intended to behave with dignity, and scarcely a day has passed and already I'm weakening. And yet, Charles, I had every reason to be angry. What must I think when I see you run away from me, if it is not that you are thinking of the other woman, whose black face and black soul have come between us? I feel humiliated and insulted. Were it not for the respect I have for you I would curse you. I would like to see you suffer. I am being consumed with jealousy, and can't be reasonable at such times. My friend, I hope you never have to suffer like this. What a night I passed, and how I cursed this cruel love. . . .
>
> Bonjour, Charles. How is what remains of your heart? Mine is calmer. I'm calling it to reason, in order to spare you its weaknesses. You will see! I shall persuade it to cool down to the temperature you desire. I shall certainly suffer, but, to please you, I shall resign myself to enduring all possible pain.[9]

La Présidente was as good as her word. Baudelaire would remain a close friend for the rest of his life.

One cannot help feeling intense sympathy for the unfortunate woman who became involved in a situation with which she was too normal, healthy, and mature to cope. The White Venus earned her title precisely because she had no inkling of the kind of emotional stresses and distortions that informed Baudelaire's inner life. She gave herself to him, immediately and generously, without flirting or teasing. Nothing could have been more fatal than such a direct appeal to respond in kind.

The poet had manufactured a certain emotional situation through his letters and poems. It was of the essence of this situation that it should have no basis in reality. Free of the restrictions of real life, he could create an emotional fire storm of feeling which reality could not destroy. But destroy it it did. As long as Mme Sabatier remained an idol, emotion could endure; once she became flesh, the dream vanished and

Baudelaire was called to account for emotions which were now all too firmly rooted in reality. They had become an obligation, a debt—the necessity to match her passion with his own in a normal love affair.

Baudelaire found such obligations intolerable. Real relationships lacked the intensity of imagined emotions which could float free in a fantasy world, a world in which he could control them. Just as he had always had an intense inner creative life full of ideas and projects that he could never turn into real work because he lacked will, so he could never convert emotional fantasies into a mature emotional and physical relationship. Here too he suffered from paralyzing emotional inertia. When threatened by the sense of a real obligation imposed by reality upon his inner life, ideas and feelings alike would go dead in him.

Whether or not Mme Sabatier became a "mere woman" simply because he may have slept with her is unclear. But Baudelaire had no need to do so to experience emotional flatness, a flatness compounded by the knowledge that his fantasies had got out of hand, leaving him not a happy and requited lover, but a cornered rat. Whether he actually made love or not, Baudelaire was a constant prey to *post-coitum triste*, that sense of staleness and emotional emptiness experienced when the adrenaline has ceased to flow and you are left alone, coldly conscious, with the responsibility for whatever it is you did to procure that flow in the first place. In this instance Baudelaire had to bear the responsibility for breaking the heart of his White Venus. Her only consolation is that his poetry immortalized her, and his contact with her has displayed her to future generations as the supremely honest, kind, generous and emotionally responsible person that she was.

12

I N 1854, SHORTLY after his last anonymous letter to Mme Sabatier, Baudelaire became involved with the so-called Green-eyed Venus, the third woman to inspire a poem cycle of *Les Fleurs du Mal*, the actress Marie Daubrun. The poems are, on the whole, weaker than those inspired by Mme Sabatier, and they do not tell us as much about the nature of the poet's relationship, more perhaps about his sense of his own decline.

Marie Daubrun was seven years younger than Baudelaire. She had been acting since 1846. One of her better known roles was that of a pansy in a vaudeville called *Les Fleurs animées*. Her most famous part was the lead in *La Belle aux Cheveux d'Or* in 1847. One of the poems she inspired, "L'Irréparable" was first called "La Belle aux Cheveux d'Or." It is a desolate poem about the worm of remorse which eats the poet away, and about his failure to achieve the oblivion which will make him forget his failures. His inner life is black as pitch, beneath a low muddy sky. Hope is dead. Once in a "banal theater" he had seen a fairy light up an infernal sky, and a creature of light, gold and gauze overthrow Satan. His own heart is an empty stage, where he waits in vain for the creature with wings of gauze.

This is the only direct reflection of the actress in his poetry. It suggests that he saw her across the footlights as the image of beauty, magic and grace, an image promising redemption. His recollection of her becomes the symbol for a salvation which would never come to him.

Baudelaire's interest in Marie Daubrun dates from a time when she was appearing at the Théâtre de la Gaîté in a play entitled *The Wild Boar of the Ardennes*. His courtship is beset, inevitably, with financial problems. We find him writing to his mother asking her for money to buy flowers for Marie's name day. To convince her that the cause is worthy he informed his mother that Marie had stayed up all night to watch over her dying parents, "after playing her five stupid acts." He also asked for money to take her out to dinner. He could put Marie off with a lie, saying that he was ill, but actually he would not mind eating out himself as the food in his hotel had become appalling. The reader may care to remember that the author of these letters is thirty-three years old.

Baudelaire tried to use what influence he had to advance her career. He wrote to journalists asking for good notices—reminding one that her performances varied according to the state of her nerves and the direction of the wind, but that she responded to encouragement. She was not easy to work with; she fell out with every theater manager in Paris—no doubt because the wind blew often from the wrong quarter.

The Baudelaire who considered literature a form of prostitution— and remained a writer—was not averse to "whoring" to secure favors for Marie. The writer George Sand was among those he approached. She was having a play put on at the Odéon, and Baudelaire wrote to ask her to have Marie considered for the lead. It is a detailed and deferential letter, ending with professions of timidity, explaining that he did not know how to address his letter—since George Sand was also the Baroness Dudevant. Although afraid of displeasing her, to use the latter name seemed an impertinence. She was a genius and he thought she would prefer the "name in which you reign in the heart and mind of your age."[1] George Sand answered him kindly, though nothing came of the request, and Baudelaire wrote to thank her.

Typically, Baudelaire could not stand George Sand. Her feminism, her mawkishness, her sentimental socialism revolted him. As he wrote in later years:

> . . . She has never been an artist. She has the famous *flowing style* dear to the bourgeois.
>
> She is stupid, she is heavy, she is loquacious, she has, in her moral ideas, the profundity of judgment and the delicacy of feeling of concierges and kept women. . . .
>
> The fact that men could fall for that latrine is proof of the debasement of men in our times. . . . Look at the preface to *Mademoiselle de la Quintine*, where she claims that true Christians do not believe in Hell. La Sand is for the *God of good people*, the God of concierges and pilfering servants. She has good reason to wish to suppress Hell.[2]

Baudelaire himself started to write a play in which there would be a part for Marie Daubrun. It focussed on appetite—as usual. Entitled *L'Ivrogne* [*The Drunkard*], it was to be a study in delirious violence, as a drunkard yields, exultantly, to the temptation to murder his wife. An early experiment in the theater of cruelty, it is a pity that Baudelaire never got beyond the outline.

The poems inspired by Marie are in part a celebration of her majestic sweeping person, in part overtly sexual. "Le Poison" describes the pleasure of her terrible "biting" saliva, which plunges his soul, free of all remorse, into forgetfulness and a current of vertigo that bears him to the very shores of death. He also addresses to her what is perhaps his most famous poem. "L'Invitation au voyage" is an invitation to join him in a foreign seaport. The lyric is an evocation of the exotic, sensuous rocking of the ship, the calm, the leisure that they would enjoy there, the old polished furniture, and the scent of amber which would await them. It is less a longing for a dream boudoir situated in a Holland combining the exoticism of the Spice Islands and old Europe, than a longing for order, peace and sensuous pleasure. The mood is set by the despairingly nostalgic refrain:

> *Là, tout n'est qu'ordre et beauté,*
> *Luxe, calme et volupté*

"There everything is order and beauty,/Luxury, calm and sensuous pleasure." These lines tell us what it was that he sought through Marie Daubrun, but they also have a wider resonance. Ever since his break with Jeanne, Baudelaire had lived alone, ever slipping from one address to the next, one hotel room to another, barely managing to keep one jump ahead of his creditors. He craved for peace and a settled existence, the essential prerequisites for that calm and spiritual order which he sought above everything else. Throughout the mid-1850s the central concern of Baudelaire the man would be to build a refuge, a home; find a center where he could be safe from the crushing pressures of "Implacable Life." He knew that he was incapable of building such a haven alone. He needed a companion; and during these years we see him trying to find one—and wilting under a burden of grief and stress as his efforts failed.

He was not destined to know *"luxe, calme et volupté"* with Marie Daubrun—although he tried hard enough to find them. He persuaded his mother to allow Ancelle to advance him a little capital, to set up an apartment of his own. He was sick of living in drab furnished rooms, eating in vile restaurants which destroyed his digestion. He wondered how he had stood it for so long:

> I am tired of colds, migraines and fever, above all tired of having
> to go out twice a day, and of snow, mud and rain.

He hopes that in his own place he will no longer feel time slipping by:

That's my open sore, my huge open sore; for there is something still worse than physical pain, this fear of seeing the wearing-out, the destruction, the disappearance, in this terrible existence full of upheaval, of the magical poetic talent, the clarity of ideas, and the strength of hope which make up my real capital.[3]

Baudelaire is in dire need of peace. He sees himself frittering away and losing a second inheritance, one worth incalculably more than a paltry hundred thousand francs: the capital of his genius.

But he was not to share an apartment with his Green-eyed Venus. On returning from a nine-month tour of Italy, she rejected him and went to live with Théodore de Banville. Baudelaire lost touch with her for some years, and seems to have suffered no great sense of loss. It was the idea of living with someone sympathetic, as opposed to Marie Daubrun in particular, which had attracted him. But the cycle of poems inspired by the Green-eyed Venus does not end here. When Marie returned to Paris in 1859, Baudelaire would renew the relationship. At the time Banville was ill and had been in the hospital. The sense of decline which Baudelaire felt in those years is reflected in a poem he wrote for her, "Chant d'Automne" ["Song of Autumn"]. It is full of melancholy and awareness of imminent death, but also of the splendors of a sunset love.

There were other poems as well that Marie inspired. When Banville came out of the hospital, she went to him again, and the couple left suddenly for the south of France. Baudelaire was shattered by a betrayal, which he commemorated with one of his blackest poems, "A une Madone," which is based on the image of the Sacred Heart pierced with seven swords. This is a profane Madonna, and Baudelaire will take the swords of the seven deadly sins and drive them through her throbbing, sobbing, streaming heart.

The unremitting series of lean years had begun to mark the poet by the mid 1850s, although the man who spent two hours a day on his appearance could still look smart, and the poet-dandy still hold forth. A young writer, Emile de Molènes, recalls him:

He always wore black, a sort of smock, but of a studied and most elegant cut, a generous cravat knotted daintily beneath a large shirt collar, which showed off his smooth white neck. For that reason some of us called him "le guillotiné," others the "priest." In truth there was something ecclesiastic about him. He called us "the ephebes." . . . Sometimes he was kind to us and gave us advice with a paternal air—which was the funniest thing in the world; sometimes he insulted us and cracked savage jokes at our expense. But how we admired his dry and relaxed delivery when he condescended to talk of art, and how we listened, open-mouthed, to the theories he deigned to air. . . .[4]

Yet for all the admiration he was beginning to command, these were bad years. He found the unremitting hardship increasingly difficult:

> . . . Anyway, I am used to physical suffering, I am so good at tucking two shirts into a pair of trousers, with a torn coat that lets in the rain; I am so good at putting straw or even paper into holed shoes that almost all I feel is moral pain; —but I must admit to have reached the stage when I don't dare make sudden movements—or even walk, for fear of making new tears.[5]

His longing for a place of his own, and for peace, is understandable when one considers just some of his addresses over these years—1852: 60 Rue Pigalle; 1854: 61 Rue St. Anne, 60 Rue Pigalle, 57 Rue de Seine; 1855: Rue Neuve des Bons-Esprits, 27 Rue de Seine, 18 Rue d'Angoulême-du-Temple; 1856: 19 Quai Voltaire—eight addresses in four years, most of them hotels. That is only part of the story; in between these quasi-permanent addresses he was obliged to live on the move. In 1855 he wrote to his mother:

> IN A SINGLE MONTH I have been obliged to move SIX times, living in the midst of debris, sleeping with bugs, my letters (the most important ones) refused—pushed from hotel to hotel; I lived and worked at the printers, being unable to work at home.[6]

As usual his debts denied him any peace. Pressure made him permanently enraged and under stress. He wrote to Poulet-Malassis envying him the calm of his life, in contrast:

> *My* life, as you may imagine, will *always*, always consist of rage, *death, outrage*, and above all discontent with myself.[7]

He writes in similar vein to his mother. He is sorry that he failed to thank her for an unexpected sum of money:

> You know my strange life, you know that each day brings its contingent of rages, arguments, embarrassments, errands and work, it is not surprising that I put off, sometimes for a fortnight, letters that I consider to be duties.[8]

Occasionally his predicaments have a ring of farce. Baudelaire described a visit from his debtor-in-chief, Arondel:

Arondel has just left. He looked a real specter; luckily I had hidden in my washroom. He waited for some time, and M. Lepage [his concierge] really had the wit to say that I had just been called to the printers.[9]

The Aupicks now lived in Paris, since Aupick had been made a senator. Baudelaire's mother attempted a reconciliation. Baudelaire agreed provided that "your husband is intelligent about it,"[10] but unsurprisingly it came to nothing. Baudelaire's relations with his mother came under strain yet again, as yet again her hopes for his future seemed unfounded, his rudeness and ability to accumulate debts unaltered. His letters consisted of unremitting requests for money, accompanied by promises:

You say that I make you suffer, and suffer a lot—but if my punishment consisted simply in the need to write these intolerable letters—*explain, explain, always explain*—my punishment would suffice.[11]

Mme Aupick began to return his intolerable letters unopened. Baudelaire swallowed this further humiliation, as he had swallowed so many—and sent his next letter unsealed. Eventually he lost touch altogether, did not know her address, and had to write to her via Ancelle. By the end of 1855 she had refused to see her son for an entire year. Baudelaire begged her for a meeting:

Above all I want to see you. You have declined to do so for over a year, and I really think that your justifiable rages should be satisfied. There is in my relationship with you something absolutely abnormal, absolutely humiliating for me, which you cannot really want to maintain. If this prayer is not enough for you, at least be generous. I am not actually old, but I can grow old soon. It seems impossible that you should want to keep the situation up; I am steeped in humiliations of every description; at the very least I should not be humiliated by you. And as I said, if you agree to a reconciliation without pleasure or confidence, let it at least be out of some sort of charity. Yesterday, when about to leave . . . I began to sort a mass of papers. I found a lot of your letters, from different times, written in different circumstances. I tried to reread a few; all were filled with a profound but purely material concern, as if debts were everything, as if spiritual pleasures and satisfactions were nothing. But as the letters were all maternal, they set me thinking the most painful thoughts. . . . They all represent years gone by and gone badly by. Reading them soon became intolerable. Sometimes nothing is worse than the past. And from thought to thought I said to myself that the situation was not only monstrous and shocking, but even dangerous. Because my mind is fashioned in a certain way, which clearly appears eccentric to you, you must not imagine that I take perverse pleasure in this utter solitude and estrangement from my mother. I think I told you, just now, that I may grow old; but there is worse. One of us might die and it is really painful to think that we could die without seeing one another. . . . For a long time now I have been fairly sick in body and mind, and I want it all, at once, complete rejuvenation, immediate satisfaction, mental and physical. The years build up without either one or the other, and it is really hard.[12]

Mme Aupick was, in some ways, a hard woman; she could sustain a sense of resentment for many months at a stretch. Moreover, she failed to respond to the tender tone of her son's letter. Baudelaire had also asked her for some capital. She wrote to Ancelle agreeing to its release—which was the essential thing for him—but saying that she felt too grievously offended to be disposed to see him again.

It is an astounding response. One is led to wonder whether, for once, the money really was the essential thing for a miserable aging Baudelaire.

The threat that he might age prematurely, that his sanity and health were at risk, are not in themselves evidence to suggest that he suspected that syphilis had not really left him. He had no need of that disease to forecast his imminent decline. 1855 was an exceptionally bad year for a poet conscious of his genius and of his inability to use it. The year had started with an event which would haunt him for the rest of his life—the suicide of Gérard de Nerval.

Nerval was found hanging from a street lamp in the Rue de la Vieille Lanterne on a January morning in 18° of frost. The day before he had borrowed seven sous from Asselineau. He was down and out, penniless, and convinced that his talent had dried up, so that he could no longer make a living.

The possibility that he too might lose his talent—spend his capital —would haunt Baudelaire, utterly appalled at the suicide of his friend and fellow writer. The death cast a long shadow over 1855, and beyond. Nerval joined Poe as another of modern literature's victims—the perfect image of the modern poet. In his notes for a preface to *Les Fleurs du Mal* Baudelaire would write:

Gérard de Nerval—We are all hanged or deserve to be.[13]

138

In later years, in the depths of a paralyzing attack of depression and inertia which had led to a severe writing block, Baudelaire described himself as being attacked by:

An illness à la Gérard, in the fear that I shall be unable to think or write a line.[14]

The steadily building pressures of the 1850s obliged Baudelaire to widen the scope of his begging letters. He is no longer too proud to beg from his friends. Yet although his behavior might smack of sponging, it was nothing of the sort. Baudelaire did not have the kind of vanity that was wounded by the necessity to beg from his friends. There was nothing graceless, apologetic, cringing or spiteful about his asking. His letters were always urgent, but remained forthright enough not to be importunate. The real enchantment that could radiate from his warped and unhappy personality comes through even in his correspondence. Baudelaire's letters are essentially a depressing read. He seldom had time to be charming, informative, even reflective. They are almost all written out of need. Yet even the begging letters do not diminish one's regard for this singularly unhappy man, still legally a minor at the age of thirty-five:

My dear Malassis,
I beg you, I won't say most urgently, it would be impertinent, I just beg you, if you can, as soon as you get my letter, to post for me, in the form of a money order, ANY SUM of money. I am making it easy for you, as you can see, for obviously there can be no question of *a substantial* sum. I simply have to find a few days rest, and make use of them to finish things which will bear fruit next month. . . .
I have not A SOU to work, not for a fortnight but for a day, don't be surprised that I turned to you who have been so charming to me, and always.
P.S. WITH OR WITHOUT MONEY answer me at once; but please, my friend, no heavy excuses designed for fools; I shall be persuaded that you cannot help by the simple fact that you don't. —And also—my dear friend, don't be too witty—it would not go down well in my present state.[15]

My dear Nadar,
I don't know if it is right for me to trouble you in your new [married] life, to discuss wretched problems with you. The truth is that if you could, not help me *substantially*, I don't believe you could—but modestly—you really would be doing

something rather fine. *Oh, substantially*, that would be too marvelous; —but, to reassure you, remember what it is like to have to find substantial sums—*and not have the means with which to find them.* —I don't know if you are still at the same address; anyway I have addressed it to the old one. I beg you, do what you can, and don't be angry if I chose a bad time.[16]

When he tried to account for the disastrous quality of his life, particularly for these bad years, he was at a loss. He sometimes considered suffering a purifying process which developed his spiritual potential, but when faced with the sheer accumulation of debts, pressures and loneliness, no such optimistic explanation could suffice. He came to think of himself in Jansenist terms—as damned through no fault of his own; he had been born into a state of gracelessness and was the victim of a judgment against which there could be no appeal. He had been marked by that same *guignon* which had marked both Poe and Nerval. Once he accepted essential gracelessness the pattern of his life became crystal clear:

In short I think that my life was *damned* from the start and that it is damned *for ever*.[17]

It is characteristic of a damned, graceless and disaster-prone Baudelaire that, having at last secured an apartment, and escaped from cheap hotels, desperately tired of solitude, his chosen companion, Marie Daubrun, should have let him down. So urgent was his need for a haven that he could think of nothing better than to go back to Jeanne Duval, to try to create with her the calm that he had failed to find with Marie Daubrun. We know little about their relationship since the ménage had broken up in 1852. It would seem, however, that Baudelaire never lost touch with her, giving her whatever financial help he could. She represented for him a responsibility that he would always acknowledge and honor as much as his slender means allowed. Yet it is a dreadful testimonial to his loneliness and decline that in 1856 he should turn to Jeanne once again, in a desperate effort to make some kind of home. On all past evidence, the attempt was bound to fail; that Baudelaire hoped it might succeed indicates what little hope remained to the drowning man.

Inevitably the arrangement was a disaster, but this time it was Jeanne who found Baudelaire impossible. Being alone, in increasing despair and poverty for four years, had not made him easy to live with. Renewing long-standing liaisons once let slip is always a hazardous business. Jeanne left him very soon after their reunion and her departure caused yet more grief and distress; partly because he still felt for her, partly because he had hoped for a settled life, but most of all because it *was* a departure, the end of a relationship first started fourteen years before, in the time of his heroic youth. However impossible the partner, the loss of someone who had been part of one's life for so long is an irreparable loss. He wrote to his mother, saying that he would have told her sooner, had he been able to tolerate the "maternal delight" which the news would have inspired:

> My liaison, my liaison of fourteen years with Jeanne is ended. I did all that was humanly possible to try to prevent its end. This torture, this struggle, lasted a fortnight. Jeanne kept on answering, imperturbably, that I had a character impossible to cope with, and that anyway one day I would actually thank her for her decision. There is the great bourgeois wisdom of woman for you. I know that whatever agreeable adventures, pleasure, money or vanity may come my way, I shall always miss that woman. So that my pain, which you may not really comprehend, should not seem too childish to you, I must tell you that I had staked all my hope on her, like a gambler; this woman was my only distraction, my only pleasure, my only companion, and despite all the upheavals of a stormy relationship, the idea of a definitive separation never entered my head. Even now, when I am quite calm, I find myself thinking, when I see something beautiful, a landscape, anything nice, "Why is she not with me to admire it with me, to buy it with me . . ."
>
> . . . When it was finally proven to me that it really was *irreparable* I was overcome by a nameless fury. I did not sleep for ten days, I threw up all the time and had to hide because I could not stop crying. The idea obsessing me was anyway a selfish one; I saw before me an endless succession of years, without family, without friends, without a companion, just years of loneliness and chance, with an empty heart. I could not even console myself with pride. It was all my fault; I used and abused; I amused myself by making a martyr and was martyred in my turn. . . .
>
> I never thought that emotional pain could cause such physical torments. . . . I am alone now, really alone, for ever more than likely—for I cannot *morally* place my confidence *in creatures, any more than in myself*. Having nothing left to occupy me from now on but financial affairs and vanity, with no pleasure other than literature.[18]

Although this may sound like hysteria, the reader should remember that Baudelaire believed in his own hysteria and special pleading.

However shallow his motives may have been, however he may have overdramatized his loss, he certainly experienced it as he described it—even though he may have stolen an occasional glance at his tear-stained face in the mirror between fits of vomiting. Above all he had to face the dreadful and usual truth that he had only his own impossible character to blame for the loss which had taken self-destruction a stage further. He was perfectly right to see nothing but loneliness ahead; no other woman was to play an active role in the last years of his life.

For all his rage and illness, he was too generous to lose touch with Jeanne. He would continue to support her for the rest of his life and retain an active concern for her—and a sense of pain:

> To be perfectly sincere the thought of that girl has never left me, but I feel so reconciled to the business of living a life of lies, empty promises, that I feel incapable of falling again into those heart traps from which there is no escape. The poor child is now ill, and I refused to see her. For a long time she avoided me like the plague, for she knows my terrible temperament, all trickery and violence. I know she is to leave Paris, and I am relieved; although, I confess, that I feel sad at the thought that she might die far away from me.[19]

One might be tempted to take Baudelaire's expressions of grief lightly. After all, he had not displayed any real warmth to Jeanne for many years now; if he mourned their inability to live together so bitterly, could it not be that it was the prospect of future loneliness that was the cause of his distress? Yet this is not quite so. In their reunion he had experienced a surge of deep, almost elegiac emotion—deep enough to make him believe for a moment that the two of them might indeed share a future of *"luxe, calme et volupté."* They could not, but the reunion did inspire some of his finest, most tender and melancholic lines of prose, as seen in this evocation of what it was that he felt when they were reunited:

> Stirred by the contact of those pleasures that resemble memories, softened by the thought of a misspent past, of so many mistakes, so many quarrels, so many things to hide from one another, he started to cry; and his hot tears flowed in the darkness on the naked shoulder of his dear and ever-attractive mistress. She shivered; she too felt softened, moved. The dark reassured her vanity and her frigid woman's dandyism. These two fallen creatures, suffering yet from the remnants of their nobility, spontaneously embraced and, in the raining of their tears and their kisses, they mingled the sadness of their past with their un-

certain hopes of the future. Perhaps sexual pleasure was never so sweet for them as it was on that night of melancholy and charity; pleasure steeped in pain and remorse.

Through the blackness of the night, he had looked back into the deep years, and had thrown himself into the arms of his guilty companion to find there the pardon he granted her.[20]

THE EARLY 1850s were a time of misery for Baudelaire, but they were also the years which made him as a writer. His first translations of Poe enjoyed genuine success in literary circles—without bringing the translator much money. Baudelaire, not for the last time, failed to gain the support of his distinguished and influential friend Saint-Beuve. He had written to beg for a favorable notice, but his friend had fobbed him off with promises and done nothing. Another friend, Barbey d'Aurevilly, the Catholic writer and critic, on the other hand, had published a highly favorable piece, praising the quality of the translation in particular.

That Baudelaire was acquiring a reputation, if only as a translator, is confirmed by his presence, however modest, in the *Panthéon Nadar*. This was a huge lithograph, consisting of caricatures of all the leading literary figures of the age, nearly two hundred studies in all. The relative size of the figures is a gauge of their status—and Baudelaire is not very large. He is also mentioned in a sort of Who's Who of literary Paris.

To his contemporaries Baudelaire may have seemed no more than a translator on the fringe of literature, but it was at this time that he was composing some of his finest verse. To do so, he craved peace—not appreciating, paradoxically, that his best work was born of pressure. Poetry never came easily to him. Compared with other poets such as Victor Hugo, his output is tiny. Baudelaire was a perfectionist who hated facility. Poetry meant the intense and lucid concentration of all his energies, all that was best in him; it was the most exhausting activity that he knew. As he wrote to his mother in a letter longing for peace, in which he complained of having to change rooms six times in a single month:

As the height of ridicule I have in the midst of all these intolerable upheavals, that wear me down, to compose poems, the most tiring of all occupations for me.[1]

Baudelaire had long had a reputation as a bohemian poet, but as yet he had never published his work in any significant journal. The year 1855 altered that. Hector Buloz, the editor of the *Revue des Deux Mondes*, decided to publish a selection of his work. This was a compliment: the *revue* did not take chances with unknowns. It had a solid, intelligent, but conservative readership, which is why the editor was at pains to state that Baudelaire's poems represented his own and not the paper's values. The poems themselves, including such vital pieces as "Voyage à Cythère," "L'Irréparable," "L'Invitation au voyage," and "Le Vampire," were a fair sample of his perverse and violent imagination, his despaire, and his spirituality. They were poorly received by critics and readers alike, perhaps because of their moral anguish.

France in the 1850s was not anxious to learn about its secret passions, vices, and failings. It wanted to be amused, to get rich, to comfort itself with the thought that things were improving steadily and of their own accord, safe in the knowledge that one day science would create an earthly paradise without anyone having to stir a limb. In the meantime, the nation wanted to sit back and listen to Offenbach.

The reviews were scathing and dismissive. *Le Figaro* said that for years Baudelaire had been trading on his reputation. Finally he could not resist publishing; what he offered was short-winded, puerile, and pretentiously disgusting poems. Baudelaire would be remembered if at all as one of "the dead sea fruits" of modern poetry. The article ensured that the tantalizing prospect of a regular slot in the *Revue des Deux Mondes* would be denied him. Indeed, *Le Figaro* continued to dig its knife into Baudelaire. A year later when the novelist Duranty discussed new trends in French literature, he talked of the young "shock and death's head set"—largely inspired by Baudelaire, who used mystery and horror as a source of cheap sensationalism. He was no kind of poet, and his only legitimate claim to reputation was earned by his translations of Poe. Duranty was not disinterested. A close associate of Champfleury and the realists, he had been slighted by the scorn with which Baudelaire had treated that aesthetic, and was now repaying him in kind.

The poet was gaining a reputation for notoriety and unfulfilled promise. He was being misread by the public, misrepresented by the few journalists who wrote about him. His violent rhetoric and extravagance made him unreadable to a public brought up on platitudes. This notoriety was to linger on unchanged, even after he had become the most fashionable underground poet that Europe would ever know. For almost a century Baudelaire was to remain the extravagant devil's advocate and sexual pervert that the horrified Second Empire first took him to be. The only difference was that a later generation of ether-sniffing aesthetics would love him for it.

In April 1857 he placed nine pieces in *La Revue Française*, and three more in *L'Artiste* a month later. But the chief event of 1857—and of his whole career—was the publication of *Les Fleurs du Mal*.

Baudelaire's book had been maturing for over ten years, and would not reach its definitive form until 1861. This is because the work was a uniquely original conception, the reflection of a lifetime's experience, of an increasing maturity and understanding. Its central themes and techniques were the direct product of a slow and often unconscious process of growth and understanding over a period of fifteen years.

As we have seen, Baudelaire had abandoned his original title of *Les Lesbiennes* in favor of *Les Limbes*, which was intended to portray the spiritual crisis of modern youth in an industrial and materialistic age. As Baudelaire grew older, however, his subject shifted. It was no longer youth's spiritual crisis that preoccupied him, but man's capacity for self-destruction in the interests of seeking sensation in a modern and meaningless world.

The definitive title was not Baudelaire's. He had been forced to reject *Les Limbes* because another poet, a certain Veron, now perfectly forgotten, had published a collection under that title in 1852. *Les Fleurs du Mal* was suggested by the critic Hippolyte Babou. It appealed to the poet for its sensationalism and its appropriateness. It suggested that beauty could be born of evil, that evil and squalor could be turned into the finest poetry.

Baudelaire had hoped that the book would be published by Michel Lévy, but the firm had been discouraged by the reactions of press and public to the poems published by the *Revue des Deux Mondes*. He was obliged to look elsewhere.

For some years Poulet-Malassis had had unsatisfied ambitions. He wished to become a printer of fine books and had already under-taken the printing and publishing of Banville's *Odes funambulesques*. He had long admired Baudelaire's work, and eventually poet and printer signed a contract. It was a better one than Lévy's, with a $12\frac{1}{2}$ percent royalty on every copy printed and a guaranteed first printing of a thousand copies.

The professional relationship between poet and printer was not always satisfactory. Poulet-Malassis knew nothing of bookselling and lacked the instinctive commercial flair that might have compensated for his inexperience. He was a dreamer who loved fine printing, but a careless production manager, passing inadequate proofreading and motivated by intermittent enthusiasm. He produced and sold limited editions of beautifully printed books—which cost ten times more than the commercial products of the age. His whole approach to business tended to complicate his relationship with Baudelaire.

The poet made his own contribution to that complication and it was a substantial one. To the amazement of the often slapdash publisher, the poet who could never complete anything on time, who could not begin to organize his life, was a compulsive perfectionist in matters of literature and printing. Baudelaire once observed that editors were welcome to reject his work, but he would never countenance the alteration of a single comma.

Poulet-Malassis came up against that attitude. *Les Fleurs du Mal* took five months to produce, owing to the poet's daily letters of complaint and correction. He queried spelling, the use or nonuse of capital letters, the layout, the size of the type. He complained of the quality of the paper, of the shape of the inverted commas.

Poulet-Malassis found his friendship brought frequently to breaking point. The poet's concentrated attention to details of production left him incredulous. He sometimes suspected that Baudelaire was simply trying to make a fool of him.

Matters got to the point when the entire printing works was filled with the set type of *Les Fleurs*, and no other work could be undertaken. Baudelaire nearly brought his association with the firm of Poulet-Malassis to a close when he wrote a furious letter to de Broise, Poulet-Malassis's partner and brother-in-law, who by this time had had his fill of Baudelaire. Fortunately Poulet-Malassis intercepted the letter. It fulminated, talking of the scandalous proofs which required an "excessive" number of proof corrections with which he was alleged to burden the luckless printers.

It was not simply a question of Baudelaire interfering in the design of the book or meticulously correcting typographical errors. He changed his mind with a frequency that enraged his printers. He knew quite well what he was doing, which is why, throughout his life, he was always ready to pay for the cost of excessive corrections after the type had been set. It was his misfortune that he could never judge work in manuscript. He needed the distance that only a galley proof could provide to step back and make his final assessment.

As publication date drew nearer Baudelaire became filled with that mixture of excitement and apprehension familiar to any author. One may exult in one's work in manuscript, but as the day approaches one may equally be overtaken with the suspicion that the work has gone wrong. That the matter is out of your hands and in the hands of booksellers, critics and the public is no consolation. Certainly Baudelaire hoped for a success, a *succès de scandale*, to be more accurate, but he also had misgivings that the book would be judged as immoral. It was for this reason that he had hesitated sending his mother a copy when the

147

book finally appeared, although he himself did not regard his work as immoral:

> You know that I have never thought of literature and the arts as other than pursuing a goal foreign to morality, and that the beauty of conception and style are enough for me. But this book, the title of which, *Les Fleurs du Mal*, says it all, is clothed, as you will see, in a sinister and cold beauty. It was created in rage and patience, moreover the proof of its positive value resides in the evil people say of it. Besides, shocked myself at the horror I would inspire, I cut it by a third at the proof stage. I have been told I have nothing, not even inventiveness, or a knowledge of the French language. All those fools make me laugh, and I know that this book, with its good and bad points, will take its place in the memory of the educated public, beside the best poems of V. Hugo, T. Gautier and even Byron.[2]

It was in fact Gautier who had inspired these misgivings. Obscene enough in his private dealings, the "good Theo" had warned Baudelaire of the "scabrous nature" of the book.

At first sight it is hard to understand Baudelaire's concern. But 1857 had already seen one trial for obscenity. In January, Flaubert had been prosecuted for the alleged obscenity of his novel *Madame Bovary*. His acquittal had infuriated Billaut, the Minister of the Interior. If writing about adultery automatically secured prosecution, scarcely one nineteenth-century author would have escaped the clutches of the law. Essentially Flaubert was charged not with writing about it, but with making it sordid. Rather than use the glamorizing stereotypes to which French fiction took such monotonous recourse, he preferred to give his theme an unequivocal and matter-of-fact treatment. The prosecution founded its case on Flaubert's "vulgar and often shocking realism."

The realist aesthetic of Champfleury, and more particularly of Courbet, seemed to those it revolted to concentrate needlessly upon the ugly, mundane, and sordid sides of life, at the expense of noble sentiments and fine actions. Realism was the terror of the respectable middle classes, witness one Léon Dumont, scion of a wealthy family from Valenciennes, who in 1855 left school and rejected the bourgeois way of life; declaring himself to be a "realist philosopher," he was driven out of his home town and declared an outlaw.

This was the shockable public that Baudelaire addressed in *Les Fleurs du Mal*. The very first poem, "Au lecteur" ["To the Reader"], paints a picture of our miserable sinfulness. False repentance, hypocrisy, foolishness haunt us all. We even enjoy our own remorse. We believe that the occasional tear can wipe out past sins—and then start to sin again. We all dance to the devil's tune in our quest for pleasure. Baudelaire completes the dramatic picture of an inner life of evil, sin, and backsliding with the greatest vice of them all—the delicate monster *ennui*. The poem ends with a final insult to its reader. He should not suppose that the piece is just a portrait of the poet; it is the reader's portrait too—the reader who is no better than the poet, his brother in vice.

The impertinent suggestion that others shared Baudelaire's predicament was the first of many cues for indignation—cues which no one missed. The book went on sale on June 25. Baudelaire had worked hard on the advance publicity, ensuring that complimentary copies went to, among others, Hugo, Longfellow, Tennyson, Browning and de Quincey. Unfortunately, a review copy also reached the desk of his old enemy *Le Figaro*, which again took up the cudgels. On July 5, one Bourdin, now remembered for this piece alone, went into action:

Monsieur Charles Baudelaire has for fifteen years or so been a poet of tremendous stature for a small set of persons, whose vanity, by hailing him as a god, more or less, had been making a fairly sound speculation.

He had only published a review of a Salon [*sic*] much vaunted by doctors of aesthetics, and a translation of Edgar Poe. . . .

I have read the book, and I have no judgment to pronounce, no sentence to give, but here is my opinion, which I do not wish to impose upon anyone.

There are times when one doubts Monsieur Baudelaire's sanity; there are those when there is no longer any doubt; most of the time we have monotonous and calculated reiterations of the same words and notions—the odious is cheek by jowl with the ignoble—the repulsive joins the disgusting. You have never seen so many bosoms being bitten, chewed even, in so few pages; never has there been such a procession of demons, fetuses, devils, animalia, cats and vermin.

The book is a hospital open to all forms of mental derangements and emotional putrefaction. . . .

If one may understand a poet at the age of twenty allowing his imagination to be carried away by such subjects, nothing can justify a man of over thirty making public such monstrosities in a book.[3]

The author was the son-in-law of Villemessant, the editor of *Le Figaro*, which had the reputation of being a government newspaper. It was this review, in Baudelaire's opinion, which was responsible for his being brought to trial. A no less unfavorable piece appeared in the *Journal de Bruxelles* on July 6, 1857:

> The hideous novel *Madame Bovary* is a work of piety compared to *Les Fleurs du Mal*. The author is a Monsieur Baudelaire who translated Edgar Poe, and who, for ten years, has passed for a great man among one of those little sets which send out bohemian and realist garbage. Nothing can give an idea of the web of infamy and filth which this volume contains. The author's friends are horrified and hastily announce a failure, for fear that the police may intervene; a decent pen cannot even quote. . . .

On July 12 *Le Figaro* fired a second broadside. This time the author was J. Habans, a protégé of the Minister of the Interior. Baudelaire had hoped to escape official attention, since the minister was preoccupied with the Paris elections, but he was mistaken. Billaut took time off from politics to defend public morality. Habans writes:

> In Monsieur Charles Baudelaire's case we must use the word nightmare. . . . All these coldly displayed charnel-house horrors, these abysses of filth into which both hands are plunged to the elbows, should rot in a drawer. But people believe in the genius of Monsieur Baudelaire; the idol, long hidden, had to be revealed to the adoration of the masses. And behold, in the light of day the eagle turns into a fly, the idol is rotting and worshippers hold their nose.[4]

Such responses could scarcely have surprised the poet. He knew that his poetry would shock: indeed, he meant it to. He considered shock an essential part of the artistic experience. Yet here again we see his fatal optimism. He seriously believed that the public, or at least the critics, would see beyond shock to appreciate the spirituality and seriousness of the work; its unequivocal indictment of the vices it portrayed; and that peculiar nobility found in art of the highest order.

He had forgotten who he was writing for, forgotten that the French could only appreciate the doggerel rhymes that Béranger wrote in honor of Napoleon, and that otherwise they preferred delicately presented smut. In his own words, the public must "never be offered delicate perfumes, which exasperate it, but carefully chosen pieces of excrement."

Optimism, common sense, and the elections combined to make Baudelaire discount rumors that a prosecution was pending. Nevertheless, he begged Sainte-Beuve, who wrote for the government paper *Le Moniteur*, for support. The critic had, after all, done as much for Flaubert. Characteristically, for all his private professions of admiration, the cautious Sainte-Beuve declined to commit himself in public.

Baudelaire turned to another possible protector in Prosper Mérimée, the author of *Carmen* and a distinguished figure of the establishment. Mérimée, however, declared that he would not move a finger to prevent Baudelaire from being burnt at the stake. He found the book an indifferent work with flashes of talent. He suspected its author to be a decent fellow and probably a virgin—which is why he would on the whole be glad enough to see him escape burning!

Something may, in fact, have come of Baudelaire's approaching Sainte-Beuve, for another journalist, Edouard Thierry wrote a favorable review for *Le Moniteur*. It described *Les Fleurs* as not being for the casual reader, adding that its author neither enjoyed nor celebrated evil. Thierry judged the work highly—and correctly—by harking back to Dante:

> . . . The old Florentine would more than once recognize in the French poet his own fire, his terrifying diction, his implacable images and the sonority of his bronze verse.[5]

Baudelaire and Asselineau had entertained high hopes for this piece when they heard it was to be published. They spent hours waiting outside *Le Moniteur* while it was being set up, corrected, and approved by the editor. But since press censorship under the Second Empire extended even to literary reviews, it also had to get past the Minister of State Achille Fould. The two friends had another hour to wait before the editor returned with Fould's authorization that the piece could appear in print.

Favorable as it was, it did more harm than good. There were factions within the government, and the Minister of the Interior felt that Fould had made a serious blunder. It made him more determined than ever to prosecute. It was a determination shared by the Minister of Justice Abbatucci, who believed in moral censorship and felt that Fould should have consulted him before allowing publication. Billaut and Abbatucci joined forces. Another paper, *Le Pays*, was forbidden to publish a favorable review by Barbey d'Aurevilly. Barbey meanwhile sent Baudelaire a copy of it to help him prepare his defense. Fould could not withstand the combined pressure of two ministers, and the prosecution party got its way.

The poet Leconte de Lisle had already warned Baudelaire on July 11—a little bit late—that the edition was to be confiscated. Baudelaire wrote at once to Poulet-Malassis:

Quick, hide, really hide the entire edition; you should have 900 copies in sheets. That is what comes of sending copies to *Le Figaro*!

That is what comes of not wanting to *promote* a book properly. At least we would have the consolation had you done what was needed of having sold the edition in three weeks, and we would just have the glory of a trial—which is easy to get out of anyway.

I hope the letter reaches you in time; it will go tonight, you will have it at four o'clock tomorrow. The confiscation is not yet announced. I got the information from Monsieur Watteville [a civil servant] via Leconte de Lisle, who, unfortunately, let five days go by.

I am sure that the misfortune was caused by the piece in *Le Figaro*, and by stupid gossip. Fear did the damage.[6]

For all his precautions the sheets were duly confiscated on July 17.

The year 1857 had already brought Baudelaire sorrow and rejection of a different kind. General Aupick had died on April 27, unreconciled with his stepson and leaving no mention of him in his will. He attended the funeral, only to endure the cutting humiliation of Aupick's friends. Strangely enough, Baudelaire does not allude to his mother's bereavement in his letters; there is not even a formal expression of condolence from him. Nevertheless, he wore mourning, probably out of consideration for his mother, and he was still doing so at the time the book was confiscated. True to form, in answer to a friend who asked him about his black armband, he retorted that he was in mourning for *Les Fleurs du Mal*.

Yet still he remained optimistic. He would always believe more in his own future than in his *guignon*. He could not admit the inevitability of another disaster, and proudly told his mother that he had brought about a power fight between three ministers:

I beg you to consider this scandal (which is causing a real sensation in Paris) as the foundation of my future.[7]

Matters did not look too black. Baudelaire appeared before an examining magistrate for three hours, and found him a reasonable man. The prosecutor, Pinard, had the reputation of being a liberal; however, he had already lost his case against Flaubert, and could not afford to let history repeat itself. To his credit he did not press too hard. He actually received Baudelaire in person when the poet brought a collection of favorable reviews bound into book form.

He had been warmly praised by Asselineau in yet another article which underwent a delay in publication, appearing a month or so after it was ready. It points out that the book was not written for little girls, who have a literature of their own. Instead these were real flowers of evil, assaults on spleen, melancholy, sensuality, hypocrisy and moral cowardice. It is the most intelligent of the early reviews. Flaubert also wrote a highly complimentary letter, providing a second intelligent appreciation. He found in Baudelaire a kindred spirit who understood the intolerable burden of living and was able to sing of flesh without loving it, in a sad and detached manner. He described the poet as "resistant as marble, as penetrating as an English fog."[8]

In the meantime Baudelaire set about preparing a defense. Amazingly, he turned for support to Sainte-Beuve. One must appreciate his respect for established reputations and his readiness to be humiliated to understand the docile loyalty which Baudelaire felt for that critic. Yet it is easier for us to see the limitations of that cautious and ignoble man than it was for a luckless Baudelaire who needed all the help he could get. For all his past failures to get support of any kind from Sainte-Beuve, he once more sought his advice.

The advice was typical. He offered "little means of defense as I conceive them!" Everything worth writing about had already been exhausted. Lamartine had taken the heavens, Hugo the earth and man, Laprade the forests, Musset passion, Gautier Spain. What was left? What Baudelaire took. It was as if he were obliged to do so. The critic, who liked his pornography, went on to show that Baudelaire was not alone in immorality. Musset and even the great Béranger had written lines which a modest critic could not quote without a blush. To condemn Baudelaire for writing in a similar vein would be hypocritical. Besides, the book should be judged as a whole, and for every obscene piece there was a platonic flower.

As a defense, it takes one's breath away. As long as Sainte-Beuve was helping, Baudelaire had no need of enemies. Other friends had stressed the high spirituality of *Les Fleurs*, had talked of Dante. The greatest critic of the age could only suggest that the luckless poet was left with nothing but filth to write about. The worst thing about this truly dreadful advice is that Baudelaire thanked Sainte-Beuve and took it. The thought of his meek and grateful acceptance of such counsel from the smug and dirty-minded critic can still bring tears of impotent rage to the eyes of this biographer over a century later.

The case was heard on August 20 by a court that usually handled cases of petty larceny and rape. It took place in the sixth correctional chamber of the Palais de Justice, a dismal room with dull green paint, long dirty windows, a crucifix, and a loud ticking clock. The prosecutor opened by suggesting that on occasion *Les Fleurs* stepped over the frontiers of license. He also suggested that four poems were blasphemous. Still, he was strangely understanding and asked the judges to:

Be indulgent to Baudelaire, who has a disturbed and unbalanced nature. But, by condemning at least certain parts of the book, give him a warning that has become necessary.[9]

To defend him, Baudelaire had engaged a well-known lawyer, Chaix-d'Est-Ange, who proceeded half-heartedly on the poet's behalf. Barbey d'Aurevilly talks of his dull and monstrous baseness. His speech was three times the length of the prosecution's, a foolish enough tactic on a hot August day. He argued that for every obscenity in *Les Fleurs du Mal* there was a counterbalancing passage of beauty. He did suggest that the poet portrayed evil only to condemn it, but in essence his case was founded, disastrously so, on the existence of a "Rabelaisian" tradition in French literature. Tracing the tradition from Rabelais himself straight through to George Sand, he concluded that Baudelaire's poems were no more obscene than countless others.

The argument cut no ice. Baudelaire was found not guilty of blasphemy, but he did not escape "the accusation of offending public morality and good morals." The book was offensive, the court reasoned,

. . . since the intention of the poet, the goal he wished to attain and the route he took—whatever his efforts at style, whatever the condemnations preceding or following his portrayals—cannot mitigate the deadly effect of those portrayals which he offers the reader, and which, in the incriminated poems, are necessarily conducive to the arousal of the senses by virtue of a coarse realism offensive to modesty.[10]

In short, six poems—"Les Bijoux," "Le Léthé," "A celle qui est trop gaie," "Lesbos," "Les Femmes damnées," and "Les Métamorphoses du Vampire"—were banned. Baudelaire was fined three hundred francs, and the two printers one hundred francs a piece. The accused were required to pay costs totaling twenty francs, thirty-five centimes.

The terms of the condemnation were peculiarly sympathetic to his intentions and the punishment hardly severe, but Baudelaire was beside himself with rage:

"Did you expect to be acquitted?" asked Asselineau.
"Acquitted! I was hoping for a public apology," he replied.[11]

It was the accusation of realism that outraged the poet. No one was less sympathetic to realism than Baudelaire, who believed so passionately in the spirituality of art and felt that artists who simply reproduced slices of low-life were unworthy of their calling. Yet clearly, this was how the public had received his book. Because it dealt with the

154

sordid quality of vice, it was taken as the work of a realist who believed that the sordid was the proper subject for his pen.

There is a particular reason why his judges mentioned realism. Three days before the trial, the Count de Montalembert had addressed a large public gathering on the evils of realism, claiming that modern youth had lost its passion for noble matters and given in to the

> . . . crude lassitudes of an encroaching empiricism which invites a decadent generation to abandon good taste and morality, reason and honor, conscience and faith. Under the name of realism, a word still less barbaric than the object, this deadly influence already infests literature, art, and even philosophy.[12]

The speech had attracted much publicity and was printed by various papers three times in the next three days, the three days preceding the trial and in their judgment the magistrates were indubitably echoing Montalembert's catch phrase. The irony of it was, however, that for all the pompous rhetoric of a guardian of public morals, the speech represented Baudelaire's own viewpoint; but while the orator talked in generalities, Baudelaire had elected to portray in detail the damage done to modern man's psyche by the loss of his high seriousness.

Baudelaire was understandably enraged. His manner and appearance at this time stress that rage, and the bitterness it induced in him. Witness a portrait of him by the Goncourts:

> Baudelaire takes supper at the next table this evening. He is without a cravat, neck bare, head shaven, truly the turnout of a man about to be executed. Basically a delicate and cultivated appearance, small carefully washed hands, cared for like those of a woman. . . . And along with that the head of a maniac, a voice as cutting as steel, and a diction that aims for, and finds, the ornate precision of a Saint-Just.
>
> He defends himself obstinately, and with a certain dry rage, against the charge of offending morality in his poems.[13]

Baudelaire's contacts with the establishment had not quite ended, however. In November of that year he wrote the strangest of all his begging letters, to the Empress Eugénie herself, asking her to have his fine remitted:

> Madame:
> It requires the prodigious assumption of a poet to dare draw the attention of your Majesty to a case as small as mine. I have had the misfortune to be condemned for a collection of poems

entitled *Les Fleurs du Mal*, the dreadful frankness of my title being an insufficient defense. I had believed I had created a beautiful and great work; it was judged obscene enough for me to be condemned to rework it and remove a few pieces. . . . I must say that the courts treated me with admirable courtesy, and the very terms of the judgment imply the recognition of my lofty and pure intent. But the fine, increased by costs surpassing my understanding, are beyond the means of the proverbial poverty of poets, and encouraged by so many proofs of consideration I have received from persons in high places, and at once persuaded that the heart of the Empress feels pity for all tribulations, spiritual and material, I decided after days of indecision and humility, to solicit the kindness of your Majesty, and to ask her to intercede for me with monsieur the Minister of Justice.

I beg you, Madame, to accept the hommage of my feelings of the profoundest respect, with which I have the honor to be
    your Majesty's
                most devoted and obedient servant
                        and subject
                                    Charles Baudelaire
                                    19 Quai Voltaire[14]

The letter worked. After due and lengthy processes of consultation, the fine was reduced to fifty francs.

The piece resembles other begging letters which Baudelaire had addressed to the famous, yet there is a special twist to this one. He indulged his imp of perversity in a way unique in the entire history of petitions to the wives of heads of state. The French word for "case," *cas*, has an obscene sense which Baudelaire knew well: in a letter he once wrote that he knew the word could mean "penis," but could it also do for "backside"?[15] The meaning is a rare one, but Baudelaire must have felt ecstatic pleasure when respectfully and apologetically requesting the first lady of France to deign to notice a *cas* as little as his own.

Despite the reduction of his fine, the judgment stood: the six poems remained banned from all future editions of *Les Fleurs du Mal*. They were soon published in Belgium under the title *Les Epaves*—"the wrecks"—Belgium being free of censorship and a great center for subversive and pornographic literature. The French, however, were not inspired by the example of the Belgian press. The ban on the complete edition of *Les Fleurs* continued in France. In the early twentieth century it was still being marketed as a dirty book. A bookseller of that time, which specialized in works of distinguished pornography, the well-named "Bibliothèque de Curieux," lists a complete *Fleurs du Mal* in its catalogue as late as 1910—along with the Marquis de Sade and other pornographers of a bygone age.

The ban secured Baudelaire's reputation as a scandalous Satanist and lover of evil almost up to the Second World War. It remained a technical offense to publish *Les Epaves* in France up to June 1, 1949, when a retrial took place. That a trial was felt necessary may seem comic. The trial itself was more ludicrous still. The defense prepared a strange case for Baudelaire: a genius, he was now immortal, whereas the magistrate who condemned him was forgotten. As for the charge of immorality, works had since been published which were a great deal more immoral. The defense examined the poems and absolved their author from pornographic intent. He had exercised the liberty which was the prerogative of genius. The judge agreed that after Henry Miller it would not be easy to find Baudelaire obscene. Besides:

> The man and the poet are dead. The work remains. A concert of praise has gone up. It comes from the best: some stress the intellectual and moral probity of the poet, others the unparalleled richness of his poetry. Some, the skilled use of a word, even when it is a little strong. . . .[16]

The judgment was reversed, but it was evident that judicial attitudes had not changed much in over a century. Like his own counsel, the defense of 1949 showed that Baudelaire was no more obscene than countless others. At no point was a powerful case made out against his obscenity. No one suggested that his work is of the highest spirituality. It contains the occasional "strong" word, but is less dirty than Henry Miller; besides Baudelaire enjoyed the license of genius. The plea for revocation, indeed the need for revocation, are enduring reminders of the nature of officialdom. Looking down from his place in critics corner, Sainte-Beuve must have heaved a sigh of relief, as, on the first of June 1949, his embarrassingly disreputable friend achieved respectability at last.

Baudelaire's own public should not be dismissed as philistines for failing to understand the book. Baudelaire had been hoist with his own legend. He had been cultivating his outrageous behavior for sixteen years or more, and his reputation had paved the way for his art. Moreover, *Les Fleurs* is not an easy work: it presupposes that the reader understands what Baudelaire wishes to say before he has said it; it assumes high seriousness in its readers. The book is easily misunderstood, and has been ever since its publication. Small wonder that the opulent, crassly materialistic and strangely limited France of the Second Empire could find in it nothing but filth. Even the poet's mother, who, once she recovered from her initial shock at yet another scandal, slowly learned to appreciate the work, retained reservations to the end. After Baudelaire's death she wrote to Asselineau, who, together with Banville, was preparing a complete edition of his works. She begged him to suppress one of the poems, the blasphemous "Reniement de Saint-Pierre" ["Saint Peter's Abjuration"], saying that she felt sure that her son would have agreed; such blasphemy was a mere "youthful" indiscretion, which, she felt, the mature—and broken—Baudelaire would have disowned. It is a sad letter written by an unhappy old woman anxious to do the right thing for the reputation of her much loved dead child. It would seem that no one would ever understand. In the terrible words of one of Baudelaire's last letters to Ancelle:

> And you were *child* enough to forget that France *loathes* poetry, real poetry; that it only loves scoundrels like Béranger and de Musset; *that whoever tries to spell correctly passes for a man without feeling* (which is incidentally quite logical since passion always expresses itself badly); that finally, poetry that is profound, but complicated, bitter, coldly diabolic (in appearance), is less suited than any other to eternal frivolity . . . !
>
> Must I tell you, you who were no more able to guess it than the rest, that in this *atrocious* book I put all my *heart*, all my *tenderness*, all my *religion* (disguised), all my *hate*. It is true that I shall write the contrary, that I shall swear by the great gods that it is a book of *pure art* of *apeing* of *clowning*; and I shall lie like a patent medicine seller.[17]

How could a nation believing as much in its frivolity as in its prosperity have been expected to read Baudelaire?

IN THE FIRST edition of *Les Fleurs du Mal*, Baudelaire was still uncertain of the book's focus. Although it would not take final shape until 1861, it is appropriate to consider it in its revised, and final, form. The book is much more than a collection of poems, as Baudelaire very clearly pointed out in a letter to Alfred de Vigny. He wrote that the only praise he wanted for his work was the recognition that it was not an anthology, but a coherent work with a beginning and an end. Indeed, the work tells a story. Although it consists of poems written at various times and for various reasons, Baudelaire had rearranged them to make a kind of narrative. The restriction of his medium prevents him from achieving the kind of continuity and development we expect from prose fiction. At times the story line is very clear, at others the focus softens and the narrative element remains in the background. Moreover, the attempt to tell a kind of story through a series of individual poems makes for a certain jerkiness of narrative rhythm. It is as if we were seeing not a film, with smooth linking passages, but a series of still photographs flashed on a screen in a set order. Each picture can stand alone, but the spectator is also free to associate them and make a story out of their arrangement.

Les Fleurs du Mal is the story of a life, but not necessarily of Baudelaire's life. Baudelaire believed that art must be much more than self-expression. The artist must use his experience to pass beyond it, to try to capture the quintessence of his age through his art. It is only when poetry goes beyond the personal to achieve universality that it aspires to greatness.

Baudelaire composed many of the poems of *Les Fleurs* in response to his own experiences—his love of Jeanne, his reaction to Marie Daubrun's betrayal. But this is by no means true of all the poems. There is no reason to believe that he was ever a Satanist or that he frequently associated with lesbians. Many of the pieces were written to fit the narrative framework of the book. Even those that were initially more personal take on a new function when fitted into *Les Fleurs du Mal*. They develop the narrative, rather than act as a medium for self-expression. Although Baudelaire has integrated his most intimate and painful experiences, the book goes beyond these to become a poetic allegory. It is a *Pilgrim's Progress* in reverse, but Baudelaire is no more its hero than Bunyan was Mister Christian.

The book tells the story of its protagonist from birth to just before death. It is the story of his self-destruction and of the reasons for it. The protagonist, like Baudelaire, seeks to fulfill his craving for idealism the lazy way—through sensation. He learns, to his cost, that such intensity of sensation is subject to the law of diminishing returns—an ever-increasing dose is needed to provoke an ever-fainter response. By the time he has learned that harsh lesson he is doomed. There is nothing left for him but to try to exult in the inevitability of his own complete destruction.

The introduction reminds us that we are reading our own life story. The protagonist is not any one individual, he is modern man. Baudelaire saw the craving for sensation as the supreme characteristic of his age. Hence his freaks' gallery of lesbians, drunkards, and sex criminals all striving desperately for a fulfillment they cannot find. In short, Baudelaire has composed the first handbook on the psychology—and the poetry—of absolute addiction, "the habit." He does not tie himself down to any particular opiate; he spells out, in general and poetic terms, the anatomy of addiction of any and every kind.

The book is also a study in evil. Evil for Baudelaire was rarely so obviously the devil's work that it smelled of sulfur. Satanism as such plays a modest part in *Les Fleurs du Mal*. Satan prefers to remain behind the scenes, yet it is he who encourages our readiness to indulge our sloth, indolence, and thirst for sensation—at the expense of our spirituality and concentration. Baudelaire believed man to be a divided creature; set halfway between heaven and hell, man combines characteristics of them both:

> In all men, at all times, there are two simultaneous postulations, one towards God, the other towards Satan. The Invocation to God, or spirituality, is a desire to elevate oneself; that to Satan, or animality, a delight in descent.[1]

Baudelaire believed in the devil as he believed in his *guignon*, and in the likelihood of his own damnation for absolute gracelessness and spiritual disorder:

> . . . I have always been obsessed by the impossibility of account-

ing for certain sudden thoughts and actions in man, without the hypothesis of the intervention of an evil force external to him. There is a great confession which the entire nineteenth century conspiring against me will not make me ashamed of![2]

Indeed, it was history's refusal to recognize the intervention of the devil that made the composition of *Les Fleurs du Mal* necessary. A note he wrote for the preface reads:

> The Devil. Original sin. Man good. . . . It is harder to love God than to believe in Him. On the contrary, it is harder for the people of this age to believe in the devil than to love him. Everybody feels him and no one believes in him. Sublime subtlety of the devil.[3]

Moreover, modern man was quite capable of sinning anew, after a moment's tearful repentance, with the reassuring conviction that he was in a state of grace; believing in good, he cheerfully did evil.

Les Fleurs du Mal was divided into six sections of varying length: "Spleen et idéal," "Tableaux parisiens," "Le Vin," "Les Fleurs du Mal," "Révolte," and "La Mort."

"Spleen et idéal" opens with a birth. In a parody of the Annunciation a mother curses her son and God for having chosen her of all women to give birth to a monster. However the monster, or poet, grows up under the tutelage of a guardian angel. He knows he will have to suffer, but as a poet he will achieve nobility and spirituality through suffering.

The earliest poems of the section deal with the young poet, who is only at home when soaring above base reality. He understands the secret doctrine of correspondences, and can see the world in terms of harmony and meaning. He has a sense of idealism and spirituality.

Almost at once, however, he begins to lose a grip on spiritual truths. His imagination dwells increasingly on grotesque and violent images. He still believes in the high spirituality of art, but that art has become the art of decadence.

Degeneration goes a stage further with a series of poems, among them "Le Guignon," which describes the failure of his own art. Inspiration, high seriousness, spirituality have all left him, he can no longer sustain his efforts. But even though he can no longer create it himself, he still retains a love of beauty. Beauty, however, has grown fatally ambiguous: it could be a promise of hell or of heaven, divine or infernal. He elects, in a fatal decision, to disregard that ambiguity. Any beauty will do provided that it supplies sensations strong enough to relieve his boredom. The choice is made: he has committed himself to the dark side of beauty and henceforward his life will consist of a perpetual search for satisfaction, through sensations which can only aggravate, never satisfy, his need.

Next comes the Black Venus cycle, the poems written to Jeanne Duval, in which the protagonist has turned from beauty to sex. Their tone varies from languid sensual evocations of sexual fulfillment in pieces such as "Parfum exotique" or "La Chevelure" ["Hair"] to violent attacks upon the sexual cruelty of his woman, as in "Tu mettrais l'univers entier dans tu ruelle" ["You would place the whole universe in your alley"]. "Une Charogne" ["A Rotting Corpse"], perhaps the most remarkable piece of the cycle, reconciles the two main strains of adoration and disgust. The poet evokes a rotting carcass, legs in the air, and describes its malodorous maggot-ridden appearance in strangely gentle detail. He then turns to his woman in a blend of savagery and confidence, telling her that one day she too will rot; and yet—through the medium of his poetry—he will have preserved the form and divine essence of his decomposing lover. It is a violent and, at first sight, shocking poem, but also a superb example of what Baudelaire means by drawing beauty from horror. Its theme is the poet's ability to transcend the pathetically short life of the flesh and create immortality through great art. Its music, its texture are extraordinarily beautiful. The very savagery of the description of the corpse is mitigated by the control of artistic form. Baudelaire could create horror through his art, but he did so only to take his readers beyond that horror.

Next comes the White Venus cycle, the poems dedicated to Mme Sabatier, followed by those to his Green-eyed Venus, Marie Daubrun. The tone of individual poems oscillates: moments of ecstasy are qualified by poems which bring the protagonist down to flat and stale reality; longings for peace are qualified by professions of irrefutable sinfulness; moments of calm, by sadistic fantasies.

The focus then softens, and it is here that we find some of the poet's greatest and most melancholy poems. The protagonist is now so dulled by sensation that he can no longer either enjoy or provoke it. He is left alone with the dreadful consciousness of time's passing. He longs for death and oblivion, yet succumbs to fits of helpless rage. Overwhelmed by a thirst for vengeance, he has no victim on whom to wreak his revenge. He can only get drunk on dreams of hate and violence, but hate can never procure oblivion.

These savage pictures of spiritual and emotional devastation are succeeded by four poems with the same leaden title—"Spleen." They depict a terrible emptiness, as the clock ticks on, rain falls and a smoky log fire burns in the hearth. The protagonist is "king of a rainy country." Young, yet dreadfully old, nothing amuses him anymore—neither women, nor his jester, nor the hunt, nor even his people dying at his feet. What is the reason for his terrible condition? It is that instead of

162

blood, the waters of forgetfulness run through his veins.

This is an important comment on the quest for fulfillment through sensation. Since the addict cannot maintain a state of perpetual physical excitement, he becomes dependent on his memory, upon the ability to recreate excitement in the mind. As long as he can do so, he can, to some extent, leave his perpetual search for new stimuli by escaping into memory. Some of the finest poems in *Les Fleurs du Mal* describe peace and serenity achieved through remembrance—but now even memory has failed him. Unlike the artist, the pure sensation seeker, be he pervert, alcoholic, drug addict, or gambler, has no memory. If he could recreate in his mind the texture of past experiences he would not always be obliged to renew experience. But he can do nothing of the sort, and is doomed to take another little drink as soon as he comes round from the last bout.

The last poems of "Spleen et idéal" portray the protagonist's realization of what he has done. He has so abused his responses that he has destroyed his capacity to feel or remember. He can only long for oblivion, cultivate self-destruction to escape from the remorseless passage of time. Accordingly he wallows in sado-masochistic fantasy. He looks to pain for stimulus and is indifferent to whether he receives or inflicts it. The section culminates in the full recognition of his own damnation, a black picture with only a single point of illumination— the ironic, infernal lantern of "consciousness in evil." The last poem, "L'Horloge" ["The Clock"], is a final reminder that time is passing and life wasted. At any moment it may be too late to repent for it will be time to die.

"Spleen et idéal" is a remorseless study in the destruction of an individual through his quest for fulfillment in the world of sensation. He abuses his spirituality, commits sins, destroys his capacity to feel and to remember what he has felt, and is left a wasted, burned-out hulk waiting for death.

With the next section, "Tableaux parisiens," the focus softens. This series of poems, loosely based on the theme of the modern city, provide a backdrop to the drama just enacted. *Les Fleurs du Mal* is not the story of Everyman; it is the story of modern man living in the infernal world of the big city, a place of exile and of loss. Drawing inspiration from city life, the poems paint pictures of loneliness, loss, and hallucination. In "Les Sept Vieillards" ["The Seven Old Men"], the poet, wandering through the narrow twisting streets of old Paris in the fog, sees a succession of identical, grotesque old men, which brings him to the verge of insanity. He then evokes a chance encounter with a woman whose eyes he catches in the crowd; he knows that he could have loved her, but she is swept away before they can meet. Elsewhere he portrays a gambling den, prostitutes, grotesque statues, even an evocation of a drug-induced

163

vision of Paris as a Piranesi-like confusion of elaborate architectural shapes with still-frozen fountains.

"Le Vin" is a short section reflecting the poet's belief that drunkenness was a characteristic phenomenon of the age—and one of his own weaknesses. It opens with a favorable view of wine: wine as the working man's solace, a source of consoling illusions to the ragpicker who would be king. But wine too turns sour. "Le Vin de l'assassin" ["The Wine of the Assassin"] describes an exultant drunken murderer; the assassin is free and happy at last. Having just pushed his nagging wife down a well, he breathes deeply the air of his release and drinks to celebrate it. That night he will drink himself into oblivion and lie down in the road, only to have a cart come along and crush the life out of him. The last poem of the section, "Le Vin des amants" ["Lovers' Wine"], is the most subtle. It is apparently a splendid celebration of drunken lovers, yet they are less fulfilled than they seem. Although they believe they are in harmony, each lover pursues a parallel course.

"Les Fleurs du Mal" describes the desperate measures to which sensation seeking drives the addict. Its tone is perverse and sadistic—a love of pain and destruction of the self and others dominates. "Une Martyre" ["A Martyr"] is the strongest of all Baudelaire's evocations of secret and perverse eroticism, with its boudoir of heady perfumes, its headless, bleeding corpse, the legs spread wide, and its killer who even then could not satisfy the immensity of his desire. This note of perversion is continued with the lesbian poems, the lesbians representing aggravated and frustrated appetite.

Baudelaire takes his view of the essential hollowness of sexual pleasure a stage further with "Un Voyage à Cythère," a poem based partly on Watteau's *Embarquement pour Cythère* and the expectations those ladies and gentlemen entertain as they set off, and partly upon Gérard de Nerval's account of an imaginary voyage to the island of love, and what he found there—a three-branched gibbet. The emblem is enough to spark off Baudelaire's enduring disgust at the animality of sex and the banal fantasies of sexual expectation. His character has the highest hopes of the island of Venus, only to find it a sad, dark place—"the banal Eldorado of old bachelors"—in no way does it live up to its Watteauesque promise. A corpse hangs from the gibbet, eaten by dogs, pecked by birds. As the protagonist observes the wretched carcass he realizes that his own body is ravaged by no less painful forces; he ends the piece with a prayer to God, begging for the strength and the courage to contemplate his own heart and body without disgust.

The next section, "Révolte," earned Baudelaire the reputation of a Satanist, and procured such unwelcome admirers as the Great Beast, Alesteir Crowley. Baudelaire was nothing of the sort. "Révolte," although blasphemous, is a phase in the development not of Baudelaire, but of his protagonist. After exhausting all other modes of perversion, only to recognize the futility of sexual experience, and having damned himself in the process, the protagonist has little left. Accordingly he turns to metaphysical perversion, and adores the evil principle that has engineered his destruction. If he is irredeemably damned he may as well get what he can from that damnation. It must be said that the three poems that make up this section are not among his most successful. They are shot through with a note of hysterical strain that makes them monotonously unmodulated. One, however, "Le Reniement de Saint-Pierre" ["The Abjuration of St. Peter"], contains a line that explains the mood of frustration and dissatisfaction that runs right through *Les Fleurs du Mal*. The protagonist declares himself all too happy to leave "un monde où l'action n'est pas la soeur du rêve." "A world in which action is not sister to the dream" is the perfect description of Baudelaire's sense of the reality in which he had his being. Now he understood that that reality—the crass reality of nineteenth-century France—could never match his expectations. Hence his striving for escape and fulfillment out of this world, a striving that could only lead to self-destruction.

The final poem of "Révolte" is a prayer to Satan. It is the only piece of actual devil worship in the entire book, but it is the piece which has consolidated Baudelaire's enduring reputation as a Satanist. It is simply the poem of a loser, with nothing left but to adore the cause of his own loss. At least that can give the derisory illusion that he retains some control, some responsibility for his plight. Rather than reeking of evil and the black masses it is a pathetic poem, the work of someone with nothing else left to turn to. Satan is the only game in town.

"Révolte" was the ultimate surge towards destruction, the attempt to collaborate in the damnation of an immortal soul. Yet it is not the end. The final section, "La Mort" ["Death"], is marked by a new calm and serenity. The first piece, "La Mort des amants" ["Lovers' Death"], is a reply to "Le Vin des amants," in which death brings the couple a genuine harmony. No longer in pursuit of parallel fantasies, their two hearts beat as one; in a languorous death they find serenity and the promise of salvation. Death is also the consolation of the poor; it keeps them alive, enables them to get through their day. For artists it is the final hope. They exhaust their lives in clowning and histrionics in the pathetic attempt to capture beauty. Their one hope is that death itself may provide inspiration where life has failed them. The penultimate poem, "Le Rêve d'un curieux," reveals a last flicker of anxiety. The protagonist dreams that he dies—but death, far from providing the revelation he longs for, is yet another disappointment. Death is nothing, and he is waiting still.

The last poem, "Le Voyage," is also Baudelaire's greatest. Written while he was staying with his mother in Honfleur, and a reflection of the peace and clarity of vision he achieved there, it crystalizes the movement of the entire book, giving it that precision of focus which it lacked in its original form. Travelers set off into a world that seems great with promise, only to make the bitter discovery that it is not. They are disappointed, finding nothing to assuage their curiosity; some settle for intoxication, but the real searchers travel on, for traveling's sake. Nothing can match their restlessness because they crave for an experience out of this world, and their dissatisfaction is heroic. All they find is violent and futile appetite; delusion after delusion and never any rest. In its despair, the poetry has the tonality of Wagner's *Flying Dutchman*. Imagination makes every landfall an Eldorado in anticipation, but in reality the landfall is only a barren reef. The most glorious sunsets, the richest cities offer no contentment. The travelers see nothing but the unchanging spectacle of immortal sin: mankind living stupidly through sensation, and damning itself in the process.

Yet the traveler does achieve something—the something the protagonist has achieved in the course of *Les Fleurs du Mal*. He has learned not to be taken in by promises of satisfaction in this world. Such promises can only deceive. He will henceforward turn his back on hope and lotus eating. The lesson has been a costly one. The protagonist has been to the extremes of self-destruction, and come back. He has learned to abandon hope of fulfillment and achieved the only serenity possible, a serenity born of despair. He is now ready to greet death:

> Death, old captain, it is time! Let's hoist the anchor!
> This country bores us, Death! Let us set sail!
> If sky and sea may be as black as ink
> Our hearts, as you know, are filled with light!
>
> Pour us your poison that it may comfort us!
> We wish, so fiercely does that fire burn our brain,
> To plunge to the depths of the gulf, Heaven or Hell, what matter,
> To the depths of the Unknown to find something *new*!
>
> *O Mort, vieux capitaine, il est temps! levons l'ancre!*
> *Ce pays nous ennuie, ô Mort! Appareillons!*
> *Si le ciel et la mer sont noirs comme de l'encre,*
> *Nos coeurs que tu connais sont remplis de rayons!*
>
> *Verse-nous ton poison pour qu'il nous reconforte!*
> *Nous voulons, tant ce feu nous brûle le cerveau,*
> *Plonger au fond du gouffre, Enfer ou Ciel, qu'importe?*
> *A fond de l'Inconnu pour trouver du nouveau!*

This, the ending of *Les Fleurs du Mal*, is profoundly ambiguous. Baudelaire was reluctant to examine his truths too closely. On the one hand it suggests that the protagonist has learned nothing. Like Baudelaire himself, he remains to the end a perverse victim, indifferent to the alternatives of damnation and salvation. He simply looks forward to death as to the "big one," the definitive sensation which cannot disappoint. Yet there is another, optimistic interpretation. The protagonist has reached serenity. Free of the treadmill of sensation he has learned that life cannot satisfy his craving. In that escape from striving he has achieved release from sin itself to achieve other-worldliness. His inner being is purified and ablaze with light. Heaven and hell are simply earthly concepts, and through death he will achieve a new life which will transcend such distinctions. It is an interpretation in tune with Baudelaire's own desperate optimism, the optimism which made him attempt suicide because he had an immortal soul and "he hoped." It is not possible to make a clear choice between the two readings. Baudelaire himself is hesitant, unable to reconcile the optimism and the despair which struck such a strange balance in his being. At all events his was not the kind of ruthless personality which would destroy optimism if it threatened clarity of thought and feeling. He would rather retain ambiguity than destroy hope.

It should be remembered that the poem deals not with Baudelaire but with his protagonist. The point is important. Very early on the latter turned his back on poetry. Baudelaire has given the protagonist some but not all the aspects of his own self. He has kept back the lion's share—the ability to turn his own hopeless sinfulness and self-destruction into some of the most beautiful and spiritual poems in the language. The poet believed in all sincerity that in the writing of poetry lay his own salvation. By a typically Baudelairian paradox he tells the story of the steady self-destruction of his protagonist, and ensures his own salvation by using the fate of his protagonist to inspire a string of beautiful poems. The protagonist, or Baudelaire the man, may go under, but Baudelaire the poet is saved, redeemed by his own artistic achievement.

The secret of Baudelaire's art, and indeed of his otherwise utterly miserable life, lies in this conception of poetry. It was for him a kind of alchemy, a spiritualizing process. By dint of intense concentration of all that was good and noble in him, he believed he could convert the squalor and ugliness of his world, his circumstances, and his inner self into the spiritual perfection of art. God kept a place for poets, and as long as Baudelaire believed in poetry, the author of this "atrocious book" and the subject of this atrocious life could never be damned. This is what Baudelaire means when he calls beauty a religion. When he composed *Les Fleurs du Mal* he believed passionately in the power of art to transmute evil into good. He makes this abundantly clear in one of his projected prefaces. Addressing Paris, the infernal city and his great inspiration, he writes a ringing phrase which is also, with a little luck, his own epitaph:

You gave me your mud
And I made it into gold.

BAUDELAIRE WAS THIRTY-SIX in the year that *Les Fleurs du Mal* was published. He had not achieved manhood easily. He could look back—a long way—to a warm and enveloping childhood, to harsh years of school, to a glorious period of extravagance—the free spending of his money, his health, and his time—a period followed by some thirteen years of increasing hardship. It is much to his credit that he never recalled the glorious dandy of the Hôtel Pimodan with any nostalgia. Indeed, he came to see that period as a time of literally sinful waste and dissipation, a time when he sowed the seeds of his wretched future.

Nevertheless, for many years Baudelaire had retained his optimism. He knew that he had talent, genius even, and felt that, given the chance, genius would bear fruit and give him not just a place in French literature but riches as well. He looked forward to the end of over a decade of pressure and hardship, the regular certainty that each month would bring new obligations to be met, but nothing with which to meet them. In Baudelaire's day it was not common for genius to go unrecognized and unrewarded by a public of philistines. It was after all not just the age of Baudelaire but of Tennyson and Hugo as well. Baudelaire had every reason to expect that his genius would eventually secure not just immortality but success. How could he know that, with the exception of Poe and, in a different way, Nerval, he was the first "misunderstood" poet, ahead of his time? How could he know that he was the first of a new kind of artist who would depend on the spectacle of his own misery and self-destruction for his material, and who for the period between 1850 and the beginnings of Picasso's commercial success, was doomed to go poor and unrecognized?

In these circumstances the disastrous reception accorded *Les Fleurs du Mal* formed a watershed in the poet's life. Up to that moment he had still been able to hope. Henceforward he could not seriously look to the future with any optimism, not seriously expect that the time would come when the pen would release him from his debts. He was now without illusions as to the reception that his future works might enjoy. His optimism gone, he was now left alone with the knowledge that time was slipping by, left with nothing but regrets, rage, bitterness and a terrible burden of debt.

Baudelaire's appearance at this period radiated a despairing asceticism:

> Baudelaire was at home, working, as usual, in shirt sleeves, like a laborer . . . a soft cravat of purple silk with black stripes, loosely knotted, flouted about that solid, finely set neck he was so proud of. Clean shaven and bright as a new penny he leaned back in his vast canvas shirt, white as snow, and of old-fashioned cut. When he saw me he smiled and shook his long gray hair, slightly curly, which gave him a certain priestly air, and he looked at me with his large, intelligent and beautiful eyes.[1]

Despite that priestly appearance Baudelaire could still be a desperate clown, and unrelenting clowning made him a merciless companion. His manner found him admirers, made him enemies, but few friends. Enough of the dandy had survived for Baudelaire still to believe in sustaining style at all costs, both in his own eyes and in those of the world. Years of bitterness and disappointment, however, had turned his style into that of a bitter comic who no longer bothered about the laughter of his public. He simply persevered in his monotonous and humorless act:

> Elegant, somewhat mannered, both shy and iconoclastic, he had acquaintances but no friends, and fools could make him flee to the end of the world with their urgent observations on his own works and those of his contemporaries. His amazing self-control derived from the profound scorn in which he held those chatterboxes, who were always prepared to state their views on anything, and with whom he had nothing in common. He clearly appeared eccentric to his fellow writers, for he had the greatest respect for himself. . . . Many of the writers of the age—and still more the hacks—loathed him, in the first place for that reason, and then because he delighted in making them look foolish. Inclined to black humor, he would scorn excitement to display a false impassivity. . . . Was he ever more lugubrious than when he tried to appear jovial? His conversation was unsettling, his comic vein made one shiver. When in form he would recount, in between two bursts of laughter as rending as sobs, . . . some pro-

digious tale of the beyond which made the blood run cold, and which even terrified him, or he would, pitilessly and very skillfully, make fun of his listeners for an hour or more. . . . "Let us amuse ourselves," if he addressed you in those terms, you could be certain that his confidences would soon take a sinister turn and your flesh would start to creep. . . . If the conversation went that way you were lost.[2]

From 1857 on we find a steady aggravation of the rage and wretchedness which had already marked his earlier and happier years. Baudelaire had grown prematurely aged, yet he was still under the tutelage of Ancelle, a tutelage growing ever more distasteful. Never averse to finding scapegoats for his plight, Baudelaire blamed Ancelle for his ruin. The lawyer never understood that it was more desirable to save the man than to save his capital, and so ensured that the poet's debts would be with him always. Moreover the nervous energy that it required Baudelaire to make any kind of contact with him—and regular contact could not be avoided—cost him quite as much as the interest on his debts:

> It is useless to write to Ancelle, you know perfectly well that he is too stupid to do anything sensible on his own. . . . The poor man has been my utter ruination, without knowing it, the ruination of my fortune and my time. He will never know what an enormous restitution he owes me.[3]

Finally, his humiliating dependence upon Ancelle made him explode. Ancelle was never content to take his duties lightly. He persisted in an active interest in the poet's affairs with disastrous results—and, as we will see, some personal risk.

After Aupick's death Baudelaire's mother found herself in reduced, if not dire, circumstances. She had her widow's pension and some money from her first husband. Nevertheless, she found it necessary to move to the tiny holiday home which Aupick and she had bought in Honfleur. They christened it the *"maison joujou,"* and it was to house her for the rest of her life. The street in which it stood was later renamed the Rue Charles *Beau*delaire—a characteristic stroke of ignorance on the part of the French when it came to Baudelaire. Even more appropriately the house would become part of an asylum. The house itself was devoted to those suffering from contagious diseases: a proper way for Honfleur to commemorate France's greatest poet.

Baudelaire was desperately anxious to go there and stay with his mother for a protracted period. Honfleur became a dream for him; the chance to win a few months of real calm. To attain his dream, however,

171

Baudelaire needed money. He knew that it was useless to approach Ancelle for an advance. Instead, he turned to a lawyer friend of his mother, Jaquotot, who had shown kindness in the past. Baudelaire suggested that a lump sum be raised from the estate, sufficient to dispose of the most pressing debts. In the meantime, since in Honfleur he would have virtually no expenses, Ancelle could restore the capital out of the estate income.

To anybody unfamiliar with the dreadfully plausible quality of the poet's professions of financial intent, the scheme sounded reasonable. Jaquotot lent it his support and wrote to Mme Aupick suggesting that it was perfectly viable. To Baudelaire's delight she agreed. Nothing could give him more pleasure than the chance to lay his hands on a little of his own capital, and use it to buy a few months of peace. But unfortunately the arrangement demanded Ancelle's approval.

Baudelaire had assumed that his mother's agreement would be enough. In fact that cautious lady had not agreed altogether. Whilst her son was building castles in the air, deciding which creditors to pay off, what books and pictures to take with him, Mme Aupick was consulting Ancelle. Baudelaire grew apprehensive. As usual he had looked forward to an instant solution, immediate release from pressure. He knew with a dreadful certainty that with Ancelle's involvement any hope of instant release was gone.

The disappointment was bitter. Honfleur had come to seem a haven. Cut off from Paris, its pace, its pressures, its debt collectors, he had hoped to enjoy, for the first time since the days of the Hôtel Pimodan, a period of real calm; his first opportunity as a mature artist to do uninterrupted justice to his talent. It is scarcely possible to exaggerate the importance he placed on such a prospect of release:

> . . . I shall be able to read, read, and read, without interrupting my writing. Every day to be used in rebuilding my mind! For I must tell you, dear mother, that my wretched education was cruelly interrupted by all my foolishness and misfortune and youth is passing, and I sometimes think in terror of the years flying past; yet years are only made of hours and minutes. But while you waste time you think only of fractions of time and not of their total.
>
> These are good plans; and I do not think them impossible, since at Honfleur I shall have no excuse not to realize them.[4]

It is fascinating to see Baudelaire think of time as money—in the sense that he freely "spends" fractions of time, without thinking of the way in which he "depletes" their total, the lump sum. "Look after the minutes and the years will look after themselves" was not a precept he could follow. Now, just when peace and recovery seemed a train ride away, the threat of Ancelle's intervention made Honfleur appear just another pipe dream. He wrote to his mother imploring her to change her mind. He still longed to join her, but he realized he would have to finance the stay himself. Even if Ancelle were to propose some kind of elaborate financial arrangement, as long as the lawyer remained in control he would only make matters worse:

> Ancelle will come and kill me with his help, and when he sees me refuse his money he will want to help anyway. He will force his way in, into my affairs, force me to tell him my difficulties. Even thinking of his visit turns my suffering to rage. Seeing my persistent refusals he will try to do as much harm as possible under the pretense of helping. I cannot run away from Paris to avoid him, the cure would be worse than the disease. He will force his way into my affairs, as he did at my trial. He forced his way into conversation with my friends, whom he did not know —he is so intent on meeting people and involving himself in everything; and my friends asked me who was the grand gentleman who appeared to know me. I always kept a worried eye on him, for fear that he might compromise or make a fool of me.[5]

Baudelaire wrote that letter on the morning of February 27, 1858. By that afternoon the damage was done. The letter had been prophetic. Shortly after sending it he discovered from his landlord that Ancelle had been ferreting about. He had paid a secret call two days earlier to make inquiries. Did Baudelaire receive women? Did he keep late hours? The poet's nerves were always stretched tight and news of this investigation was enough to throw him into the greatest of all his rages. Rage had become a mode of release from tension—into hypertension; the state of "explosion" which played a major part in his life and art. On February 27 Baudelaire did not just explode, he came apart. He spent the day in a state bordering on insanity, a white hot flaring, aggravated by having no one on whom to vent it. His sole outlet was the pen, and so he began to write to his mother.

The "prophetic" letter had been written that morning. The second, announcing his discovery, was finished at 2:30 P.M. In it he threatened to beat up Ancelle in front of his wife and children at 4:00 P.M.; if Ancelle were out he would wait.

At 4:00 P.M. he wrote again. His landlord had begged him to restrain himself. Baudelaire had agreed not to see Ancelle that day, but he insisted on the humblest apologies. Otherwise he would strike Ancelle and his son. The next letter was written an hour later. By now he plans a duel, either with Ancelle or with his son, unless he gets an apology.

He is worried by the sad fact that most of his close friends are now married men with families; it might prove difficult to find a second. He writes to his mother again:

All this is disgraceful. *I want excuses. I don't give a fig for the three thousand francs that would have given me peace at last. I want excuses.* I have tears of rage in my eyes and I feel my bile rising to the point that I am going to vomit, it has to end. *Don't you feel insulted, too?* Or did you give the rascal instructions to act as he did? Where was he born, *how was he born?* Am I really fated to be insulted all my life? I shall take my revenge, unless you obtain from him a *sufficient apology made to me in person before three witnesses, one of whom will be M. Jaquotot, since he was involved in it all.*[6]

The next letter is a character sketch of Ancelle. Baudelaire had asked him for a character reference. Ancelle obliged, but gave him the letter sealed. Baudelaire broke the seal to discover that Ancelle had advised against giving Baudelaire what he asked! The last letter he wrote to his mother that day is explanatory. It describes the order and circumstances in which the five earlier ones had been composed. It apologizes for the distress they may cause, but repeats that they were necessary. He has been advised that it would be shameful to strike an old man in front of his family, but an apology he must have. The adrenaline is no longer flowing so fast, however he spent that night in a fever, his head throbbing with neuralgia, and it was only after spending most of the next morning throwing up that he recovered from this most savage of rages sufficiently to write a relatively detached seventh letter to his mother—who, incidentally, had to pay the postage on all of them!

Baudelaire had been distraught with rage before, but nothing matched this sustained fury. It was rage not just at the lawyer, but at all the forces and obstacles, all the disappointments that were conspiring to thwart his most modest hopes and dreams. With the effective collapse of any prospect of literary success Baudelaire would devote a major proportion of the remaining years to increasingly urgent attempts at negotiating at least one small oasis of peace, a time to mend himself and step aside from debts and tensions.

The extent of the need was increased, if not created, by a particularly vicious and typically Baudelarian financial arrangement that the poet entered into with Poulet-Malassis. It created a situation of an ever-increasing complication, as it drew first one friend and then another into its fragile web. The arrangement—which Baudelaire christened "the game of shuttlecock and battledore"—was essentially complex, and typically based on hope: the hope that sooner or later

Baudelaire would make some money. In the meantime he would borrow against prospects.

The optimism with which he viewed the prospects of his raising money remained unshaken. It was an optimism never based upon reasonable hope or an assessment of probabilities. It is very close indeed to the optimism of a gambler who always loses, but who never allows loss to dispel his unshakeable, irrational belief that one day he will win. It is not a belief that a gambler can afford to examine critically, for if he were to do so he would see that optimism cannot be justified and would be obliged to leave the game. Baudelaire had the mentality of a gambler, without ever needing to take to the tables. He ran life itself as one long gamble, a sustained losing streak which he hoped to ride out by doubling up. This emerges with great clarity in his complicated system of financial juggling. It could only be justified by the belief that one day he would hit the jackpot. It began in borrowing from Peter, to pay Peter, and developed into borrowing from Peter, to pay Paul, and from Paul to pay Peter again.

Poulet-Malassis would sign a promissory note which would fall due in so many months' time. Baudelaire would present it to a banker, who would discount the note at say 5 percent and give him the cash. He would use the cash to pay off an earlier debt. As the note fell due Baudelair would sign another, at three months, and Poulet-Malassis would cash it, at a discount, to meet payment on the original note. Thus essentially Baudelaire and Poulet-Malassis would put an ever-increasing amount of their own paper into circulation, ensuring that no two notes fell due upon the same day, and having to pay ever larger discounts to bankers as their credit rating declined.

In order to keep their paper in circulation and postpone the moment when they would be proved unable to meet their commitments, they gradually drew friends into the arrangement. Newcomers could raise money more cheaply with their own "courtesy promissory notes." The end result was a terrible confusion. Both men lived on borrowed time, and their only hope was Baudelaire's eventual financial success. Poulet-Malassis agreed to the arrangement with a perfect cheerfulness which is its own monument to that unfortunate man's generosity of both spirit and pocket.

The arrangement, which began in 1857, added severely to the pressures on Baudelaire, or rather brought them to a single point of worry. Its complexity, the need to keep the most careful count of who had to pay what, when and where, would have preoccupied the most methodical of financial controllers. It nearly drove Baudelaire insane. Yet it was essentially his sole means of support. No wonder he craved for a little peace.

His letters to his publisher consist almost entirely of financial detail.

He is sending money to cover one debt, he needs a fresh note to deal with a second, and so on:

> My dear friend, you make me tremble with your *penury*. And I am in the same plight. You have to pay 410 francs, 410 and 500 at Honfleur, when? I do not know. Here is a note to help you; it will be easy to cash now that there is hardly any Baudelaire paper at Alençon.
>
> Should Calonne's note be made out to *you* or *me*? Answer at once and you can cash it on the 14th. You know I'll ask you for a cut of it, even if I send the money back, for I think de Rode is going to keep his promise. . . . If you could manage the 500 at Honfleur without *me* or *Calonne* it would be better still.[7]

As time passed the amount in circulation increased from a few hundred to several thousand francs. The juggling act became more and more dangerous, as Poulet-Malassis himself teetered towards bankruptcy and both friends found their credit worthiness diminishing. Baudelaire writes to Poulet-Malassis to ask why he insists on trying to cash a note of the poet's in Alençon, where he owes fifteen hundred francs, when they still have a banker in Paris who will be happy to accept Poulet-Malassis's paper:

> You do understand don't you, that its not a question of my being timid but that since we are obliged to play the game for another six months, perhaps nine, we must make it look as plausible as we can.
>
> In a word you are playing at *shuttlecock and battledore* badly.
>
> What a torture this periodic anxiety, which comes regularly every six weeks.[8]

Inevitably, Baudelaire was sinking deeper and deeper, but he felt lucky to be still in the swim at all. When Poulet-Malassis reproached him, he replied quite sharply that all things considered he had done remarkably well:

> When you find someone who, independent at seventeen, with an excessive taste for pleasure, always without a family, enters literary life owing thirty thousand francs, and after twenty years has only increased the debt by ten thousand, and is far from feeling crushed, you just introduce me, and I will salute my equal.[9]

A fortnight later, however, he wrote to his mother in a different vein. He had come to accept his debts as a dead weight he could never be rid of. Indeed the weight could only grow heavier. The appointment of a guardian had sealed his fate for life:

> ... My debts have doubled *because all debts double in time*. ... I owed M. Arondel ten thousand and for some years now have owed him fifteen. I borrow to pay, and to give you another example, the money I earned by the production of my works in the last sixteen months has all gone to pay the interest on the renewal of a debt I contracted to go and stay in Honfleur. Besides, you should increase the total sum by the difficulty of working in the midst of such agony while the expenses keep building up. You wrack your brains, go daydreaming, in your attempt to understand, instead of just saying the words *"legal guardian"!* That terrible mistake which ruined my life, put a blight upon every single day, and colored all my thoughts with hate and despair. *But you do not understand.*[10]

As usual Baudelaire was borrowing short to pay long. The money he finally raised to buy peace at Honfleur had simply added to the burden. He had proposed to join his mother early in 1858; alas the time and energy devoted to the enterprise had left him distraught and behind in his work. He had to finish his translation of *Arthur Gordon Pym* for Michel Lévy. He was four months late and had lost his proofs. It was typical of the conditions in which he worked, conditions partly of his making, that he eventually had to go to the printers outside Paris to correct his proofs on the premises. Even then he could not leave Paris. He was too intent on trying to place other work, and fulfill other overdue obligations. Although constantly hoping to join his mother, he finally realized that it would not be possible until after the beginning of the new year.

There was another factor contributing to his inability to join his mother at that time. By November of that year he was again living with Jeanne Duval, in Neuilly at 22 Rue Beautreillis. It was to be his third, and final, attempt. Little is known about their relationship after 1852, when they first parted, yet it is clear, judging from their attempted reunion in 1856 and from their present coming together, that Baudelaire had never altogether broken with the only companion he had ever had, the only person with whom he had shared a home of any kind. He would continue to live with her intermittently until 1861, but the relationship was now further complicated by Jeanne's declining health. In 1859 she showed the first symptoms of paralysis, a paralysis which we shall see weaving its extraordinary pattern right through the final pages of Baudelaire's biography, to destroy both him, his woman, and all his closest relations.

Baudelaire was not with Jeanne at the time of her first attack, in April 1859. He was staying with his mother in Honfleur, having finally managed to get there in late January of that year. But on hearing the news of Jeanne's ill health he returned to Paris and arranged for her to enter a nursing home where she spent six weeks.

The only one of Baudelaire's letters to Jeanne that has survived was written during her stay in the home. It is tender, paternal almost. Patiently he explains that he has had trouble raising money, but he is anxious that she should not go short. He encloses a note that she should forward to Ancelle, suggesting that if she feels embarrassed to write with her left hand (paralysis made it impossible for her to use her right), she should ask her nurse to address the envelope. The letter ends with the touching injunction that she not go out alone on the slippery roads.

Having done what he could for his sick companion, Baudelaire returned to Honfleur for May and June. United for the first time with his mother since his suicide bid fourteen years before, Baudelaire found the last peace of his life. Initially he intended to do no more than write six new poems which would fill the gap left in the first edition of *Les Fleurs du Mal* by the pieces that had been banned. But a newfound ability to work enabled him to do much more than that. He produced a considerable number of pieces of great quality, including "Le Voyage," his spiritual testament.

Inevitably, Baudelaire's stay in Honfleur had its problems. His mother's respectable friends regarded him as a suspect, not to say notorious, figure, and this enraged him. He, on the other hand, had his own views about the Honfleurois:

Local news story: some laborers who were working in the garden told me that some time ago someone surprised the mayor's wife, being fucked in a confessional stall. They told me when I asked them why St. Catherine's church was shut when there were no services on. It would seem that the priest took his own measures to prevent sacrilege. She is a monstrous woman, who recently informed me that she knew the painter who painted the front of the Panthéon—But she must have a magnificent backside. This tale of provincial lechery in a holy place has all the classic spice of French dirty stories.

Take care not to tell people who might spread it around Honfleur that you heard it from me; I should have to leave my place of rest.

It is since then that the mayor has had to rub out the horns that people draw on his door.[11]

On returning from Honfleur, Baudelaire put up at the Hôtel de

Dieppe, Rue Amsterdam, his last permanent address in Paris. He would stay there until 1864. He twice tried to go and live with Jeanne, again, late in 1860 and early in 1861. She did not improve with the years, however, and still did all she could to exploit and cheat her lover. She would pretend not to have received money he had sent her for her nursing home, in the naive expectation that he would simply send more. Baudelaire greeted such actions with resigned sadness, not with rage. His final attempt to live with her was ruined by the presence of her brother. Baudelaire had hoped that her brother might begin to provide for her, but instead, it was the brother who expected Baudelaire to provide for him. Baudelaire complained bitterly that he could never be alone with Jeanne; the brother was always there. He had lived with her off and on for nineteen years, and believed that they could still talk— were it not for the brother. The irritation Baudelaire felt, the hopes he had of sharing the companionship of the dipsomaniac Jeanne, aging and crippled, selfish and stupid, say much for his optimism, but more for his enduring warmth, generosity, and kindness towards Jeanne. She was constantly shown a side of him which many were not given to see. Writing apart, she was the only responsibility which he never shied from.

He asked her to make her brother leave, whereupon the latter announced that he would do nothing of the kind. As for the suggestion that he support his sister, Baudelaire should never have taken a mistress if he could not afford one. Understandably, Baudelaire flew into a rage. He learned that Jeanne had been supporting her brother for over a year; small wonder that she was so poorly dressed and could not afford medicine. But even now he was unable to vent that rage on her:

So many tears on that aged face, all that indecisiveness in a weakened creature moved me; my rage vanished. But I am in a state of constant irritation which my financial situation does not alleviate.[12]

Baudelaire moved out and never returned. Yet later that year he saw her again, after she came out of a pauper's hospital. He continued to do what he could for the crippled, dishonest, drugged, and drunken figure that had once been his Black Venus. She borrowed money in his name—and he met the debts. She sold the most private treasures he had given her—and he was never offended. He accepted each monstrous betrayal, and eventually resorted to sending her money in a disguised way. He remained to his end anxious that his mother provide for her—a wish which that God-fearing lady did not respect. Jeanne now sinks from sight, except for a final glimpse of her in 1870 by Nadar, who

179

mentions that he saw her painfully dragging herself along a boulevard on crutches.

Baudelaire's own health was deteriorating. For most of the 1850s he had supposed himself to be cured of his disease. He had never linked his bouts of leaden lethargy to his old infection. Yet from 1857 on, he had increasing grounds to suspect that he still carried the infection in him. The first hint came late in 1857 during a puzzling attack of extreme depression:

Indeed my health gives cause for complaint, and my condition both perplexes and worries me. Perhaps I need a change, I don't know. Is it illness which saps the intelligence and the will, or is it spiritual cowardice which tires the body? I don't know. But what I feel is an immense sense of discouragement, a feeling of intolerable isolation, constant fear of some vague disaster, complete lack of faith in my powers, total lack of desire, total inability to amuse myself in any way. . . . A passing serious state of mind for a man whose profession is to produce and dress up fictions. I keep asking myself, "What's the point of this? What's the point of that?" It is a veritable state of spleen. . . .

Although he had known such moods before they had never been so prolonged or so acute:

. . . And to tell the whole truth there have been strange shortages of breath and stomach and intestine troubles for a month.[13]

Things grew more serious the following year. His handwriting which had not changed for some eight years began to show a very marked decline. It had become chaotic to the point of illegibility, suggesting deterioration of mind, hand, or both.

The sense of suffocation continues, and is treated with liberal doses of ether and opium, which do not contribute to his general well being. From then on his health begins to deteriorate steadily, but with no specific symptoms. He complains of lethargy, and of nervous and digestive troubles. At first he does not suspect syphilis, does not recognize a mild bout of paralysis for what it was—a curtain-raiser for the final attack which would nail him nine years later.

Quite understandably, Baudelaire was not aware of the pattern that fate was weaving round him, developing paralysis like a musical theme. Baudelaire had now had a brief taste of it. The next to suffer, as we saw, was Jeanne. We have no record of any medical diagnosis of her paralysis. Yet when we recall that Baudelaire already had syphilis when he met her, and that they had lived together on and off for the better part of sixteen years, it seems more than likely that he had communicated his infection to her, and as his consort it was logical that she should suffer so. Yet no reason, other than fate's having a strange sense of humor, can explain the theme's next variation: the paralysis of Baudelaire's sanctimonious half-brother, Alphonse. Baudelaire had not seen him for years, and there is no way in which the poet could have infected him. But, in 1860, he too was smitten with a paralysis from which he died. All Baudelaire could do was observe that, although he does not wish Providence to think him ungrateful for small mercies, Providence would have done better to have cured Jeanne. But is it *Providence* that he is dealing with?

In the meantime he had taken another turn for the worse, and had begun to suspect the cause. In 1860 he wrote to his mother telling her not to worry about his dreadful health:

> *Except for the thing you know.* Of course I am horribly displeased with my health, but the body would be well were the soul well. The soul will never be well. Those wretched bouts of vomiting that I talk of so often have become a regular feature of my life, even on an empty stomach. Even when I am not angry, afraid, or worrying. Worst of all I can find amusement in nothing, and I feel *my will* and my *capacity for hope* greatly weakened.[14]

None of the medical studies on Baudelaire have isolated these aspects of his decline as being directly attributed to his infection. Yet the studies do suggest that syphilis contributed largely to the deterioration of his mental health, his loss of vigor, his feeling that he was falling endlessly into a black pit. During 1860 and 1861 his moods became increasingly frequent. Whether they were caused by pressure or by a disease now entering its tertiary stage is not important. What matters is the effect upon his sanity. He continues a letter he started to his mother as follows:

> The preceding page was written a month, six weeks, two months ago. I don't know. I have subsided into a kind of enduring nervous terror; sleep is dreadful, waking dreadful—impossible to do anything. My complimentary copies [of the second edition of *Les Fleurs du Mal*] spent a month on my table before I could find the courage to wrap and address them. I haven't written to Jeanne, I haven't seen her for three months; of course, since it was not possible, I have sent her nothing.[15]

He tells her of falling victim to trivial hallucinations:

181

I am ill again with laziness, horror, and fear. I was physically ill two or three times but one of the things I really can't stand is when, going to sleep, or asleep even, I hear voices with the greatest clarity, complete sentences, but very banal, very trivial, and bearing no relation to my affairs.[16]

The first hint that he is really sick comes when he collapses in the street in early 1860. Mosselman, Mme Sabatier's protector, had found him tottering along the street in search of a cab:

The day before yesterday I had a peculiar fit. I was out; had hardly eaten, I think I had something like a stroke. A kind old woman got me round using rather odd means. But when I felt all right another fit occurred. Sickness and such weakness and giddiness that I couldn't climb a single step without feeling I was going to faint. I got home yesterday evening; I am quite all right, but tired as after a long journey.[17]

This is the first clear sign that he had never been properly cured. Ironically the account of that collapse was written a few days after a letter to Poulet-Malassis about the latter's syphilis. Baudelaire had urged his friend to follow his advice on treatment, recommending potassium iodide for stiffness in the joints. A few days later he wrote again, telling Poulet-Malassis that his doctor was a fool, and asking him for a complete account of the symptoms "I once had myself":

None of this is serious *provided that you are not taken in by an apparent cure.* And you should know that no one is fitter than someone who has been cured of syphilis. All regimental doctors and prostitutes know that. It is a veritable rejuvenation.[18]

Little did he know that no one in that pox-ridden age ever *was* completely cured.

Baudelaire was forced to admit finally that he himself had not been cured. Although he still preferred to believe that most of his troubles were nervous ones, he could no longer pretend that all was well in more fundamental respects. In one of the finest of all his letters to his mother, in which he confesses himself at length, talking of his childhood and his love for her, he also makes another kind of confession:

But my physical health, which I need for you, for myself, for my obligations, that is yet another problem! I must tell you about it since you pay so little heed to it. I don't mean those nervous afflictions which destroy me day by day and which break my spirit, vomiting, insomnia, nightmares, fainting fits. I have talked of those too often. But it is pointless to be modest with you. You know that when very young I caught a venereal infection, which I later supposed to be totally cured. In Dijon after 1848 it erupted again. It was made to subside once more. Now it has returned in a novel form, marks on the skin, and extraordinary stiffness in all the joints. You may believe me; *I know about it.* Perhaps in the state of sadness in which I am plunged, my terror makes it worse. But I need a strict regimen, and the life I live will not permit it.[19]

This is the worst of all his flashes of optimism: his belief that syphilis can be cured by a "strict regimen"!

Money troubles, concern over Jeanne, bad health, and lack of success continue to pressure Baudelaire relentlessly between 1857 and 1861. He bends and buckles beneath the pressure, without ever collapsing completely. He gives in to surges of rage, accompanied by vomiting, which could last a fortnight. At other times he meditates, with horror, on his wasted youth and on a present that is slipping from him. His only answer at such times is to pull the blankets over his head and long for oblivion. In the course of these years he fears more and more for his sanity, and begins to look again to suicide.

His youthful bid had been a piece of histrionic bravado. He saw suicide differently now, considering it with a calm that comes from knowing the extremes of despair, from knowing that he was not using his talents, that pressures were forcing him to let himself slip and waste his most precious asset:

. . . When a man's nerves are greatly weakened by a multitude of worries and sufferings, the Devil, despite all resolutions, insinuates himself into his mind, every morning, with his thought; why not rest for a day, and forget it all! Tonight I'll do all the urgent things, and at once, and then night comes, the mind is horrified by the multitude of matters delayed; a crushing sadness brings impotence, and the next morning the same comedy is enacted in good faith, with the same confidence and awareness.[20]

The idea of suicide became increasingly attractive in such circumstances. Baudelaire confesses to his mother that he had been on the brink of killing himself for some time—although he feels, alas, condemned to live through years as long as centuries.[21] He has allowed the misery to build until he could write to her, without shame, as a son to a mother, begging her to pray for him; he is so unhappy and beset by disaster. If she thinks prayer will help, then he needs her prayers urgently. The only thing that stops him from killing himself is his sense of responsibility for Jeanne, and for his mother; also a strange pride, the determination not to leave a confusion of unpaid debts and unfulfilled obligations.

In other words, at his very worst moments, we see Baudelaire retaining his dignity, retaining his sense of obligation to others, and to himself. It was that dignity which was the most enduring and important characteristic of his metaphysical dandyism. He never let himself go entirely, never altogether gave in to the temptation to write off his whole existence as a failure and follow the luckless Gérard de Nerval.

Yet suicide continues to persist as a dream of peace. He writes to his mother that he prays fervently for the strength to go on living. He and she are the only forces that keep one another going. He foresees, rightly, that she will not survive him by long. Were she to die first he would kill himself, for if she did die, Ancelle would still be his guardian and he would be utterly alone. He knows that suicide is a sin, but although he believes in the devil, he cannot bring himself to believe in God. He would love to think that an exterior and invisible force takes an interest in his fate but, in the circumstances, how can he? Suicide haunts him not because of his debts but:

> Because of a fearful weariness, which results from an intolerable situation that has gone on too long. Every minute proves to me that I have no appetite for life.

He knows that although he will never enjoy success in his lifetime, he will leave a great reputation behind him: ". . . provided that I have the courage to live."[22]

For the moment Baudelaire is reviled, insulted, without honor or money. Every penny he earns goes towards paying the interest on his debts, and the business leaves him crushed and discouraged. He can see no point in continuing. By 1861 Baudelaire is broken. Only a sense of spiritual decorum and good order, his obligations to his mother, Jeanne, and his creditors keep him alive.

16

BAUDELAIRE MAY HAVE been fighting a perpetual, losing battle with his *guignon*, but he was also continuing his attempts to live by the pen. His main literary staple, the translations of Poe, no longer sold well; his obsession with the American had outlived the enthusiasm of his readers, and *Arthur Gordon Pym* had not been well received. As usual the translator had asked Sainte-Beuve for a favorable review and as usual his friend remained silent. Baudelaire was also working hard on the second edition of *Les Fleurs du Mal*. It was an agonizing process, for poetry made extreme demands upon him. Moreover, he was trying to get the artist Bracquemond to design a frontispiece based on some medieval woodcuts, and he was growing increasingly exasperated by the artist's inadequate efforts.

He was also in the midst of composing *Les Paradis Artificiels* [*Artificial Paradises*], his treatise on opium and hashish, for which, as usual, he had high expectations. Fragments finally appeared in *La Revue Contemporaine* early in 1860, after months of squabbling with the editor Calonne, with whom Baudelaire found it difficult to work. Calonne presumed to edit his copy, an interference which he found intolerable. The editor finally brought him to one of his paroxysms of rage, during which he longed to "smash everything like an explosion at a glazier's." Rage had become his almost habitual mood, obliged as he was to depend, forever, on the goodwill of incomprehending editors who did not even like his writing.

His work on Poe was encountering further difficulties. He had quarreled with *La Revue Internationale* of Geneva, which had suspended his translation of *Eureka*—and suspended payment as well. He had also failed to publish a collection of his relatively meager critical writings and was finding it increasingly difficult to place work of any kind. He had paid a heavy price for his reputation, and papers such as *Le Figaro* lost no opportunity to attack him. "What sort of society, what sort of literature would accept Monsieur Charles Baudelaire as its poet?" wrote one critic.

Although never seriously disturbed by the criticism of such fools, he finally wearied of this barrage of stupid vilification. Writing to Nadar, he uttered a real *cri de coeur*:

It pains me to pass for the Prince of Putrefaction.[21]

The plaint was his response to a cartoon of Nadar's showing Baudelaire in those very terms.

For all his disappointments, he was well pleased with the second edition of *Les Fleurs du Mal* when it finally appeared in 1861. Curiously, Baudelaire, who had only received a few small grants from the government for his translations and criticism, actually received two hundred francs from the Minister of Education in recognition of *Les Fleurs du Mal*!

But both physically and morally he was in bad shape. He derived pleasure neither from sleeping nor waking. It was at this time that he removed the hands from his clock and wrote upon its dial: "It's later than you think."

He did retain his capacity for generosity, however. Baudelaire was always eager to help persons whom he believed to have real talent, and this generosity is very apparent in his relationship with the artist Charles Meryon. At a time when the poet was ill, unhappy, and above all tired, he devoted time and energy to helping Meryon place his own work. A retired naval man, Meryon had produced a remarkable series of etchings of Paris which portray the city in a strange, Gothic style, evoking both its present aspect and medieval antecedents. The etchings also hinted gently, like Baudelaire's own poetry, that it was a place of madness and hallucination, an approach that derived in part from the fact that Charles Meryon was himself perfectly mad.

Baudelaire complained bitterly of the problems of dealing with a lunatic. Meryon insisted on featuring eagles in his pictures, since he was convinced that the government of Napoleon III consulted their entrails for omens. He was obsessed by signs and portents to be detected in patterns of light and shade. He exasperated Baudelaire by asking him if he had heard of one Edgar Poe. When Baudelaire replied rather shortly that he knew his work better than anyone, Meryon asked him, with some urgency, whether he believed that Poe had really existed, for he had a faint suspicion that he might have written the books himself. Yet for all Meryon's madness and remarkable obstinacy, Baudelaire never lost patience. He saw in Meryon, as in Nerval, the terrible image of what he might so easily become:

186

After he left me, I asked myself how I, who have always had in my mind and my nervous system all it needed to go mad, have managed to remain sane. Seriously, I thanked heaven with the prayers of the pharisee.[3]

The second artist to absorb Baudelaire in these years did not make his appeal through madness, although little can be said of his mental stability. Wagner was the last great artistic love of the poet's life. Although his response to the composer was less studied than his response to Delacroix, for Baudelaire knew relatively little about music, it was no less immediate and intense. Baudelaire had understood the richness and tense excitement generated by Delacroix's use of color and twisting form at a time when the painter was almost universally unpopular. Now, when Wagner was considered in France to be a brassy Teutonic joke, Baudelaire responded instantly to the rich color of his harmonies and to that element of wistful nostalgia that rang through his work. Delacroix he understood both intellectually and emotionally; his response to Wagner was entirely emotional and yet he wrote so accurately of that response that his account of *Tannhäuser* remains one of the great pieces of Wagner criticism.

The German's repeated attempts to be accepted by the Parisian public are well known. He had first visited Paris from 1839 to 1842, and failed to find recognition. In 1860 he renewed his efforts, giving a now famous concert at the Théâtre des Italiens. All Paris attended to hear the music which its composer claimed would revolutionize the art. The response was lukewarm to hostile. Berlioz, whose own orchestral coloring and harmonies had come as close to Wagner's as a Frenchman would ever get, was conspicuously indifferent to the whole performance.

Yet where Berlioz was unable to respond, Baudelaire did—with the utmost enthusiasm and intuitive understanding. In the aftermath of the concert he wrote Wagner the most authentic and unsycophantic of his fan letters. The poet described with the utmost eloquence the feeling that all Wagner lovers know, when that rich and soaring music finds a resonance so deep within the listener that it seems to make one's very entrails vibrate in sympathy. Baudelaire, like so many after him, could not believe that this music had been created by a being as imperfect and limited as a man. To those who know Wagner well the quality of this response is understandable. What made it remarkable was that Baudelaire was not only writing his first piece about music, but that this, the finest of all amateur accounts of Wagner, was based on hearing fragments of *Lohengrin* and *Tannhäuser* performed in concert.

Baudelaire was soon to hear more. In 1861 Wagner returned to produce *Tannhäuser* in person. The emperor himself had given reluctant permission for the piece to be staged at the Opéra. The production

187

would cost 100,000 francs and require 165 rehearsals! Wagner was an exacting producer, a lunatic perfectionist in fact. He required huntsmen and ten pairs of hounds on stage. He clashed with the artists, who found his music unsingable. The reception accorded the performance was mixed; many members of the audience enjoyed it but their pleasure was marred by the actions of certain members of the Jockey Club. They kept not just horses, but also dancers in training, and when they discovered that there was no ballet in *Tannhäuser*, they decided to signify their disapproval by filling the opera house with the sound of hunting whistles, purchased by them during the intermission.

Wagner never tried to produce his work in Paris again. Yet he was, in a sense, rewarded by Baudelaire's superb piece of intuitive criticism, *Richard Wagner and Tannhäuser in Paris*, published in 1861 by *La Revue Européenne*. Of no real technical value to the musicologist, it remains the most splendid of all introductions to the moods and tones of that sublime music.

The vision we have of Baudelaire at this time—a sick man, reeling with metaphysical vertigo, feeling that he is falling forever downward into some dark pit—is strangely incomplete. For these years also saw him producing much of his most distinguished and revolutionary work. The additions he had made to *Les Fleurs du Mal*—poems such as "Le Gouffre" ["The Gulf"], "Receuillement" ["Recollection"], and "Plaintes d'un Icare" ["The Complaints of an Icarus"]—were among its most profound, most spiritual poems. He had written a study of Gautier, expounding his delicately balanced view of the relationship between beauty, truth, and morality. He also published *Les Paradis Artificiels*, and two of his most important pieces of art criticism, the *Salon of 1859* and *Le Peintre de la vie moderne* [*The Painter of Modern Life*] in 1863. It may seem surprising that he produced such work in these intolerable circumstances, yet it was anything but a coincidence. It takes us to the heart of his creativity: Baudelaire would always thrive on pressure. It procured a strange excitement for him, building up until he would explode in an ecstasy of anger and release. Indeed, pressure, the quest for intensity and the warping of the psyche which it brought about, was the central theme of his work. In sum, Baudelaire was an early version of the modern artist who courts and compounds his self-destruction in order to write of it. Yet Baudelaire can not be charged with wallowing in his plight while contemplating it with a morbid curiosity; he believed passionately in the redemptive power of high art, and felt seriously that he could redeem his own wretched life by turning it into art of the highest spiritual aspiration. Baudelaire the damned would be saved by his own poetry, which brought balance to his lopsided life.

He eventually conceded that he needed his intolerable existence, just as he had earlier seen that he had been shaped by leisure, debts, and dandyism. He came to recognize that his circumstances, dreadful as they were, provided him with the incentive to continue working. It was in this light that he finally admitted to his mother that, after so many years of complaint against Ancelle, he did not want him removed; nor did he want his debts settled all at once, since *"beatitude creates idleness."* Ancelle should only go when Baudelaire was confident that he could continue working without the pressures of financial need.[4] He recognized that his art was born of pressure and that his temperament required it:

> I am and always have been at once both perverse and reasonable—alas! Perhaps I need to be whipped like children and slaves.[5]

Baudelaire, in premature middle age, was at last achieving that self-knowledge which informs his remarkable confessional notebook, the *Journaux intimes*.

Yet self-knowledge for Baudelaire was never absolute. Fortunately for him, he could never admit to himself at all easily that his genius was quite unsuited to his public. He had entertained his usual high hopes of *Les Paradis Artificiels*, which appeared in May 1860, but, as usual, the work was a flop. Poulet-Malassis lacked the funds to launch it properly, and, also as usual, Saint-Beuve failed to respond to a humble request for a review. The work was as misunderstood as *Les Fleurs du Mal*. Essentially a condemnation of drugs, it was taken as another piece of Satanic sensationalism, a celebration of decadence. One critic even suggested that for Baudelaire swallowing a pellet of hashish was like swallowing Satan.

Yet Baudelaire's study is calm, responsible, and at times almost detached. He had long been interested in opium and hashish, since drugs were part of modern man's desire to distort consciousness in the quest for excitement. Just as he had used aspects of himself for his poetry, so he did in *Les Paradis Artificiels*. He was a steady drinker, had made unremitting use of opium, and although he was not a regular user of cannabis, he had taken enough to speak knowingly about it. It is important to realize that Baudelaire—the alleged father of drug culture, distorted consciousness and the strange visions afforded by narcotics—felt an essential hostility toward drugs, a hostility that had a strong moral and spiritual basis. Shortly after the publication of his study (the title of which is moral enough), he wrote to a young and enthusiastic friend about the dangers of addiction; warning him off stimulants of any kind, he went on to describe a woman who drank champagne regularly to cure herself of depression and now could only "return to normal" with its assistance. Champagne was an innocent corrupter compared to morphine, laudanum, or cannabis!

> I have come to loathe all stimulants because of the way they expand time, and of the exaggeration with which they endow everything. It is impossible to be not only a practical man, but a writer in a sustained condition of spiritual debauch.[6]

Baudelaire himself, as we have seen, was quite dependent on opium, which he took to remedy depression! There is a paradox here, but no contradiction. He was able to advise against stimulants which sapped the will, because he knew all too well what they had done to his own.

Les Paradis is essentially a moral work. Critics recognized this, but dismissed it as hypocrisy. Baudelaire took this obtuse critical lunacy, so typical of the Second Empire, in his stride:

> Nothing astounds me at a time when a minister declares that the function of the novel is to improve *the conscience of the masses* and the police, which supposes itself to be Morality incarnate, turns prostitutes out of cafés when they are too well dressed.[7]

Les Paradis Artificiels consists of two parts. The first, "Le Poëme du haschisch," is Baudelaire's own study of the experience of taking cannabis. The second, "Un mangeur d'opium," is his adaptation of Thomas de Quincey's *Confessions of an English Opium-Eater*. The first part mounts an attack upon hashish because it gives the *illusion* of paradise. Under its influence one feels onself in a world of plenitude and meaning, the world of correspondences, yet the experience is an illusion procured by chemistry. It is typical of modern man that he should accept this illusion, this stage-set paradise, as an adequate substitute for the real thing. Rather than devote himself to the long and difficult process of developing his spirituality, he wants instant results: "to gain paradise at a stroke." Drugs promise a world of debased and instant mysticism, and to seek an illusion of plenitude through them was to give in to weakness, appetite, laziness: in short, to the forces of evil. Hashish provides a "false ideal"—it was a series of such false ideals which had destroyed the protagonist of *Les Fleurs*.

The essay knowledgeably describes the hashish experience. It begins by discriminating between leaf and resin. It discusses the various ways of absorbing it—smoking or eating it in an aromatic paste. It then describes the experience itself. In passages of great beauty and also of great accuracy, the author relies on his superbly rich, rhythmic, and sensual prose to recreate in his reader the very texture of the experience.

190

Some of his biographers have suggested that Baudelaire knew little or nothing of hashish, that he wrote from hearsay and misrepresented it. They are certainly wrong. The response to hashish can vary enormously, according to the quality of the substance, the circumstances of its consumption, whether or not the subject is a habitual user, and finally (and perhaps above all) the subject's temperament. There are enough variables to accommodate a very wide range of response. Baudelaire writes intimately about the drug, like someone who is no longer a beginner for whom "nothing happens." He chronicles convincingly the various phases of the experience, starting with compulsive giggling and turning to the beatific contemplation of objects which become endowed with glorious significance. He tells us that music sounds superb under its influence. He talks of sudden surges of appetite, or, more trivial and more convincing still, of the way one can become strangely overaware that one's teeth are pressing together. His account of the morning after is equally accurate. There is no hangover, just the feeling of intense weariness. Standard enough this—but less standard is another detail: that sometimes one awakes to find onself still mildly and pleasantly under an influence that can return in little surges all the next day. Only a user or ex-user would have known about and bothered with such details.

Baudelaire's veracity has been doubted because he seemed to exaggerate the effects of the drug. He claimed to attain almost mystic heights of contemplation, and the absorption of the self into the object contemplated, achieving finally the illusion that one has become God. Such intense ecstasy is not normally consonant with the experience of the average user; but Baudelaire was not an average user. His art and also his criticism bear witness to an extraordinary sensitivity, a vast capacity for emotional and aesthetic response. It is arguable, for example, that the Delacroix paintings he re-created in his criticism are infinitely richer and more tortuously exciting than the actual works. Similarly, the effect that hashish has upon Baudelaire was infinitely richer than its effect upon a normal user; so too was the way in which he was able to write about his experience. The "Poëme du haschish" reminds us that in all these ecstasies our visions are limited by our own selves, an illusion for which we pay dearly.

It is strange that Baudelaire wrote from personal experience when dealing with hashish, which he did not take regularly, but turned to de Quincey for opium, which he did. Perhaps it was out of self-defense—the reluctance to admit his own addiction—perhaps too because de Quincey is such a superb text. At all events, here too he stresses that the most serious effect of opium is to sap the will and make one incapable of work.

Les Paradis Artificiels is an important work because of its influence.

Future generations of aesthetes and addicts would look back to Baudelaire as the inaugurator of their tradition. It is more important still in the way that it fixes the peculiarly ambivalent relationship which Baudelaire the man enjoyed with the self-image he projected. The work establishes him as one of the founding fathers of the drug culture, and yet it consists of an indictment of the use of drugs. The artificial paradise is the perfect exemplification of modern man's capacity to destroy his spirituality through the cultivation of sensation, to use sensation as a substitute for spiritual perfection. So has Baudelaire been misread and misunderstood? The answer is yes and no. It is true that he condemns drugs as opposed to celebrating them. Yet he chooses to write about them, and writes about them as an insider; he understands their temptations, the possibility of self-destruction which they afford. We should never forget that if much of his art consists in the condemnation of modern man's destructive urges, that art is born of his own experience, of the capacity for self-destruction that runs right through his own wretched life. However serious may be his condemnation of drugs, those who see the legend and not the text may not be altogether wrong if they detect an odd strain of complicity with the vice which runs through his indictment of it.

The other major piece that Baudelaire wrote at this time is very different, free of complicity and self-destruction. It is vitally important for the history of aesthetics since it is the first full-length formulation of what would become the aesthetics of modernism. Indeed, *The Painter of Modern Life* is without doubt Baudelaire's most important critical essay. Ostensibly it is the study of Constantin Guys. Guys had worked for the *Illustrated London News*, for which he had covered the Crimean War. He had a great talent for making sketches, gouaches, and watercolors which captured the essence of a scene. In Paris he concentrated on portraying high and low society: the Bois de Boulogne, ladies and gentlemen at home and in public, high- and low-class courtesans. He used an informal, casual medium, closer to a sketch than to a highly finished Academic painting.

Baudelaire sensed that the Academic tradition, founded in stable and enduring values, was dead. The values which underpinned it, values and assumptions that stretched back to the High Renaissance, concerning man's relationship to his world, his culture, and finally to God, had lost their significance by the middle of the nineteenth century. In the final analysis Academic art represented a belief in metaphysical certainties and the continuity of high culture, and Baudelaire sensed that such a belief had died: so that painting founded in this tradition was either sterile, or, at the least out of touch with contemporary reality. Above all, painters could no longer use traditional techniques or traditional subject matter, for as he saw it the task of the artist was to capture the spirit of his age, an age of triviality and high fashion: the age of modernity. It was no longer enough that the painter capture its feeling tone through traditional images, as Delacroix had done in his *Death of Sardanapalus*. The modern artist must hold up a mirror and portray modern subject matter, seize life as it happened and not compromise the accuracy of his work by sacrificing immediacy to formal painterly elaboration.

With this view Baudelaire makes out a case for a modern art which would supplant the Academic tradition, rendering contemporary subjects in a loose and informal manner. The essay becomes a work in praise of modernity itself. The modern artist must concern himself with street scenes, crowds, and characteristic figures such as the dandy and the whore. Indeed, in his aloofness, his elegance, his style, the artist must himself be a dandy. He must understand women and fashion, from the duchess to the street walker. He must know about carriages, be able to put the right saddle and bridle on the right horse, tell a thoroughbred from a cob. The work continues with a hymn to high fashion. Woman seeks to transcend her natural and sinful condition through fashion, which makes a woman into a work of art. Cosmetics in particular receive the poet's approval, since the aesthetic transformation which they effect is a source of spirituality.

It is an extraordinary essay which captures the feeling of modernity, with its recognition of constant change in the detail of fashion and social behavior. Baudelaire calls for an artist sensitive to its every modulation, who will possess all the flexibility and informality of response which the world of the Second Empire demanded. In short, *The Painter of Modern Life* is the culmination of Baudelaire's longing for an artist who would present nineteenth-century man in his boots and black frockcoat. It is a work that has often been said to anticipate Manet and the impressionists.

Indeed, the work develops ideas that he had held for years, but it is also a new departure. To date, his hero had been Delacroix, the last great artist of the Academic tradition. Now he champions Guys, an artist who, in comparison, must be considered trivial for all his talent and elegance. Next to Delacroix, Guys was a lightweight and Baudelaire knew it. The essay implies that the age of Delacroix was dead, because his culture and tradition were dead. Support of Guys is a recognition of the triviality of the modern age. Henceforward the language of the Academy would by definition create ossified, dead work, because the values supporting that language had perished. This is the fundamental, and unhappy, message of *The Painter of Modern Life*. It is a message echoed in Baudelaire's own creative work, for henceforward, as we will see, he would turn his back on verse and seek to express himself through the low-key and informal language of the prose poem.

Some art historians have wondered why Baudelaire should have chosen the relatively insignificant Guys. It would have been so much more appropriate, they feel, had he chosen Manet. When the essay was published, in 1863, Baudelaire knew the young painter quite well, well enough to borrow money from him freely; but the essay was, in fact, composed between 1859 and 1860, almost certainly before they had met. Manet was only twenty-seven at the time and had just had his *Absinthe Drinker* refused by the Salon; and Baudelaire did not review it in his *Salon* as he never reviewed works that were not actually exhibited.

The relationship between Baudelaire and Manet is a puzzling one. The painter was a fervent admirer of the poet's work. He painted Jeanne Duval and *Olympia*, another tribute to Baudelaire, which with its Negress and cat so inexplicably scandalized contemporaries. He also did studies of the poet and featured him in one of his own great paintings of modern life, *La Musique aux Tuileries*.

Yet Baudelaire, close friend though he became, remained insensitive to Manet's work. His criticism mentions *Le Guitariste* and *Lola de Valence*, but its tone remains lukewarm. Baudelaire did not approve of Manet's approach. He considered his work to be crude. It lacked elegance and lapsed into vulgarity and realism. Hence his rejection. He considered Manet to be typical of the *decline* of modern art, as it turned away from spirituality and elegance. He once wrote to the artist, telling him that he was the "leading painter of the decrepitude"—that is to say, the best of a bad bunch of aesthetic degenerates.

Guys, on the other hand, was an artist-dandy who in the midst of the trivial age in which he found himself was not himself trivial, managing to sustain a self-made elegance of style. Manet, with his emphasis on naturalism and technical roughness, seemed in comparison something of a vulgarian.

Les Paradis Artificiels and *Le Peintre de la vie moderne* were two of the most original essays written in nineteenth-century France. In their various ways they had a tremendous influence upon the evolution of modern art. The first piece would encourage Rimbaud and countless other artists of future decades to cultivate disorder of the senses, though Baudelaire scarcely intended that. The second piece marks the moment when painting in France freed itself of its hidebound tradition; Paris was about to become the art center of the world, and would remain so for almost a century. The essays establish Baudelaire as one of the founding fathers of modernism. But although they may have helped to establish his reputation in the eyes of posterity, at the time they were of absolutely no material benefit to him.

T HE BALANCING ACT set up by Baudelaire and Poulet-Malassis was becoming increasingly precarious. Baudelaire's associate was a lamentable businessman, producing beautiful, expensive and unprofitable books; although it must be said in his defense that he published some of the most distinguished authors of the age—authors such as Baudelaire, Banville, Gautier, Champfleury, and Sainte-Beuve. His brother-in-law de Broise complained bitterly at the firm's involvement with Baudelaire. At one point Poulet-Malassis ventured to suggest that such was Baudelaire's improvidence that they should perhaps sever their relationship, but Baudelaire replied generously that he would not hear of such a thing.

Early in 1861, in an attempt to restore his fortunes, the printer decided to open his own bookshop and cut out the middleman. He took expensive premises on the corner of the Rue Richelieu and invested generously in furnishing, creating a prestigious bookshop hung with portraits of his authors. Needless to say, the enterprise was an expensive failure. Poulet-Malassis was no better at selling books than he was at publishing them, and the business soon degenerated into a coffeeshop and free eating-house for hangers-on and friends.

De Broise was not delighted. He realized that Poulet-Malassis would not stay afloat for long, and had no wish to go down with him. He suggested they dissolve the partnership. He would keep the printing works and the nonliterary side of the business, leaving his partner with the shop and the publishing. Poulet-Malassis was a bad enough businessman to agree. With the loss of the commercial side of the partnership he lost all goodwill, and saw his credit disappear overnight. Even Baudelaire realized that his friend and publisher must be on the verge of bankruptcy. This meant that all his works would either be pulped or remaindered, and other publishers, knowing the poet's plight, would wait to dictate their own terms to a starving Baudelaire.

It was this threat to his future earnings which late in 1861 made Baudelaire embark on the strangest enterprise of his life. Only a blend of despair, need, and manic optimism could have made him seek election to the French Academy! The Académie Française was, to French eyes, the most prestigious assembly of artists and savants in the world. To become one of the forty "immortals" brought instant recognition and also, of course, financial security. Whenever one of its forty seats became vacant through the death of its occupant, candidates were free to propose themselves for election. The procedure involved a formal process of canvassing, whereby all surviving members of the institution had to be visited and solicited for their vote, regardless of whether they were the candidate's close friends or bitter enemies.

The Academy has always been a conservative institution, the embodiment of French high culture. At no time was this truer than under the Second Empire when the emperor used government control over the arts as a political weapon to reinforce the stability of his regime. In these circumstances Baudelaire's decision to stand calls for comment. True, he was beginning to gain some recognition. A critic had kindly described him as better than Banville, although, of course, he would never match Gautier. Yet he was still considered an immoralist. With his reputation there could be no question, by any stretch of the imagination, of election to the Academy.

His friends thought he was joking, but to their consternation he declared himself to be a serious candidate. Two seats were vacant at the time: one had been occupied by the dramatist, author of some 350 plays, Eugène Scribe; the other by the Dominican monk Lacordaire. At least, his friends supposed, Baudelaire would not present himself as the successor of Lacordaire? But this was precisely what he proposed. Scribe was, after all, no more than a light-weight playwright, and Baudelaire, with his deep sense of his own spiritual high seriousness felt it would be more appropriate were he to attempt to follow the monk.

For once Baudelaire was not clowning. He had a clear idea of his own genius and of the nullity of the competition. Yet it seems inconceivable that he should have had the slightest hope of getting elected. He knew his reputation too well, knew how greatly he was misunderstood. His decision to stand must be seen as the supreme example of his gambler's optimism. A gambler always hopes to win, even though he knows that the odds are against him. Gamblers don't believe in odds. Long odds are just the chance of an even bigger win, and the gambler always knows he will win—until he loses. Multiply such optimism and blindness to reality tenfold, and we begin to gain some idea of Baudelaire's motives. But there was yet another order of motivation, a more sinister one. Baudelaire had long enjoyed being obsequious to the famous, had long supported humiliations of every kind. Although humiliation never became for Baudelaire the drug it was for Dostoevsky, the prospect of total and humiliating rejection at the hands of thirty-eight "immortal" representatives of official French culture had its own insidious appeal.

If it was humiliation that Baudelaire sought he was not to be disappointed. He wrote to his mother that he proposed to stand since becoming an Academician was the only honor a writer could decently aspire to. He realized that he would have to call on persons hostile to him, but would try to do so when they were out. As it turned out, he would have been wise to call on most of the immortals in their absence. By 1862 Baudelaire had come to cut a sorry figure. No longer the dandy, he wore shabby threadbare clothes, and only his sparkling white shirts prevented him from appearing a complete down-and-out. He had to trudge from visit to visit on foot, rather than by carriage, and on arrival he was either humiliated or not admitted. The experience of relentless rejection became intensely painful. Finally he told his mother that he could only face going on because he wished to please her, but election would require a miracle. He goes on to describe his reception at the hands of various members. Mérimée, whom he had always thought a friend, had refused to see him. Others had been perfectly vile. There had been, however, two exceptions: his fellow poets Lamartine and Vigny, both of whom received him with kindness and understanding. Lamartine, for years one of France's leading writers, had had his moment of political glory under the Second Republic. The coup d'état had ruined him politically and financially, condemning him to years of literary forced labor to survive. He had tasted bitterness enough to sympathize with Baudelaire, and warned him not to stand and expose himself to humiliation. He then signified appreciation of his work with a compliment so gross that not even Baudelaire could bring himself to repeat it. Baudelaire found him "something of a whore," but appreciated his kindness.

Alfred de Vigny was different; another leading poet of the romantic age, he had known great unhappiness which he faced with resolution. He too had experienced rejection, having failed six times to get elected to the Academy. When Baudelaire called on him he found a dying man, dying in great pain of cancer of the stomach. Nevertheless, Vigny greeted the younger poet with the greatest kindness. He too advised him not to stand, but his was the advice of a friend. Despite terrible pain he talked to Baudelaire for three hours, and asked him to call again.

Baudelaire was very moved by his warmth. On his return home he sent him a letter of thanks and all his published works, including *Les Fleurs du Mal* and *Les Paradis Artificiels*. He felt instinctively that Vigny was not only a friend, but a real poet who would appreciate the true temper of his work. In this respect he was right, for Vigny would declare himself deeply moved and impressed by his poetry. However, here once again Baudelaire's letter writing takes a strange turn. Greatly concerned by Vigny's dreadful health and anxious to help if he could, he suggested that Vigny treated his stomach cancer with very old English ale of the highest quality—Bass is best—and with a special kind of meat jelly! The imp of perversity seems always at work in Baudelaire even when he tries to repay kindness with kindness.

The story of Baudelaire's attempt to gain immortality is not complete without a brief word about the part played by Sainte-Beuve. Hitherto he had never used his influence to give Baudelaire support of any kind, and the omission had not gone unobserved. Some time earlier Hippolyte Babou had published a ferocious attack on Sainte-Beuve blaming him for praising a cheap novel of adultery by Ernest Feydeau, and remaining silent about *Les Fleurs du Mal*. It was suggested that he acted out of prudent self-interest. The critic was understandably enraged—but so too was Baudelaire! He was furious with Babou for alienating Sainte-Beuve's ever-potential support. He wrote to the critic assuring him of his innocence. Sainte-Beuve was after all the most influential critic of the age and Baudelaire could neither afford to alienate him, nor to admit to himself that his so-called friendship with "Papa Beuve" was worthless. It was a blend of optimism and a readiness to humiliate himself that made him disown Babou, and even accept the critic's monstrous suggestion that both Sainte-Beuve and *Baudelaire* had been offended by the article.

When Baudelaire presented himself as a candidate, Sainte-Beuve could remain silent no longer; he had to take a stand. He wrote a vile article suggesting that Baudelaire was a little-known artist who had decided to run as a joke. At no time did he let it be known that "Monsieur Baudelaire" was a close friend. He termed him a minor romantic poet, the author of mysterious and elegant works, inspired by narcotics and other strange poisons. Although such work did not get one into the Academy, the poet himself was a nice, polite, well-bred young person, in every respect a gentleman.

Amazingly the article did not enrage Baudelaire—it delighted him. He actually wrote an anonymous analysis of the piece in the *Revue Anecdotique*, quoting with approval the very sentences that might have seemed most wounding. Sainte-Beuve was delighted. He thanked Baudelaire and confessed he had been a little worried, for "when you tickle you can never be certain that you are not scratching." Indeed.

It was Academician Beuve who finally convinced Baudelaire not to stand. He pointed out that his candidacy was an embarrassment to all and advised him to withdraw. Baudelaire obliged and the critic congratulated him:

Your withdrawal did not displease, but when they heard your last sentence of thanks, couched in such polite and modest terms, they said out loud *"very good"*! So you left a most favorable impression. Is that not something?[1]

Baudelaire left a good impression; his manners were excellent; the Academy had murmured its approval! Of all the vices, meanness of spirit is the hardest to conceal, and the luckless Sainte-Beuve could have had no inkling that in those few lines to Baudelaire he was putting his mean inner life on permanent display to posterity.

A BIOGRAPHER OF BAUDELAIRE is faced with the alarming fact that nothing ever gets better in his life. Each chapter must begin with the observation that "next year things took a turn for the worse." From the high dandy of the Hôtel Pimodan to the threadbare would-be Academician, the story of his life is the story of unremitting decline punctuated by bursts of manic optimism.

On the face of it, the next years, 1862 to 1864, are no exception. They bring their share of failure, procrastination, and loss. Yet it is wrong to see his life in terms of failure only, and at no time does the point emerge so clearly as now. As Baudelaire declined, he developed that kind of spirituality that may only be reached through despair, a despair deriving from one's own hopelessness and total guilt. Over the years he had had proof enough of his shortcomings: his sensuality, his rage, his deadly procrastination. His readiness to admit these weaknesses, his refusal to pretend they were not really there, had taken its toll, yet it had also matured him. We can see this now essential despair develop into a spirituality which takes on an ever richer and mellower resonance. Believing, as he did, that redemption could come only from himself and his art, Baudelaire felt utterly and solely responsible for his predicament; the greater his sense of personal failure, the greater became his sense of spiritual responsibility. Unlike the younger man, the mature Baudelaire no longer deludes himself with hope, or blinds himself with rage. He achieves a clearer understanding of what he is and has become, reaching that desperate, serene spiritual calm that made him, at forty, already an old man, with gray hair and the understanding expression of an unfrocked priest.

He had reason enough for despair. His failure to reach the Academy was a failure among many. He had also planned to become a theater manager; the project would have required considerable funding, but it would make him rich within a year. Needless to say, the plan came to nothing. He was increasingly in need of funds, since now in 1862 it was clear that Poulet-Malassis was on the verge of financial ruin. In November of that year the printer was arrested, declared bankrupt, and sent to prison. Thus ended the poet's commercial association with the one man who had had the patience and understanding to work with him. Even down-and-out he had remained a hopelessly tyrannical author, rejecting editorial interference of any kind, capable of withdrawing a whole piece rather than change a comma. As a result editors found it impossible to work with him, and he found no work.

Baudelaire was on the run once more. He found it harder and harder to open letters, and his capacity for procrastination grew at an alarming rate, thanks to "the state of anguish and terror in which I live perpetually." To avoid his creditors he had once more to live on the move, changing hotels virtually every night. Inevitably his health was deteriorating, too. He had dreadful fits of vertigo which brought him to the edge of madness, and which were the foretaste of his final breakdown:

> Morally and physically, I have always had a sense of the gulf, not just the gulf of sleep, but of action, of dream, of memory, of desire, regret, remorse, beauty, number, etc. I have cultivated my hysteria with enjoyment and terror. Now I suffer continuously from vertigo, and today, January 23, 1862, I had a strange warning, I felt pass over me a wind from the wing of madness.[2]

Such moods produced his deepest, most metaphysical poems— "Le Gouffre," "Examen de minuit," "Les Plaintes d'un Icare." They ring with panic and spirituality and are some of the finest and most mature verses in European literature.

It was the maturity of a broken man. Baudelaire knew that he was living in an age of spiritual decline. With his own spirituality turned into a despairing artistic dandyism, he was a voice crying in the wilderness. He knew he had achieved understanding late, wasted much of his life, and could only hope to make amends through work:

> The great and sole aim of my life now is to produce work, the hardest and most boring thing in the world, the thing which you only enjoy out of habit. I feel myself criminally guilty, having wasted life, talent, health, having wasted twenty years in day dreams, the which makes me inferior to a crowd of brutes who work every day.[3]

Yet he knew, as well, that his kind of work was not welcome in France, in the age of Offenbach:

To be over forty, to pay one's debts and get rich by literature, in a country which only likes vaudevilles and dancing. What a dreadful fate.[4]

On his good days he could still consider failure and humiliation as the grace of God, the way to maturity. In the same mood he could think of work itself as a kind of prayer, a reservoir of strength which brings out the best in one. He wrote, and prayed for salvation—release from debt, and the joy of at last giving his mother the satisfaction he had always longed to provide. One of his saddest and most touching notes read:

> Pray to God every morning . . . to my father, Mariette and Poe, as intercessors, pray them to give me the necessary strength to fulfill all my obligations, and to give my mother a long enough life to enjoy my transformation.[5]

He worked, and prayed, for spiritual good order, but he could never live up to his own standards of perfection; he could not stop sinning, nor could he ever reconcile himself to the harsh truth that his art, his lifeline to good order and redemption, was born of, and profoundly rooted in, the very disorder that he hated in himself.

It was his loathing of his own nature, tained by weakness and disease, which now made him further refine his conception of the dandy. No longer just a detached, self-made aristocrat who achieved perfection through aloofness, the dandy becomes a saint who achieves sanctity through self-mastery and triumph over his own nature. He writes, in English, of the dandy's "self-purification" and "anti-humanity." The two go together, and yet loathing of his own humanity never collapses into total self-hate because he believed in the redeeming power of his genius.

Inevitably his evolving spirituality was not appreciated. To the public he remained the Prince of Putrefaction. He had contemplated going into retreat, to the Benedictine monastery at Solesmes. A friend mentioned the plan to one of the monks, who answered: "If he comes we shall receive him. We would even receive convicts."[6] Baudelaire was sardonically amused, and distressed, by another example of the public's total incomprehension of him.

Baudelaire's belief in art as redemption inspired his second and final collection of poems, variously known as *Le Spleen de Paris* and *Les Petits Poèmes en Prose*. He had been writing prose poetry for some years, and by late 1861 had a large batch ready for publication. He negotiated a contract for an illustrated edition with the famous publisher Hetzel, who felt it essential that the poems first be serialized in a newspaper if the illustrated edition were to be a success. Hetzel had recognized in Baudelaire the most original poet and prose writer of his age. It was arranged that the poems appear in a periodical edited by Arsène Houssaye. Houssaye did eventually publish them, but reluctantly, and at Hetzel's most urgent insistence.

Unfortunately, the relationship with Houssaye deteriorated when the latter was informed that some of the poems had already appeared in other journals. This was only a partial truth. Baudelaire had indeed published six of the poems in *Le Présent* in August 1857; but despite the announcement that more would appear in the following issue, no others were published. He also published a few in 1861 in *La Revue Fantaisiste*—which soon afterwards duly went bankrupt. Baudelaire did not feel that he had acted improperly. Not only was *La Revue Fantaisiste* a journal with a tiny circulation—and defunct into the bargain—but he had considerably reworked the poems since their original publication. Houssaye, however, was enraged. He broke the contract, suspended payment, and Baudelaire failed to patch up the quarrel. As a result he only succeeded in publishing the odd poem in 1862 and 1863, although he finally got a substantial number into *Le Figaro* early in 1864. He would continue to write prose poetry for some years, but no edition of this work in book form appeared in his lifetime. We do not know how he would have arranged such an edition, but it is safe to say that the arrangement of the poems would not have been as vital to the book as it was to *Les Fleurs du Mal*, a work of high art, ordered and designed with a splendid and rigorous architecture. The prose poetry was very different. Prose was an informal, low-key medium; indeed, the very idea of prose poetry approaches a contradiction in terms. Just as Baudelaire's criticism had moved from the celebration of high seriousness and Academicism in Delacroix to the trivial and dandyish Guys, the "Painter of Modern Life," so his own art shifted to the slighter form of the poem in prose.

In the prosaic age of the modern city, high art and poetry seemed dead. Modernity could only be caught by a more flexible and less beautiful medium; hence the adoption of prose and rejection of verse. The result is a more desperate kind of writing than we have seen before. The subject matter of the poems is no longer redeemed by the voluptuous rhythms of Baudelaire's verse. They are often sensuous enough, but sensuousness is tempered by violent changes of mood, paroxysms of rage or sadistic fantasy. They depict a modern urban society, and the pressures it exerts upon one's consciousness. Intoxication is no longer condemned, the poet's advice is to "Get drunk—on anything, wine, virtue, art, anything, as long as it takes you out of yourself."

Other poems are studies in modern psychology; man under pressure allowing himself the luxury of violent explosions. Lovers turn to importunate mistresses to address them in dark sadistic tones which express all the hostility they feel for their sexual partners. A poet calls a glazier to his attic, and sends him down again when he is unable to provide glass through which one would see "la vie en beau." When he emerges onto the street, the poet drops a flowerpot on him, smashing his wares, then laughing hysterically. Such jokes are expensive but worthwhile, since "a second of infinite pleasure is worth an eternity of damnation."

That is the message of the work. High seriousness, spirituality, beauty, none of these matter anymore, all that matters is to find a sensation strong enough. The moralistic framework of *Les Fleurs du Mal* has been abandoned. It is typical of Baudelaire that at the time of his greatest spiritual awareness he should produce a work reflecting defeat and misery. He makes the point in a piece entitled "Perte d'auréole" ["The Loss of a Halo"]. While crossing a busy street the poet's halo had fallen off and remained stuck in the mud. He declined to retrieve it and went instead to a brothel, leaving his halo in that mud of Paris which his art had once turned to gold. The poem suggests that he now doubts the redemptive powers of art. This is confirmed by another piece, "Le Confiteor de l'artiste" ["The Artist's Confession"]. It describes, superbly, a rich artistic daydream, which turns sour and begins to exasperate the dreamer, to stretch his nerves too tight. The perfection he had been contemplating had become a source of misery and despair, impressing upon him his own hopelessness. Art could never overcome the perfection of nature. "The study of the beautiful is a duel in which the artist cries with fright before being conquered."[7]

This profession of inadequacy and doubt was probably inspired by a painting, one of the greatest of the century. The poem was composed shortly after Baudelaire had seen Delacroix's murals at St. Sulpice, one of which portrayed Jacob wrestling with the angel. The painting is both a religious depiction and an artist's allegory. Jacob, the stubborn, muscular, obstinate man, is locked in permanent frozen struggle, shoulders bearing doggedly into the angel's side. The angel unmoved has not even bothered to shift the weight off his heels. Jacob, a mere man, is utterly absorbed in his fight with perfection. His caravan, the practical side of his life, sweeps past him unnoticed. All his excellence, all his humanity are concentrated in a struggle he can never win, but which he will not lose. The painting has all the serenity and understanding of a mature and mellow artist who has fought perfection all his life. He knows he will never conquer it, but he also knows that from that persistent struggle is born a great calm. It is in an exasperated response to the calm achieved by Delacroix, that I believe, Baudelaire wrote his own unhappy "Artist's Confession."

The failure of art to satisfy leads the poet to artificial paradises. One of the most exotic pieces in the book, "La Chambre double" ["The Double Room"], describes an opium-induced trance interrupted by an intruder who jerks the poet out of a fake eternity back to his squalid hovel, back to implacable life, time, and the prospect of damnation. The book also has its studies in black humor, such as "Assomons les pauvres" ["Let's Beat Up the Poor"], and also contains evocations of the poetic consciousness, studies in daydreaming which are among the finest bits of poetic prose in the language.

The most important poems, however, are those which paint modern city life. This is no longer the old Paris of twisting streets; it is the re-developed city that has undergone the barbaric devastations of Haussmann, a place of broad pavements and jostling crowds enjoying public celebration. It is also a place of victims, urban derelicts, bent old women, and aging acrobats no longer able to ply their trade. There are more sinister victims still. "La Corde" ["The Cord"] describes the suicide of an artist's model—a young boy. The boy's mother asks the poet for the rope and nail with which he hanged himself. She intends to make up for her loss by selling these relics for a decent price. As it stands the poem is unsettling, but it becomes worse still with the knowledge that the painter was Manet, and the hanged model the delightful child who posed for his painting *L'enfant aux cérises*.

The most sinister figure of all is the prostitute and sexual hysteric "Mademoiselle Scalpel." Obsessed by medical men and blood, she gives herself free to surgeons and rather hopes they will visit her in their blood-stained operating gowns, with their instruments. The poet ends his study with a despairing plea. Life swarms with "innocent monsters":

> Lord, my God, you, the Creator, you the Master, you who made Law and Liberty; you the ruler who disposes, the judge who pardons; you who are full of motive and cause and who have perhaps placed a taste of horror in my mind to convert my heart.
> ... Lord take pity on mad men and women. O Creator, can there be monsters in the eyes of He alone who knows why they exist, how they *were made*, and how they *might not* have been made?[8]

With this plea the poet comes to question God's design, considering the city as a place foresaken by Him, a dreadful wasteland peopled by psychological cripples and innocent monsters. No wonder that the key note to the collection is founded in the English title of one of its most important pieces—"Anywhere out of the world."

It is typical of Baudelaire that this collection should speak only of defeat, escapism, and moral indifference. He now seems reconciled to living out his life as a failed anachronism, happy to seek intoxication and court damnation, since for him there was nothing else left. Yet the note of surrender running through the poems could only be born of that self-awareness which he had once termed consciousness in evil. It had taught him that art was not, as he had earlier supposed, a mystic communion with the ideal: such was the view that had formed the metaphysical underpinning of *Les Fleurs du Mal*. Art was just another source of sensation; to think otherwise was a delusion. He had now rid himself of that delusion, had achieved that terrible intellectual and spiritual honesty, which is reflected in later portraits of him. They show Baudelaire free of illusion, free too of hope. He understands now that to take a moralistic stance about vice will never be enough to achieve virtue. Yet he knows that he is different from, better than, the rest of the world of losers, cripples, and vulgarians in which he has his being. Art may not be a mysticism, but it is the highest form of work. For all his hopelessness, his failure to achieve perfection, to wrestle with the angel, Baudelaire remains an artist. He finishes a terrible examination of conscience in the poem "A une heure du matin" ["One O'clock in the Morning"], with a fervent and desperate prayer:

Discontent with everyone and with myself I would dearly like to redeem myself, and restore my pride a little in the silence and the solitude of the night. Souls of those I have loved, souls of those I have sung, strengthen me, support me, drive away from me lies and the corrupting vapors of the world; and you my Lord God! Grant me the grace to produce a few lines of beautiful poetry to prove to myself that I am not the lowest of the low, that I am not inferior to those I despise![9]

B Y 1864 BAUDELAIRE has only one thing left—faith in work. He had devoted a lifetime to trying to escape from his sense of time passing through pleasure, indolence, distraction. Only now did he realize that he was proceeding the wrong way:

> Every minute we are crushed by the idea of the sensation of time. There are only two ways to escape that nightmare, to forget it: pleasure and work. Pleasure wears us out. Work strengthens us. It is obvious.
>
> The more we use one of those means, the more the other fills us with disgust. You can only forget time by making use of it. Everything is built little by little.[1.]

Baudelaire had come to understand the hollowness of pleasure, had learned the hard way that work was its own reward. He achieved this final moralistic stance via a lifetime of pleasure seeking, and if he condemned pleasure it was as an insider that he did so. He cannot be compared to the reformed addict—gambler or alcoholic. Any such person given a single dose of his particular addiction will relapse into hopeless commitment to his vice. By 1864 Baudelaire was much more than a dried-out addict. He had freed himself of pleasure altogether and come to see its essential hollowness. But he never realized, in his quest for spirituality and good order, that to understand one's vice is not enough. His greatest error, a very Catholic one, was to believe that ruthless honesty in self-knowledge redeemed one's shortcomings; that a sense of guilt created innocence. Consciousness in evil seemed an adequate substitute for virtue, so he had always remained content to *aspire* to purity and look to work for salvation. Yet he was sufficiently contaminated by his habit of seeking distraction in pleasure to regard work as no more than a superior form of distraction, and hence his whole-hearted commitment to work was short-lived:

> All that I am going to do, or hope to do this year should and could have been done last year. But I am assailed by a terrible sickness which was at its height this year, I mean daydreaming, *slough of despondency, loss of heart, indecision.* Certainly I regard a man who manages to cure himself of a vice as infinitely braver than a soldier or a man about to fight a duel. But what is the cure? How can one turn despair into hope, cowardice into strong will? Is this sickness real or imaginary? Could it derive from a physical weakness, or an incurable melancholy deriving from so many years full of upsets, spent without consolation, in loneliness and discomfort? I don't know. What I do know is that I feel complete disgust for everything, and the only feeling which keeps me alive is a *vague* longing for fame, revenge, and fortune.[2]

Despite prayers and professions of faith in work, Baudelaire in 1864 saw himself once more a back-sliding and unhappy man. The collapse of Poulet-Malassis and sundry quarrels with editors had left him without means of support. It was this, together with a broken spirit, that dictated his last and silliest plan. For some months Poulet-Malassis, now out of prison, had talked of settling in Belgium. For a printer of his sort the plan had much to commend it. In those days Belgium, scarcely twenty years old, had a strange role in French-speaking civilization. It was essentially a liberal country, with a strong republican and democratic tradition. It acted as an asylum for the hordes of republican refugees that had left France at the time of the coup d'état. It had no censorship, and its printing presses were the source of great numbers of politically subversive and pornographic publications which were smuggled into France.

For all its liberal traditions, Belgium, in those days, had a frightfulness all its own. Brussels was a tiny provincial town, inhabited by provincial persons. The Belgians displayed great spiritual and physical vulgarity, combined with a provincial cockiness born of inferiority: Brussels was as good as Paris, and anyone disagreeing would be proved wrong by having his block knocked off.

Brussels, nevertheless, was an ideal haven for the destitute Poulet-Malassis. With his taste for spicy literature, he had been in constant trouble with the French authorities for his publications on both political and moral grounds. It was a taste which the alleged immoralist Baudelaire condemned absolutely, but notwithstanding he decided to accompany his friend to Belgium.

He hoped to make money by lecturing to Belgian provincials about the arts in France, as both Dickens and Thackeray had done to great effect in America. He also hoped to find a publisher who would not be afraid to handle his work. In particular he had his eye on the successful firm of Lacroix and Verboeckhoven. Optimism led him to hope for a mutually profitable association. But more important than any specific motive was the need to escape—if only to Belgium. He felt his will to work bending under the pressures of creditors and correspondents that made every postal delivery a misery. Hopeful as ever, he looked to Brussels for release. A friend asked him why he went:

How do I know? I came to find peace, a chance to work, to escape the pressures of Paris life. . . . Besides I am sick, sick.[3]

If "*luxe, calme et volupté*" was what he wanted, he could scarcely have made a worse choice. Brussels was a town in which everything and everybody conspired to drive him to the height of irritation.

Even getting there was a problem. He had to raise the necessary funds and attempted to do so by requesting the Minister of Fine Arts for a subsidy. When his request was turned down he penned a letter of quite remarkable indignation. He devoted nine long months to finding a way of financing his departure. Poulet-Malassis had left before him and Baudelaire had asked him to arrange a series of lectures for him, but he failed to do so. Finally the poet sold Hetzel all his rights on *Les Fleurs du Mal* and the prose poetry for five years. He received a modest advance, the balance to be paid on completion of the second book. He also sold the rights to his translations of Poe to Michel Lévy.

The translations had earned him a steady income of four or five hundred francs a year. He had hoped that outright sale of his rights might bring some thirty thousand francs. The estimate was wildly optimistic, since return on capital for such an investment would be in the region of $1\frac{1}{2}$ percent. Nevertheless the actual sum received from Michel Lévy was shameful. Even granted that Lévy was sharp and Baudelaire desperate, it is hard to understand how he could have relinquished his rights in perpetuity for *two thousand francs*; giving Lévy a princely return of 25 percent. Incidentally, Baudelaire never saw the money; it went straight to creditors.

He finally went to Brussels in April 1864. All too soon he discovered that it was no haven. He put up at the Hôtel du Grand Miroir, which was reasonable—and hence beyond his means. As always, financial decisions were dictated by his optimism: Belgium, he felt, would soon make him rich. His room, however, was modest enough:

We went up two stories by a narrow staircase, the steps painted yellow and varnished. Baudelaire stopped and unlocked a little door with the number 39 on it in black. We went into the poet's room. I was struck by the modesty of its furnishings; a bed in imitation mahogany with a red eiderdown, a cupboard, a commode, a threadbare sofa, a worn armchair, two other chairs, a small rug. No clock on the chimney piece, instead a lamp with a shade. A table covered with books and papers against the wall, which sports faded wallpaper.[4]

In Brussels the poet sought to maintain his aloofness, his detachment from the truly horrible surroundings, with a resurgence of dandyism—at least initially, while he still had funds:

Walking slowly, with a slightly feminine roll, Baudelaire crossed the open space in front of the Naumur Gate, meticulously avoiding the mud, and, if it rained, dancing along on tiptoe, wearing shining patent-leather shoes. Clean-shaven, hair swept back in a wave behind the ears, a soft shirt of absolute whiteness coming over the collar of his long overcoat, he looked like a blend of clergyman and actor.[5]

Financial optimism stemmed from a lecture series which the clergyman-actor had been engaged to give. There were to be four lectures paid a hundred francs each, or so he had been promised. The plan to lecture and later to give a poetry reading may have been inspired by the example of Poe. In his brief study of the American's life Baudelaire talks of his idol giving public lectures as a commercial venture: a practice unknown in France. Conscious or unconscious identification may have prompted him on a similar course. But more likely it was his identification with Poe's *guignon* that might explain how Baudelaire managed to turn yet another enterprise into an act of self-destruction.

His first lecture was well attended. It was not the subject, Delacroix, that had packed the Belgians in. They had come to see the scandalous author of *Les Fleurs du Mal*. Instead of a degenerate shocker of the bourgeoisie, they found a lucid, intelligent lecturer, who, although no orator, delivered a highly honorable lecture on the painter.

Next time was different. For his second lecture, on Gautier, Baudelaire had a different kind of audience. News traveled fast in Brussels. It was soon known that the poet was respectable, not obviously a Satanist, in touch with Parisian taste and fashion, and a person of striking appearance. His second lecture was attended by a considerable number of respectable Belgian ladies and parties of schoolgirls. Baudelaire's lecture series looked as if it was going to be a success. He had not just retained his audience, he had increased it: the rarest of achievements for a public speaker. He was visibly delighted, and began by thanking his hearers for their reception. But here, not for the first time, another Baudelaire takes over. The imp of perversity draws a red haze across his eyes, and like the gentleman who smashed the glazier's wares, the poet yields to destruction in the interest of a joke. He proceeds to thank his public:

> I am particularly touched by your welcome since it was with you that I lost my virginity as a speaker—a loss which, incidentally, I regret no more than I do the loss of the other one.[6]

That was enough. Belgian ladies, Belgian teachers, Belgian schoolgirls departed en masse, scandalized and delighted. They had been amply rewarded. Assured that the Satanic poet was respectable, they had been able to attend his lecture without risk to reputation. He had scandalized them with his first sentence, enabling them to leave gratified, and without having to sit through an hour or so of literary criticism.

Meanwhile a young schoolboy poet, Claude Lemonnier, one day to become a famous Belgian writer, was hurrying to the lecture hall, worried that he was late. He hoped to squeeze in at the back:

> The staircase was empty as I raced up, silence reigned under the Gothic arches; I felt a bit ashamed at the thought that a crowd had already been that way, and that I was the last. I imagined a solemn, hurrying throng, which had gathered as if for a gala. An usher opened a leaf of the door, I heard a thin, biting, high-pitched voice; it swelled and rang like the voice of a preacher, syllables were clearly enunciated as it praised another king of poets: "Gautier, the master and my master . . ."
>
> I slipped into the hall. After all those years, I am still bemused by the emptiness of that great space where I feared I would be unable to find a seat, and which displayed serried ranks of empty benches receding into the darkness at the back. Baudelaire spoke that evening, for about twenty listeners, he spoke as he would have spoken to a court of princes and revealed to them a sublime Gautier, one of the great pontiffs of art. . . .
>
> There was a little table in the middle of the platform; he stood by it in evening dress, in a pool of light. Light played on his delicate gesturing hands; he displayed them with some pride— they possessed an almost feminine grace as they sorted his few pages of notes, casually, as if to create the illusion that he was improvising. Those patrician hands, used to using the lightest of tools, sometimes traced slow evocative patterns through the air; or else they accompanied the musical cadences of his sentences with halting, hovering gestures that were like mystic rites.

In fact Baudelaire was reminiscent of a churchman, and the eloquent gestures of the pulpit. His soft cuffs waved like a vestment. He rolled his sentences out with almost evangelistic unction. He declared his love of the master he worshipped with the liturgical voice of a bishop. Certainly he celebrated, for himself, a mass of splendid imagery; he possessed the grave beauty of a cardinal of letters. . . .

After an hour the scanty audience grew scantier still. The emptiness surrounding the magician of the Word grew still emptier; there were only two rows left. . . .

The poet appeared not to notice this desertion, which left him talking alone, under a high ceiling in an ill-lit hall. A last phrase rang out: "I salute in Théophile Gautier, my master, the great poet of the century." And he bowed, stiffly from the waist, three times, impeccably, as if before a real audience. Rapidly a door banged. Then an usher took the lamp away. I remained alone in the darkness where the voice of that father of the literary church had died away.[7]

As Baudelaire had written, a sudden surge of black humor can prove costly. In this case it cost him his nerve. By the third lecture it had cracked, and he shook uncontrollably, unable to raise his head from his notes. He did not complete the series. One good joke had finished him, but no doubt it had seemed worth it at the time.

As usual disappointments accumulated. When he requested his fee he was sent just one hundred francs. The contract had stipulated a hundred francs a lecture, but subsequently he had agreed to accept a greatly reduced fee. On receiving the money he forgot this, flew into a rage, and declared, frequently, that the Belgians had cheated him.

He was anxiously trying to contact the principals of Lacroix and Verbeockhoven. Unfortunately the principals displayed little eagerness to contact him. Baudelaire was not very welcome in Belgium. At first, because he did not live up to the image of *Les Fleurs du Mal*, he was taken for an imposter. Later, his reputation confirmed, it was rumored that he was a French government spy. He had, in fact, given the lectures in order to meet Lacroix. When that attempt failed he tried again. Were it not for his efforts to enter the Academy one might regard his new plan as the maddest of all his schemes. In order to launch himself and meet Lacroix, Baudelaire decided to give a party. He would invite a number of Belgian gentlemen of commerce, wine them, dine them, and win them over by subjecting them to a poetry reading! He invited fifteen guests, his fellow host and owner of the apartment another fifteen. Of the poet's guests two excused themselves, five came, and the other eight, Lacroix included, simply stayed away:

Imagine *three huge salons*, lit with *chandeliers*, *candelabra*, decorated
with magnificent pictures, *an absurd* quantity of cakes and wines;
all for ten or twelve *very sad* people.

A journalist leaned over and said, "*There is something Christian
in your work which has not been noticed enough.*" At the other end of
the salon on the stockbroker's sofa I heard a muttering . . . "*He
says we are cretins.*" There you have the Belgian intellect and
manners. Seeing that I was boring everybody, I stopped reading,
and started eating and drinking; my five friends were ashamed
and horrified, I was the only one laughing. . . .

I am in an intolerably nervy state; but I think of the terrible
future, and want to have God and luck on my side.[8]

At least he understood that he needed more than hope to see him
through. His stay was proving a disaster: Lacroix and Verboeckhoven
turned him down out of hand; his Paris literary affairs had to be
administered at long distance; and, above all, Belgium was beginning
to jangle his nerves. It has been suggested by some that Baudelaire
deliberately sought pain, although it seems preferable to suggest that
it was more a case of his not being averse to pain when it was the only
game in town. Yet how else can one explain Baudelaire, the dandy with
overtaut nerves, moving to Brussels, if not as an act of arrant masochism? Once there he could not even console himself with the thought
that he could escape its vulgarity by returning to France. Increasingly
he realized that Belgian culture was simply an exaggerated version of
French civilization, and that the two shared the same vulgar essence.

Something was born of his rage, however—not great poetry, but
satire of considerable quality, the most forceful expression of his disgust
with a segment of the human race, the Belgian segment. Belgians
actually made him violent. The author of "Let's Beat Up the Poor"
came to practice what he preached:

My friend, you are quite right, I am always getting into trouble.
Can you believe that I have actually struck a Belgian? Un-
believable, is it not? Absurd that I could strike anybody. And
what makes it even more monstrous is that I was utterly in the
wrong. I ran after the fellow to apologize, but I couldn't find
him.[9]

He loathed the Belgians in the street, as they would jostle you off
the pavement to prove that they were your equal. He could not stand
their cooking; their gluttony; their lack of table wine (Belgians only
drank wine to show off); their dreadful beer—*la gueuese*, which he
described as piss, or more delicately "beer drunk twice over." He found

relationships between the sexes intolerably crude. There was none of that slightly flirtatious consideration for one another mingled with good manners that the French referred to as *"galanterie."* The sight of a Belgian lady made the poet want to faint. It would be enough, he said, to cool the ardors of Eros himself. The men were no better. One day he saw an actress slip and fall on an icy road. As Baudelaire was helping her to her feet, a prosperous Belgian passed by and said, "Don't forget this will you," and proceeded to deliver a mighty kick to the actress's muff, which Baudelaire had not yet retrieved. . . .

He began composing a satire, *Pauvre Belgique* [*Poor Belgium*], which he never finished. A study of Belgians going about their lives, in the long run it is a monotonous and unmodulated read. In small doses it is bitterly funny. The poet is especially concerned with Belgian women, who piss in groups in the middle of the street, or keep the lavatory door open in order not to interrupt a conversation with their children. He looks at Belgium and sees the way France would have developed had the July Monarchy not fallen. He also sees it as hell on earth—the only conceivable explanation for its existence:

> One becomes a Belgian through having sinned.
> A Belgian is his own hell.[10]

It is not surprising to learn, in his own words, that he was "chaste" in Belgium. It is interesting that he bothers to make the point. It seems to give the lie to the theory that he died a virgin, since he clearly considered that doing without sex in Belgium was yet another reflection on that country, and a point remarkable enough to note.

Not surprisingly, the Belgians drove Baudelaire to some distinctly desperate clowning. He was fascinated by their credulity, a credulity deriving from two principles: never be had for a mug and always believe the worst. They would believe anything of Baudelaire:

> I have passed here for a *police spy*—for a pederast—I spread that rumor myself *and they believed me*! Then for a proof corrector sent from Paris to proofread *dirty books. Maddened by being always believed*, I spread the rumor that *I killed and ate* my father; if I was allowed to leave France it was because of services rendered to the French police. And they believed me! *I swim in infamy like a fish in water.*[11]

Baudelaire, the weaver of defamatory legends about himself just to see if anyone believed them—it is a figure which he has not cut for nearly twenty years, but Belgium was enough to bring out his childish dandyism again. As he wrote on another occasion:

Chaste as paper, sober as water, as given to religion as a communicant, as harmless as a victim, it would not displease me to pass for a lecher, a drunkard, a blasphemer and a murderer.[12]

The revelation that he was a pederast had an unexpected consequence. It explained to Belgian musicians his otherwise inexplicable admiration for Wagner. Baudelaire was queer, Baudelaire admired Wagner; conclusion: Wagner was queer, too!

It is not surprising to learn that the poet made few friends in Belgium. He occasionally called on members of Victor Hugo's family, in Brussels, notably his daughter-in-law Mme Charles Hugo. She had installed that most beautiful of French pianos, an Erard, in their apartments, and Baudelaire would shamelessly ask her to play Wagner after dinner, regardless of the feelings of the rest of the assembly. Among the few friends he did make were the Stevens brothers, Arthur, Joseph, and Alfred. The first was an art dealer; the latter two, painters. More important by far was his very real friendship with the artist Félicien Rops. Baudelaire had known his work before going to Belgium. He was to design the frontispiece to *Les Epaves*. Rops, who lived in Namur, was married, but only, it was said, in Namur: in the rest of Europe he was a bachelor. Baudelaire liked him enormously and described him in a letter to Manet as the only real artist in the whole of Belgium.

He was not entirely cut off from his French friends. Nadar made frequent trips to Brussels. The author-turned-photographer had now found another vocation. He had become a balloonist and took his favorite balloon, La Géante, to give a demonstration in Brussels. It was hoped that Baudelaire would make an ascent, but the plan came to nothing. He also kept in contact with Paris through the enormous number of letters he wrote at this time. One correspondent in particular, a Mme Paul Meurice, received a whole series of warm, charming, gallant letters, which are a delight to read. Her own replies urging him to return at once are no less charming. Baudelaire also wrote to Sainte-Beuve partly because he needed his help and advice, partly out of warmth for an old friend. Sainte-Beuve replied, partly because Baudelaire was an old friend, partly because that pillar of the literary establishment wanted something: Could Baudelaire please send him some dirty books? The spectacle of Baudelaire, the damned poet who detested pornography, sending de Sade to Sainte-Beuve, the virtuous critic of an "incurable curiosity," is a little ironic.

Belgium for Baudelaire was a period of hanging on, just, and waiting for something to happen—with absolutely nothing in view. He only stayed for psychological and financial reasons; he was simply unable to leave. Inevitably he ran up debts. He owed his hotel so much that the landlady came to see him whenever he received a letter in case it contained money. Eventually he had to have letters sent *poste restante*. The debts incurred by his needless lingering made it harder and harder to cut his stay short. But still worse, there remained the terror of a return which would require him to face once more the problems left behind in Paris, problems not solved but compounded by his departure. He described to Ancelle an abortive trip to Paris. He had arranged a series of meetings but failed to turn up:

> At the last moment, the moment of departure, despite all my longing to see my mother again, despite the profound boredom of my life, a boredom greater still than that brought on by French stupidity which I *endured* for so many years—*I was assailed by terror; I was as frightened as a dog*, the horror of seeing my hell again—of crossing Paris without being sure to be able to hand out enough money to secure me real rest at Honfleur.[13]

He tried to tell his mother why he felt pinned to Brussels. He was terrified of failure, facts, debts, realities, of "implacable life." It was the same terror that, in Paris, used to make him unable to face going home for a week at a time, for fear of finding bad news. Such terror of life was the price he had paid for a lifetime lived beyond his financial and psychological means. Mme Aupick was not pleased. She too felt that time was passing; her son's fear of time and failure took on a different complexion for her. She wrote to Ancelle, detailing her feelings about her son in Belgium:

> I cannot get over my astonishment at the amount of money wasted on this trip. I ought to be used to that strange and utterly unconventional life, and *resign myself*. But I cannot, sticking foolishly, stubbornly to the thought that I must, before I die, get a little satisfaction out of him. And now it is urgent, I am growing old and distinctly weak. There is not much time left for the contentment I aspire too. I will never have it. I could have consoled myself with his great literary successes (since I think that he had what was needed), but there again, cruel disappointment (since Charles chose a form as bizarre and absurd as himself, which won him few admirers). It is true that he had his *originality*; that is something. He can never write anything ordinary. He will never borrow the ideas of others, since he has his own rich store. I think he would like to see us take his literary affairs more seriously. He claims that although they make slow progress, hardly any indeed, progress they do a little.[14]

216

Surrounded by Belgians, afraid to go home, and with his only relative seeing him as she did, small wonder that Baudelaire continued to evolve his capacity for spite and bitterness. As he walked through the streets of Brussels, seeing all the wretched, talentless books on display, he thought with rage of his own works. If only he could manage a small edition, reprinting each year, he would have enough to live on. "I do declare that destiny has never *spoiled* me." Indeed, he came to believe with increasing conviction in his *guignon*, his evil star, and to suppose that he was disaster-prone. No one, neither the public nor even his mother, appreciated him, and yet he knew how good he was. Now, at the age of forty-five, with a "disagreeable and unpopular talent," he was too old to make his fortune:

> Perhaps it is already too late to be able to pay off my debts and preserve enough for a free, honorable old age. But if I could only recover the energy and vitality that I once enjoyed, I would purge my rage in horrifying works. I would like to set the entire human race against me. It would be a pleasure that would make up for everything.
>
> In the meantime my books *sleep*, lost assets for the moment. Besides they are forgetting me.[15]

Once again he aspires to release from rage through a surge of destruction and spite—yet even this is denied him. He never wrote the works of vengeance that he dreamed of. Instead, as he got poorer and his appearance deteriorated Baudelaire sought oblivion with increasing conviction, through hard liquor and opium, and they took their toll:

> I feel a bit fuddled, fog, absent-mindedness. It is the result of a long series of crises, also of opium, digitalis, belladonna, and quinine—a doctor I summoned didn't realize I had taken a lot of opium in my life. He underprescribed and I had to double or quadruple the doses. I managed to delay the crises; that was really something, but I am very tired.[16]

Drugged and ill Baudelaire hung on, a reluctant self-exiled remittance man, virtually without remittance. Dependent on the occasional small sum that Ancelle sent him, he was trying desperately to set up a new edition of his work. The enterprise had its difficulties. Publishers were in Paris, Baudelaire in Brussels; they could wait to get their price, he could not. Moreover, he did not even own all his work. He had sold his Poe translations outright to Lévy; Hetzel temporarily had rights over both books of poetry. This left him the criticism, *Les Paradis Artificiels*, and, in progress, the book on Belgium. All his most attractive works had passed out of his control, temporarily or for good.

In 1865 the tiring poet acknowledged that to place his own work was beyond him. He engaged the services of an agent. A good agent is the best friend an author can hope for; a bad one can make life a misery. So, inevitably, it was with Baudelaire. The reader will have guessed that his choice of agent was a disaster. Julien Lemer was what might today be termed a literary hustler. He had been a publisher in a small way. Now he agented writers, had a loud mouth, drank and ate too well, tended to overplay his hand, and was fundamentally dishonest. He had a reputation for being aggressive and ineffectual. He was the last person in the world who should have handled Baudelaire. Indeed, he was determined *not* to find him a publisher, hoping that when the price had fallen enough, he would publish the poet himself.

Baudelaire placed his trust in Lemer, hoping that he would get him a contract with the great house of Garnier. Lemer did nothing. In the meantime a new crisis occurred. In 1862 Baudelaire had mortgaged to Poulet-Malassis *Les Fleurs du Mal*, *Le Spleen de Paris*, and *Les Paradis Artificiels* for five thousand francs. Should he fail to repay the money by July 1865 Poulet-Malassis was free to dispose of the works as he wished. An ex-employee of the printer, Pincebourde, knew that Poulet was in severe financial difficulties. Accordingly he offered him two thousand francs for the mortgage. If Pincebourde were to get absolute control over Baudelaire's most saleable assets, the poet would be utterly ruined.

Baudelaire made a lightning trip to Paris. At the Gare du Nord he ran into a young poet, Catulle Mendès, who described his arrival— without any luggage. Mendès put the older poet up. As they talked into the night, Baudelaire did some calculations and revealed to his horrified hearer that the sum total he had earned for a lifetime's writing amounted to 15,982 francs, 60 centimes. Later Mèndes was awakened by the sound of Baudelaire, in the next room, weeping hopelessly into the night. He left the next morning before Mendès was up.

He looked to Lemer to extricate him from his predicament, but Lemer had nothing to offer. He did suggest that if he had *Les Fleurs* and *Le Spleen* to give Garnier, he might find it easier to get a contract. Baudelaire managed to persuade Hetzel to relinquish his temporary claims over these works, although he had to repay the advance to do so. Now only the threat of Pincebourde remained—and only five days in which to meet it. Baudelaire went, in despair, to his mother, and poured out his heart. For once she was sensible enough to see that he could not be allowed to lose his only assets. She suggested a loan—and in one magic moment the most crushing burden ever to have weighed upon Baudelaire was miraculously removed.

He returned to Paris in a state of elation. He entertained Banville and Asselineau with tales of Belgium, a blend of bitterness and charm itself. It was the last time that his Parisian friends were to see him like that. The next day he had to return to Brussels, to his local debts and to the Belgians. He felt honor-bound to wait there until Lemer could clinch the Garnier contract. He could easily have cut and run, indeed Ancelle advised him to do so. But Baudelaire the dandy who had gambled his whole life away on a single unremitting losing streak, was too much a gentleman ever to welsh.

The year 1865 dragged itself out with no news from Lemer. Even the optimistic Baudelaire began to have doubts. In recent years he had been growing closer to Ancelle. Their correspondence had become positively warm; Baudelaire, at last, could give the old lawyer his due, and Ancelle, in turn, repaid his ward's kindness by taking an ever-increasing interest in modern literature. There is something very touching in the turn the relationship now took. For over twenty years each had considered the other to be the bane of his life. Yet the chain that linked them had never broken, and now in the very last moments it drew them together. Baudelaire had come to trust his guardian sufficiently to ask him to act on his behalf; to check on Lemer. Ancelle rapidly discovered that he was a rogue, who had gone to great lengths to ensure that Garnier would not handle Baudelaire. Baudelaire's response was immediate; he changed agents, finding a replacement for Lemer in none other than Ancelle himself! The latter took up the delicate business of reopening negotiations with Garnier. His position was complicated by the earlier maneuverings of Lemer, and by the fact that the whole publishing world knew that Baudelaire had his back to the wall.

It was becoming clear that Baudelaire might prove a good investment. He had a considerable following among the younger generation of poets, such as Mendès, and more importantly Verlaine and Mallarmé. Swinburne had written warmly of his work in *The Spectator*. Sainte-Beuve informed Baudelaire that he had become something of a cult figure among a group of perfectly civilized, but very green, young writers. Baudelaire did not entirely appreciate their admiration, but at least it was something to be proud of. It also suggested that the publisher who got Baudelaire cheap—Michel Lévy had done so once— would pull off something of a coup. No one was in any hurry to move, however, for the longer they waited the cheaper the price would be.

In these last wretched months in Belgium, Baudelaire grew more and more miserable, enduring a poverty so absolute that even a postage-due letter from France would cause him severe embarrassment. He was also becoming more moralistic. On one occasion he even prevented Nadar's secretary from taking a girl upstairs in a brothel; the author of *Les Fleurs du Mal* proceeded to drag the young man from the place bodily.

He was still waiting for his final hope to be realized: for Ancelle to complete a deal with Garnier. The lawyer failed. His attentions had only managed to alienate the Garnier brothers completely. He had let them see that his client was desperate, which encouraged them to play a waiting game. The news of the failure shattered Baudelaire. As usual he had thought that the deal was a good as done. Now once again he had to abandon hope and start from scratch. He suggested that Ancelle approach other publishers, but the old lawyer proceeded so ineptly that soon every publisher in Paris knew that the poet had reached the end of his tether. If he were to retain any hope of success he clearly had to act himself—even if it were to kill him.

20

THROUGHOUT HIS STAY in Belgium Baudelaire had complained
of poor health. The difficulty he found in concentrating his
energies and working had been increased by the well-founded
suspicions that his body was letting him down. He suffered
from acute stomach disorders, and these—or his treatments—created
alternating bouts of astounding constipation and diarrhea. Rather more
sinister was the increasing stiffness in his joints, a stiffness optimistically
diagnosed by the sufferer as arthritis, as opposed to tertiary syphilis. He
also suffered from dreadful bouts of neuralgia, which by the end of 1865
had become almost continuous. By early 1866 his "rheumatism in the
head," as he termed it, had developed into something worse:

> In January, and even now, on an empty stomach, for no
> apparent reason, suddenly, a vague feeling, absent-mindedness,
> giddiness. Even when seated I cannot help falling over. Then a
> cold sweat and I throw up bile, a white scum. Fairly protracted
> stupor. . . . Perpetual forgetfulness and stupor—heaviness in
> the head. Great clumsiness, great awkwardness, great weakness.[1]

Even at this stage his letters never diagnose syphilis, perhaps because this would admit the inadmissable. Baudelaire simply notes the
pills which he takes in an attempt at treatment before diagnosis. He
notes symptoms but does not look for conclusions. Still a pleasure seeker
of sorts, he is disgusted to find he no longer enjoys smoking. This depri-
vation weighs much more than the unimportant fact that he has to keep
lying down, because he is afraid of falling and knocking the furniture
about. His letters are matter-of-fact and utterly free of self-pity; they
are even cheerful. He does not complain of the appalling difficulties
involved in continuing to work and administer his affairs. Yet there is

one terrible cry from the heart of an ex-pleasure seeker—in a letter to his old friend Poulet-Malassis:

> In my life I have had many desires. But I did not know the desire
> to vomit and to stop falling over.[2]

The worst thing about these bouts of giddiness and falling for a sensitive introspective such as Baudelaire was that he need only think about vertigo to bring on an attack.

It is rather dreadful to think of Baudelaire's syphilis as "the wages of sin." Yet it is strangely appropriate that Baudelaire should have suffered from terrible bouts of vertigo. All his life he had described the quest for vertigo and the destruction of cold, dull consciousness through intense experience; finally and dreadfully he seems to have found it.

Poulet-Malassis had been worried about Baudelaire for some time. He was visibly declining day by day, his nervous system, as he put it, "severely compromised." Yet he refused to take his symptoms seriously and alter his way of life. Despite the advice of friends and doctors, he persisted in taking huge amounts of laudanum and drinking a lot of brandy. He had lost all strength of will. When he came to dinner Poulet-Malassis would remove the brandy decanter because Baudelaire would drink all night if given the chance.

He was expected to return to Paris on March 15, 1866, but he failed to appear. Just before leaving Belgium he had gone with Rops for a last visit to the church of Saint-Loup at Naumur, the one place in Belgium that appealed to his sense of beauty. It was tragically appropriate that he should have described it as a "beautiful and sinister catafalque." As he walked round with Rops and Poulet-Malassis, he collapsed and had to sit down. He pretended to have sprained an ankle, and his friends were friends enough to believe him. Yet the next morning he gave clear signs of mental disorder. On the way back to Brussels in the train he asked Rops to open an already open window. The shivering man had meant to say the opposite. This most lucid and eloquent of poets had begun to suffer brain damage affecting his powers of speech.

Back in Brussels things got worse. A friend, the photographer Neyt, met Baudelaire one evening in a café, drinking heavily, often at a loss for a word or checking his hand in mid-movement, pausing for unbearably long intervals, and otherwise proceeding with a deadly slowness; all the time he was shivering uncontrollably. He eventually summoned up the strength to leave and tottered out of the restaurant, telling Neyt that he would see him in the evening. It was already late at night. The photographer began to worry about his friend, went to his hotel but he had not returned. He went the rounds of Baudelaire's regular haunts to try to find him, which he finally did, at one in the morning, sitting alone in a bar, dreadfully dazed. Neyt persuaded him to let him take him home. When they arrived at the hotel it became clear that Baudelaire could not walk upstairs and Neyt was obliged to carry him. He laid him on his bed and tried to undress him, but Baudelaire ordered him at the top of his voice to go away.

The next morning Neyt visited him in his hotel and found him, stretched fully dressed on his bed, unable to speak. Although he eventually recovered his speech for a while, the whole of his right side was now paralyzed. He dictated a letter to Ancelle, begging for funds to settle his hotel bill. When the news reached his mother she grew terribly alarmed and sent Ancelle to Brussels to do what he could. In the meantime her son had written her his last letter, which, like so many others, was more concerned about her health than his own. Inevitably the letter is optimistic, Baudelaire was looking forward to a complete recovery.

He had been taken to a kind of charity nursing home, the Institut de St. Jean et de Ste. Elizabeth, run by nuns. The choice was not judicious. As always Baudelaire's reputation preceded him. The situation was aggravated by the poet's renewed inability to speak. His eloquence was restricted to two words, or part words *"cré nom"*—for *"sacré nom de Dieu."* With this abbreviated oath, Baudelaire had to express the full range of his needs and feelings. Although the spectacle of the poet struck dumb is a terrible one, there is something profoundly moving about the effort of will which enabled him to force out these words, of all words, to express his needs. The choice was also strangely appropriate. In none of his poems had Baudelaire achieved such a profound expression of his craving for spirituality; but it was a craving which, like those poems, could all too easily be mistaken for a blasphemous oath.

Mistaken it was. The nuns interpreted his words as a perpetual blasphemy, and their reactions stoked his enduring capacity for rage. His mother came to Brussels to look after him, and found that not all was well. Baudelaire was clearly a "difficult" patient. The nuns soon abandoned attempts to "convert" him and instead would cross themselves whenever they saw him. Both approaches exasperated him. The mother superior eventually informed his mother that he was no longer welcome. She fought for her son, accusing the mother superior of lacking Christian charity. At all events Baudelaire left the institution—which was immediately exorcised.

He remained in his hotel for another three months, fairly comfortably, and in varying degrees of lucidity. Yet it was obvious that the damage was severe and chances of recovery small. On July 2, 1862, he returned to Paris after an absence of two and a half years. Friends met him at the station, and when Asselineau saw the frail white-haired man, broken in body and mind, and leaning on a stick, he wept. Baudelaire, unable to speak, tried to console his friend by attempting a tender laugh—he could still laugh—but it came out as a dreadful Satanic mockery of mirth.

He was taken to the clinic of a certain Dr Duval in the Rue du Dôme. It was a modern establishment using hydrotherapy as its basic treatment. Baudelaire was housed in a comfortable ground-floor room which contained two Manets, one of which was his copy of Goya's lovely portrait of the Duchess of Albi. Baudelaire was comfortable there:

> He neither reads nor speaks, but he can walk and recognize his visitors and indicates by signs that he understands them. His face is transformed by a completely gray beard—he had always been clean-shaven—and by the sun-tanned forehead which he leaves exposed to the July sun, apparently without ill effects. Paralysis has blinded one eye, and affected the tongue, which at certain painful moments such as shower time, articulates with effort, a little series of oaths. . . .
>
> But do not suppose that this makes him insensitive to gentler emotions. Never has he enjoyed music and flowers so much. The sound of a piano fills him with delight. He can spend a quarter of an hour looking at the most recent rose to come from the clinic garden.[3]

His mother wrote to all his friends asking them to visit him in the clinic. Most did, Sainte-Beuve was an exception—he was recovering from an operation at the time. Other friends visited him often. Mme Meurice and Mme Manet were particularly welcome, as they would play Wagner for him. Sometimes he would leave the clinic and take a meal with someone. He was as fastidious and dandyish as ever. Nadar recalls an occasion in his apartment when Baudelaire conveyed by urgent signs that he would like a manicure. He appeared profoundly satisfied with the result; half an hour later he requested another one.

His friends sought a state pension for him. For once Sainte-Beuve, who was genuinely concerned by the plight of his friend, used his influence, suggesting that the case was especially worthy since the translator and journalist—not poet—was the son of a former ambassadress! Baudelaire did not get a pension; instead he was given a single paltry allocation of five hundred francs.

During the early days in the clinic he remained lucid and capable of intense interest and enjoyment. He was also courageous enough to conceal pain and distress from his mother and friends. He would go into raptures over a plant, or a piece of music, signify rage when he heard of Courbet's latest painting, *La Femme au Perroquet*, which was hung in the Salon of 1866. To his mother he was exceptionally tender, trying to express in long gentle stares all the warmth which he felt and had never been able to express. Yet lack of speech made their long tête-à-têtes dreadfully wearying for both of them, consisting as they did of uninterrupted silence charged with feeling.

Late in 1866 the patient showed signs of improvement. He found it possible to utter a few phrases, such as *"bonjour, monsieur,"* and once asked, with great clarity, to be passed the mustard. Yet he did not altogether convince his hearers that he knew the meaning of what he said, and his mother feared that he was talking parrot fashion. Nevertheless, doctor and patient alike hoped for a cure. Baudelaire had marked the last day of March 1867 as recovery day, and looked forward to joining his mother in Honfleur in early April. This, his last plan, was also to fall through.

His mental health suddenly began to deteriorate. Asselineau once tried to get him to sign a receipt. Baudelaire remained, pen in air, visibly trying to recall his own name. To remind him Asselineau put a copy of one of the poet's books in front of him, and painfully Baudelaire traced out the name of its author. On another occasion a lady visitor brushed out his hair and combed his beard for him. When shown his reflection in the glass, he failed to recognize himself and bowed a polite greeting to the bearded apparition in the mirror.

Asselineau had been sending regular reports to Mme Aupick in Honfleur. In the third week of May 1867 she grew so alarmed at their tenor that, old and frail as she was, she returned to Paris and put up at a hotel. Her son's mental condition was getting worse. He seldom recognized his friends anymore.

In his final days, despite great discomfort and dreadful bed sores, Charles Baudelaire became calm and resigned. He appeared to be sleeping with his eyes open for the last two days of his life, although he may have regained consciousness towards the end. He died peacefully on August 31, 1867, in his mother's arms, and he died smiling. The smile lingered on after death, and perhaps it was a sign that this luckless man, the greatest poet that France has known, finally found in death that serenity that had persistently eluded him throughout the forty-six short years of his life.

He certainly did not find it before death. A strange sidelight is cast on Mme Aupick with her love, her obstinacy, her narrowness. She adored her son, yet never understood him, never took his most urgent requests seriously, considering them frivolous. He had expressed to her the great irritation caused him by her maid, Aimée, and yet Mme Aupick had her sit with her as she watched over her dying son. It was as if, even on his deathbed, the shortsightedness of his mother would deny him peace. We must hope that the dying poet was too far gone to identify this final source of irritation.

Theses have been written on the disease and death of Baudelaire.

Doctors conclude that the principle cause was brain damage caused by syphilis, drugs, and drink, or in medical jargon:

> Softening of the brain by thrombosis of the middle or left sylvain cerebral artery, with hemiplegia of the right side, aphasia and possible alexia.[4]

Yet it would be wrong to see his disease, his brain damage and paralysis, as no more than the consequence of his dissolute youth, his poisoned wild oats. His life and death form part of a pattern, the work of coincidence or something stranger still. It will be recalled that Alphonse his half-brother, and no relation of Mme Aupick, had died in 1862 of a cerebral hemorrhage and hemiplegia of the left side. Jeanne too suffered from paralysis. The pattern is completed with a fourth paralysis. In 1871 Madame Aupick herself would fall into a state almost identical to that of her son Charles. She would retain some mental lucidity but would lose her powers of speech almost entirely. Paralyzed, she died later that year.

If there is an explanation it points to Baudelaire's father. He is the only common factor. He was after all the father of both Charles and Alphonse, and the husband of Caroline. Whatever the hereditary factors, any family weakness was of course compounded in Baudelaire by alcohol, opium, and syphilis. At all events, however one explains this run of identical deaths, the odds against the pattern are long enough to suggest that Baudelaire was not so very mistaken when believing that he had been damned at birth by his *guignon*.

The reports of Baudelaire's death in the press projected the usual aura of distortion and misinformation which surrounded the poet in life. The funeral was also in character. As France's most distinguished critic, Sainte-Beuve had been asked to give the oration but, staunch to the last, poor health prevented him from attending. A great many people were variously so prevented. The hot weather had emptied Paris, and a number of friends had failed to get their invitations in time. Heat made others drop out before the procession reached the graveside. There were no official representatives of any kind. Only some sixty people were present to hear Banville's lament for a lost friend and poet. Asselineau kept his own speech short, because the poor turnout made him choke with rage. Everyone seemed in a hurry for the ceremony to end. There was another burial taking place at the same time, vastly better attended. The dead man was a successful tradesman. Baudelaire would have had a laugh at that. As the cortège entered the cemetery there was a clap of thunder. By the time the speeches were over it was raining heavily. People were anxious to leave and some made a run for it. Nobody said much.

EPILOG

One day Baudelaire, applying for a passport, was asked his profession. "Lyric poet," he announced with pride, and that is what he was. One of the greatest poets of his age, of any age; the creator of modern art, the first writer to map modern man's unhappy consciousness.

In the course of his own unhappy life he made many mistakes, but the greatest mistake of all was to overestimate his public. He gave himself a bad name and it hanged him. He was too proud and private to make his high seriousness, his morality, his values, instantly available to his readers. Instead he clowned, in the belief that an intelligent public would see through his clowning. He was wrong, for France, the country of eternal frivolity, loathed real poetry.

Yet at last the lyric poet has outlived his legend. His tight, sensuous, sometimes diabolic verse has evoked stress, beauty, nostalgia, despair, sensuality. It has conferred immortality on his women, made the name of an ignorant mulatto into an incantation which evokes ideal beauty and dusky sensuality. Baudelaire could work with words to confer eternal life; he could use them to create "intensity, sonority, limpidity, profundity, echoing in space and time."[1]

As a man and an artist he had the capacity to charm, and to shock. He understood the texture of beauty and also the textures of desire and self-destruction. Above all, he understood how to live with the overwhelming knowledge of one's own unworthiness. As a poet he preyed on the self-destruction and decline which he endured as a man. His art was born of his own surrenders, and the artist, he believed, would ever redeem the defeated man. It is a short move from Baudelaire to the disorder of the senses cultivated by Rimbaud, not a far one to the pitiful series of alcoholics, addicts, and suicides that litter the twentieth-century artists' hall of fame.

Yet Baudelaire never allowed the man to destroy the artist. He believed too passionately in work as balance and redemption. Work was the only good he could create, his only chance of salvation, his only escape from time and the hollowness of pleasure. This savage faith in the absolute value of work was another belief he would share with later artists. All writers know those dreadful moments when their faith in work is eroded; perhaps that work is too facile, too easy, not a spiritual discipline but a simple indulgence. Yet if that faith goes, one might as well cut one's throat. At such moments it helps to remember Baudelaire, remember the sum total of beauty and insight that he left behind him as his name rings down the ages and his glorious writing floats free of his miserable fated life; a life fated to make great art. Faith flows back with the sure and certain knowledge that Baudelaire did redeem his life with the beauty he made of it. Perhaps he was simply proud and conscious of his powers and did not know that he was composing his epitaph when he wrote:

> You gave me your mud
> And I made it into gold.

NOTES

All translations from the French are by the author. Dates refer to the first publication of any work. Following is a list of abbreviations of works cited in the Notes.

Baldick   Baldick, R. *The First Bohemian. The Life of Henry Murger*. London, 1961.
Bandy   Bandy, W. T., and Pichois, C. *Baudelaire devant ses contemporains*. Monaco, 1957.
Crépet   Crépet, J. and E. *Baudelaire*. Paris, 1907.
Corr. I or II   Baudelaire, C. *Correspondance*. 2 vols. Paris, 1973.
Journaux   Baudelaire, C. *Journaux intimes*, in his *Oeuvres Complètes* (see OC below).
LAB   *Lettres à Baudelaire*. Neuchâtel, 1973.
OC   Baudelaire, C. *Oeuvres Complètes*. Paris, 1963.
Pichois   Pichois, C. *Baudelaire, Études et témoignages*. Neufchâtel, 1967.
Poe   Edgar Allan Poe. *Oeuvres en Prose*. Trans. Baudelaire. Paris, 1965.

CHAPTER ONE
1. Crépet, p. 13.
2. *Journaux intimes,* OC, p. 1259.
3. Aupick, in Crépet, pp. 264–5.
4. *Réflexions sur quelques-uns de mes contemporains* (1859), OC, p. 737.
5. *Journaux*, OC, p. 1312.
6. *Ibid.*, p. 1287.
7. *La Fanfarlo* (1847), OC, p. 492.
8. *Journaux*, OC, p. 1259.
9. Letter to Poulet-Malassis on Apr. 23, 1860: *Corr.* I, p. 30.
10. Letter to Mme Aupick on May 6, 1861, *ibid*, p. 153.
11. *Salon de 1859*, OC, p. 1041.
12. *Journaux*, OC, p. 1257.
13. *Les Drames et les romans honnêtes* (1851), OC, p. 621.

CHAPTER TWO

1. *L'Art philosophique* (1859), OC, p. 1102.
2. Letter to Alphonse Baudelaire on July 3, 1832: *Corr.* I, p. 8.
3. Letter to Mme Aupick on May 6, 1861: *ibid.*, p. 153.
4. Letter to Alphonse Baudelaire on Mar. 25, 1833: *ibid.*, pp. 16–17.
5. Letter to Alphonse Baudelaire on Oct. 20, 1834: *ibid.*, p. 31.
6. Letter to Aupick and Mme Aupick on Feb. 25, 1834: *ibid.*, pp. 26–7.
7. Maxime du Camp, *Souvenirs littéraires* (Paris, 1882), p. 55.
8. Letter to Mme Aupick on Nov. 6, 1837: *Corr.* I, p. 45.
9. Crépet, p. 14.
10. *Ibid.*
11. Letter to Mme Aupick on Apr. 23, 1837: *Corr.* I, p. 39.
12. Letter to Aupick on July 17, 1838: *ibid.*, p. 59.
13. *Ibid.*, p. xxix.
14. *Ibid.*, p. 709.
15. Bandy, p. 41.
16. Letter to Alphonse Baudelaire on Nov. 2, 1837: *Corr.* I, p. 43.
17. *Journaux*, OC, p. 1258.
18. Letter to Aupick on June 18, 1839: *Corr.* I, pp. 72–3.
19. Letter to Aupick on June 18, 1839: *ibid.*, p. 72.

CHAPTER THREE

1. Crépet, p. 20
2. Bandy, p. 16.
3. Crépet, p. 23.
4. *Ibid.*, p. 22.
5. Letter to Alphonse Baudelaire on Nov. 20, 1839: *Corr.* I, pp. 83–4.
6. Letter to Alphonse Baudelaire on Dec. 2, 1839: *ibid.*, p. 80.
7. Letter to Alphonse Baudelaire on Dec. 31, 1840: *ibid.*, pp. 83–4.
8. Letter to Alphonse Baudelaire on Jan. 20, 1841: *ibid.*, p. 85.
9. Letter to Charles Baudelaire from Alphonse Baudelaire on Dec. 2, 1839: *ibid.*, p. 741.
10. *Ibid.*, *loc. cit.*
11. Letter to Charles Baudelaire from Alphonse Baudelaire on Jan. 25, 1841: *ibid.*, pp. 731–3.

CHAPTER FOUR

1. Letter from Aupick to Alphonse Baudelaire, undated: *Mercure de France* (Mar. 15, 1937), pp. 631–2.
2. Letter to Ancelle from Mme Aupick, undated: Crépet, p. 26.
3. Letter to Alphonse Baudelaire from Aupick on May 4, 1841: *Mercure de France* (Mar. 15, 1937), p. 633.
4. Letter to Asselineau from Mme Baudelaire in 1868: Bandy, p. 50.
5. Letter to Aupick from P. Saur on Oct. 14, 1841: Crépet, pp. 221–2.
6. Anonymous memoir published in *Chronique de Paris* (Sept. 1867): Bandy, p. 53.

7. *Ibid., loc. cit.*
8. Letter to Aupick on Feb. 16, 1842. *Corr.* I, p. 90.
9. Bandy, pp. 56–7.

Chapter Five

1. *La Fanfarlo*, OC, p. 483.
2. Letter to Mme Aupick, April 1842: *Corr.* I, p. 92.
3. Crépet, pp. 35–6.
4. *Le Peintre de la vie moderne* (1863), OC, pp. 1178–9.
5. *Journaux*, OC, p. 1272.
6. Crépet, p. 44.
7. *Ibid.*, p. 44.
8. *Ibid.*, pp. 65–6.
9. Bandy, p. 271.
10. *Ibid.*, p. 273.
11. Crépet, pp. 296–7.
12. *Ibid.*, p. 64.
13. *Journaux*, OC, p. 1251.
14. *Journaux, ibid.*, p. 1288.
15. *Salon de 1859, ibid.*, 1056.
16. *Journaux, ibid.*, p. 1255.
17. Bandy, pp. 128–9.
18. *Journaux*, OC, p. 1248.
19. *La Fanfarlo, ibid.*, p. 509.
20. "Les Promesses d'un visage," *ibid.*, pp. 146–7.
21. Untitled, *ibid.*, p. 200.
22. *La Fanfarlo, ibid.*, p. 508.
23. *Journaux, ibid.*, p. 1247.
24. Bandy, p. 139.

Chapter Six

1. Letter to Mme Aupick on Jan. 5, 1844: *Corr.* I, p. 104.
2. *Journaux*, OC, p. 1291.
3. Letter to Mme Aupick on Jan. 5, 1844: *Corr.* I, p. 104.
4. Letter to Mme Aupick, summer 1844: *ibid.*, pp. 108–10.
5. Letter to Mme Aupick on June 6, 1862: *Corr.* II, p. 249.
6. Letter to Mme Aupick, summer 1844: *Corr.* I, p. 113.
7. Letter to Mme Aupick, summer 1844: *ibid.*, p. 113.
8. Letter to Ancelle on Jan. 10, 1850: *ibid.*, p. 158.
9. Letter to Ancelle on Jan. 10, 1850: *ibid.*, pp. 162–3.
10. Pichois, p. 17.
11. Letter to Mme Aupick, early in 1845: *Corr.* I, pp. 120–1.
12. Letter to Mme Aupick on June 30, 1845: *Corr.* I, pp. 124–5.
13. Letter to Mme Aupick on Dec. 25, 1861: *Corr.* II, pp. 200–1.
14. Bandy, pp. 68–9.

CHAPTER SEVEN

1. Crépet, pp. 278–9.
2. *Salon de 1845*, OC, p. 866.
3. OC, pp. 472–3.
4. *Ibid.*, p. 952.
5. *Journaux, ibid.*, p. 1266.
6. Crépet, p. 290–2.
7. *Journaux*, OC, p. 1271.
8. Letter to Mme Aupick, 1847: *Corr.* I, p. 141.
9. Letter to Mme Aupick on Dec. 4, 1847: *ibid.*, pp. 143–7.
10. Poe, pp. 1017–8.

CHAPTER EIGHT

1. OC, pp. 946–7.
2. Crépet, p. 70.
3. Bandy, pp. 95–100.
4. *Ibid.*, p. 101.
5. *Journaux*, OC, p. 1273.
6. Baldick, p. 106.
7. *Théophile Gautier* (1859), OC, p. 697.
8. *Journaux, ibid.*, p. 1271.
9. Crépet, p. 82.
10. Letter to Mme Aupick on Dec. 8, 1848: *Corr.* I, p. 155.
11. Letter to Ancelle, Dec. 1848: *ibid.*, pp. 157–8.
12. Letter to Ancelle on Mar. 5, 1852: *ibid.*, p. 188.
13. OC, p. 186.
14. *Journaux*, OC, p. 1444.
15. Letter to Edouard Manet on October 28, 1865: *Corr.* II, p. 539.
16. Sketch for a prose poem, OC, p. 316–7.
17. *Journaux*, OC, p. 1274.

CHAPTER NINE

1. Letter to Mme Aupick on Jan. 9, 1851: *Corr.* I, pp. 168–9.
2. Letter from Mme Aupick to Asselineau, Nov. 1868: Crépet, p. 268.
3. Letter to Mme Aupick on Aug. 30, 1851: *Corr.* I, p. 178.
4. Letter to Mme Aupick on Mar. 26, 1853: *ibid.*, pp. 210–17.
5. Letter to Mme Aupick on Dec. 26, 1853: *ibid.*, p. 240.
6. *Ibid.*, p. 241.
7. Letter to Mme Aupick on Mar. 27, 1852: *ibid.*, p. 193.
8. Letter to Madame Marie, early 1852: *ibid.*, pp. 181–2.

CHAPTER TEN

1. Crépet, p. 95.
2. Letter to Théophile Thoré on June 20, 1864: *Corr.* II, p. 386.
3. Letter to Fernand Desnoyers, late 1853: *ibid.*, p. 248.

CHAPTER ELEVEN

1. Gautier's daughter, Judith, in Crépet, p. 115.
2. *Ibid., loc. cit.*
3. Bandy, pp. 136–7.
4. Letter to Mme Sabatier on Dec. 9, 1852: *Corr.* I, p. 205.
5. Letter to Mme Sabatier, May 1853: *ibid.*, p. 224.
6. Letter to Mme Sabatier on Aug. 18, 1857: *ibid.*, pp. 421–3.
7. Bandy, p. 134.
8. Letter to Mme Sabatier on Aug. 31, 1857: *ibid.*, pp. 425–6.
9. Bandy, pp. 134–5.

CHAPTER TWELVE

1. Letter to Mme Aupick, Oct. 31, 1853: *Corr.* I, p. 232.
2. *Journaux*, OC, pp. 1280–1.
3. Letter to Mme Aupick on Dec. 10, 1853: *Corr.* I, p. 237.
4. Crépet, pp. 130–1.
5. Letter to Mme Aupick on Dec. 26, 1853: *Corr.* I, p. 242.
6. Letter to Mme Aupick on Apr. 5, 1855: *ibid.*, p. 311.
7. Letter to Mme Aupick on Dec. 16, 1853: *ibid.*, pp. 238–9.
8. Letter to Mme Aupick on Dec. 4, 1854: *ibid.*, pp. 300–1.
9. Letter to Mme Aupick on July 28, 1854: *ibid.*, p. 285.
10. *Loc. cit.*
11. Letter to Mme Aupick on Dec. 4, 1854: *ibid.*, p. 303.
12. Letter to Mme Aupick on Dec. 20, 1855: *ibid.*, p. 325.
13. "Projets de préface pour," *Les Fleurs du Mal*, OC, p. 184.
14. Letter to Poulet-Malassis on Mar. 20, 1861: *Corr.* II, p. 136.
15. Letter to Poulet-Malassis on Dec. 16, 1853: *Corr.* I, pp. 238–9.
16. Letter to Paul Saint-Victor on Oct. 14, 1854: *ibid.*, p. 294.
17. Letter to Mme Aupick on Dec. 4, 1854: *ibid.*, p. 303.
18. Letter to Mme Aupick on Sept. 11, 1856: *ibid.*, p. 356.
19. Letter to Mme Aupick on Nov. 4, 1856: *ibid.*, p. 360.
20. *Journaux*, OC, pp. 1261–2.

CHAPTER THIRTEEN

1. Letter to Mme Aupick on Apr. 5, 1855: *Corr.* I, p. 311.
2. Letter to Mme Aupick on July 9, 1857: *ibid.*, pp. 410–12.
3. Bandy, p. 31.
4. *Ibid.*, p. 48.
5. Letter to Mme Aupick on July 9, 1857: *Corr.* I, pp. 412–3.
6. Letter to Mme Aupick, July 9, 1857: *Corr.* I, p. 412–3.
7. Letters to Mme Aupick on July 27, 1857: *ibid.*, p. 419.
8. *Lettres à Baudelaire* (Neuchâtel, 1973), p. 150.
9. *Revue des Science Humaines* (Jan.–April 1957), pp. 103–4.
10. Crépet, p. 109.
11. *Ibid.*, p. 110.
12. Pichois, p. 136.
13. Crépet, p. 110.

14. Letter to the Empress Eugénie on Nov. 6, 1857: *Corr.* I, p. 432.
15. Letter to Poulet-Malassis, July 1860: *Corr.* II, p. 57.
16. *Revue des Sciences Humaines* (Jan.–April 1957), p. 105.
17. Letter to Ancelle on Feb. 18, 1866: *Corr.* II, p. 610.

CHAPTER FOURTEEN
1. *Journaux*, OC, p. 1277.
2. Letter to Flaubert on June 26, 1860: *Corr.* II, p. 53.
3. "Projets de préface pour *Les Fleurs du Mal*," OC, p. 184.

CHAPTER FIFTEEN
1. Crépet, p. 241.
2. *Ibid.*, p. 238–9.
3. Letter to Mme Aupick on Feb. 9, 1857: *Corr.* I, p. 372.
4. Letter to Mme Aupick on Feb. 19, 1858: *ibid.*, p. 452.
5. Letter to Mme Aupick on Feb. 27, 1858: *ibid.*, p. 465.
6. Letter to Mme Aupick on Feb. 27, 1858: *ibid.*, p. 469.
7. Letter to Poulet-Malassis on Dec. 11, 1859: *ibid.*, p. 625.
8. Letter to Poulet-Malassis on Sept. 27, 1860: *Corr.* II, pp. 94–5.
9. *Ibid.*, *loc. cit.*
10. Letter to Mme Aupick on Oct. 11, 1860: *ibid.*, p. 96.
11. Letter to Mme Aupick on Dec. 22, 1865: *ibid.*, p. 552.
12. Letter to Mme Aupick on Jan. 5, 1861: *ibid.*, pp. 118–9.
13. Letter to Mme Aupick on Dec. 30, 1857: *Corr.* I, p. 438.
14. Letter to Mme Aupick on Aug. 7, 1860: *Corr.* II, p. 72.
15. Letter to Mme Aupick on Apr. 1, 1861: *ibid.*, p. 140.
16. *Ibid.*, *loc. cit.*
17. Letter to Mme Aupick on Jan. 15, 1860: *Corr.* I, p. 660.
18. Letter to Poulet-Malassis on Feb. 10, 1860: *ibid.*, p. 665.
19. Letter to Mme Aupick on May 6, 1861: *Corr.* II, pp. 152–3.
20. Letter to Mme Aupick on Feb. 19, 1858: *Corr.* I, pp. 450–1.
21. Letter to Mme Aupick on Apr. 20, 1860: *Corr.* II, p. 25.
22. Letter to Mme Aupick on May 6, 1860: *ibid.*, p. 152.

CHAPTER SIXTEEN
1. Pontmartin in *La Revue des Deux Mondes*. *Corr.* I, p. 932.
2. Letter to Nadar on May 14, 1859: *ibid.*, p. 573.
3. Letter to Poulet-Malassis on Jan. 8, 1860: *ibid.*, p. 656.
4. Letter to Mme Aupick on May 8, 1861: *Corr.* II, p. 159.
5. Letter to Mme Aupick on June 21, 1861: *ibid.*, p. 175.
6. Letter to Poulet-Malassis: *ibid.*, p. 68.
7. Letter to Barbey d'Aurevilly on July 9, 1860: *ibid.*, p. 61.

CHAPTER SEVENTEEN
1. LAB, pp. 342–3.

Chapter Eighteen

1. Letter to Mme Aupick on Dec. 25, 1861: *Corr.* II, p. 200.
2. *Journaux*, OC, p. 1265.
3. Letter to Mme Aupick on Nov. 25, 1863: *Corr.* II, p. 333.
4. Letter to Mme Aupick on Mar. 29, 1862: *ibid.*, p. 238.
5. *Journaux*, OC, p. 1269–70.
6. Letter to Hippolyte Lejosne on Jan. 1, 1863: *Corr.* II, p. 281.
7. OC,,p. 232.
8. *Ibid.*, p. 303.
9. *Ibid.*, p. 241.

Chapter Nineteen

1. *Journaux*, OC, p. 1266.
2. Letter to Mme Aupick on Dec. 31, 1863: *Corr.* II, p. 341.
3. Crépet, p. 152.
4. Bandy, pp. 209–10.
5. Crépet, p. 166.
6. Bandy, p. 211.
7. *Ibid.*, pp. 211–3.
8. Letter to Mme Aupick on June 17, 1864: *Corr.* II, p. 384.
9. Letter to Nadar on Aug. 30, 1864: *ibid.*, p. 401.
10. *Pauvre Belgique*, OC, p. 1450.
11. Letter to Mme Paul Meurice on Jan. 3, 1865: *Corr.* II, p. 437.
12. OC, p. 188.
13. Letter to Ancelle on Dec. 18, 1864: *Corr.* II, p. 425.
14. Bandy, pp. 120–1.
15. Letter to Mme Aupick on Dec. 23, 1865: *Corr.* II, pp. 552–3.
16. Letter to Ancelle on Dec. 26, 1865: *ibid.*, p. 556.

Chapter Twenty

1. Letter to Mme Aupick on Feb. 6, 1866: *Corr.* II, pp. 588–9.
2. Letter to Poulet-Malassis on Jan. 29, 1866: *ibid.*, p. 578.
3. Bandy, pp. 223–4.
4. Pichois, p. 232.

Epilog

1. *Journaux*, OC, p. 1256.

BIBLIOGRAPHY

The Baudelaire industry has been expanding rapidly for many years, producing enormous numbers of books of enormously variable quality. We have simply listed some of the better ones; readers wishing to know more should consult the excellent bibliography provided by the late Enid Starkie, in her outstanding study of Baudelaire.

Asselineau, C. *Baudelaire, sa vie et son oeuvre*. Paris, 1869.

Baudelaire, C. *A Self-Portrait*. Selected letters and a commentary by C. B. Hyslop and F. E. Hyslop, Jr. London, 1957.

Banville, Th. de. *Mes Souvenirs*. Paris, 1882.

Benjamin, W. *Charles Baudelaire*. Frankfurt, 1969.

Blin, G. *Le Sadisme de Baudelaire*. Paris, 1948.

Champfleury, J. *Souvenirs et portraits de jeunesse*. Paris, 1872.

Delvau, A. *Histoire des cafés et des cabarets de Paris*. Paris, 1862.

Du Camp, M. *Souvenirs littéraires*. Paris, 1882.

Gautier, Th. *Portraits contemporains*. Paris, 1874.

———. *Portraits et souvenirs littéraires*. Paris, s.d.

Mansell-Jones, P. *The Background of Modern French Poetry*. Cambridge, 1951.

Pommier, J. *La Mystique de Baudelaire*. Paris, 1932.

Prévost, J. *Baudelaire*. Paris, 1953.

Putter, M. L. *The Paris of Baudelaire*. Columbia University dissertation, 1958.

Quenell, P. *Baudelaire and the Symbolists*. New edition. London, 1955.

Ruff, M. *Baudelaire l'homme et l'oeuvre*. Paris, 1955.

———. *L'Esprit du mal et l'esthétique baudelairienne*. Paris, 1955.

Starkie, E. *Baudelaire*. New edition. London, 1971.

Sartre, J-P. *Baudelaire*. Paris, 1947. Also available in English.

INDEX

Names with the particle *de* or *d'* have been alphabetized under the main element of the name: e.g., for Alfred de Vigny, *see* Vigny, Alfred de. For page references to works by Baudelaire mentioned or quoted in the text, consult the separate listing at the end of the Index.

WORKS BY BAUDELAIRE REFERRED TO IN THE TEXT

240